I0793342

IMAGES
of America

MASON COUNTY
1850–1950

On the Cover: This threshing crew is taking a break after working at the Stillson place in Amber Township around 1880. In 1878, Charles Hackert joined with James Fluery and purchased the first threshing machine in Mason County; after Fluery passed away, his interest in the thresher was purchased by his son-in-law William Pittard. (Courtesy of Lois Dumas.)

IMAGES
of America

MASON COUNTY
1850–1950

David K. Petersen

Foreword by Dr. William Anderson

ARCADIA
PUBLISHING

ISBN 978-1-4671-1445-5

Published by Arcadia Publishing
Charleston, South Carolina

Printed in the United States of America

Library of Congress Control Number: 2015934790

For all general information, please contact Arcadia Publishing:
Telephone 843-853-2070
Fax 843-853-0044
E-mail sales@arcadiapublishing.com
For customer service and orders:
Toll-Free 1-888-313-2665

Visit us on the Internet at www.arcadiapublishing.com

I dedicate this book to my beloved granddaughter
Genevieve Rose Petersen, the light of my life.

Contents

Foreword

When we think about older parts of the world, the history of Mason County seems so recent, yet perhaps we are reminded that everything is relevant to other reference points. So it is with this county on the shores of Lake Michigan with its founding date of 1855.

The Northwest Territory was organized in 1787, Michigan became a state in 1837, and Detroit, its largest city, was incorporated in 1701. In all places where settlers put down roots and units of government were organized, there are events that mark the origins of history at a place and time.

The first recognized place settled in Michigan is Sault Ste. Marie in what became Michigan's Upper Peninsula. It was founded in 1673 by Fr. Jacque Marquette as a Jesuit mission. Just two years later, that famed priest is said to have died very near the future site of the city of Ludington, chartered in 1873.

What are sources for knowing our history beyond what is chronicled in history narratives? Those who research and write about local history know that the newspaper is an invaluable resource, along with diaries, letters, documents, photographs, artifacts, and much more.

Author David Petersen is a constant searcher and collector of these historical resources. He has the tenacity and ability of a bloodhound to sniff out an opportunity. Other people are commonly called pack rats, sometimes in derisive terms, yet all local historians honor the so-called pack rats because they have saved what most others have thrown away.

The Mason County Historical Society is dedicated to the preservation of our history. People recognize that it is the primary repository of historical resources that are made available to all of us. In recent years, there has emerged a growing cadre of local historians who are engaged in research—several of whom have now written published histories.

The organization of Mason County Cultural Trails, featuring our lumbering and agricultural heritage, with the story of our maritime history on deck, is another preservation initiative. Added to all of this is the much-appreciated growth of public art, in this county's case 13 sculptures, many of which celebrate our county's history. This new pictorial history will surely be read by a large audience and promote a new level of understanding and appreciation.

— William M. Anderson

ACKNOWLEDGMENTS

I would like to acknowledge the contributions of several people and organizations to my efforts to bring *Mason County: 1850–1950* to print. First, I would like to thank the staff at Arcadia Publishing, and Maggie Bullwinkle in particular for her assistance, as I worked to meet deadlines and find photographs that were needed to bring this volume to life.

The Mason County Historical Society (MCHS) was invaluable in helping to fill the void of images in my collections for some of the outlying areas in Mason County. Without their assistance, it would not have been possible to illustrate fully those areas with unique images. Thank you William M. Anderson, who shares my passion for history, for writing the foreword.

There were many other individual people and families who helped by providing one or more images, some from their personal family albums and some from their collections, and I would like to collectively say thank you for helping me bring our story to print.

Finally, for those who have ever taken on one of these projects who also have spouses, a heartfelt thank you goes to the better halves for allowing time and space to spread out images and other memorabilia while researching. Accumulators and collectors, we are a testy bunch as we sort through our treasures, and I am forever grateful for my wife's indulgence of my hobby and support for the projects that I undertake.

INTRODUCTION

As we go through old newspapers and photographs, especially those that contain stories and images of places and businesses that no longer exist, it is easy to wax poetic about days long past. We remember familiar faces that have passed and old places that no longer exist except for in the memories of those of us who are left behind. January days with their gray demeanor and nights that seem to linger endlessly make those memories seem larger than life. Those memories tend to take up more space in our thoughts as we age, more so than they did in the heyday of our youth. In those days, the business of living prevailed: working, raising families, and sharing laughter and the tears. As we travel our paths in life and youth gives way to advancing years, we are given the opportunity to reflect more and cherish those memories.

It becomes our responsibility to preserve and share those memories of our past, what once was present in our communities. Our personal and collective history is not lost lest we forget to share and record the memories of our community and its people. Lord Acton once said, "History is not a burden on the memory but an illumination of the soul." *Mason County: 1850–1950* strives to bring together those special memories and hopes to illuminate and awaken the soul of the reader and our communities here in this place. Mason County has a rich past extending back to the days when the area was inhabited by tribes of the Ottawa and the Mascouten Native Americans. In those early days, before Pere Jacques Marquette passed on our shores, there was a great battle between the tribes of the Mascouten and the Ottawa, which some say the Pottawattamie also took part in. The battle waged along the shoreline of what would eventually be called the River of the Black Robe.

A peaceful group of Mascoutens was passing through the area south of present Custer and fearing that there was an ill intent toward them were trying to leave the area. The Ottawa to the north swarmed down and attacked the Mascouten as they traveled down the river toward Lake Michigan. The battle raged for days, and when it was over the heads were severed from the defeated Mascouten and placed on sticks used to line the river and lakeshore as a warning to all who would come. It was then that the area around Pere Marquette Lake became known as No-Ti-Pe-Ka-Gon, meaning "heads on sticks." Another place near the mouth of the river that was a burial ground of the Ottawa was known as Nin-De-Ka-Tun-Ning, or "place of skulls."

Father Marquette, the Jesuit missionary, came to New France in 1666. He explored the Mississippi with Louis Joliet, and when traveling through our area on his way back to the mission at St. Ignace, he passed away on a sandy knoll on May 18, 1675. Two centuries later, the sandy point would become known as the Buttersville Peninsula after lumber baron Horace U. Butters. Around 1835, William Quevillion came to the area to trap and trade; other trappers followed and then shingle makers and those who stripped bark for the tanneries.

Burr Caswell is cited as the first permanent settler of European descent, and he settled in Pere Marquette Township. Mason County was named to honor Steven T. Mason, who at age 19 was appointed to be the secretary of the territory of Michigan and also twice-elected governor after

Michigan was admitted to the Union in 1837. Originally, Pere Marquette was the name of the little lumbering village that began to emerge after Burr Caswell arrived in 1847.

The river itself was unofficially known as the River of the Black Robe before claiming Pere Marquette as its official title. Even as late as 1867, after the sound of the lumberman's axe and saw filled the air, the area was considered desolate. On December 22, 1867, at lumbering Camp Danaher in Pere Marquette (Ludington), local lumberjack John Jameson wrote to his friend to say that he was working in the pinery 40 miles up the River from Ludington, and "it is almost like being out of the world to be here as it is nothing but woods, and the only company that we have is the howl of wolves, the leaping of deer and the smoke of Indian Wigwams." The area soon began to be noticed for its rich lands filled with large tracts of virgin pine, and men of wealth and influence started to divide the spoils. Eber Ward took control of large tracts of lands in the early 1850s. He did not have a means to harvest or transport the timber, but he had a plan. He became the president of the Flint & Pere Marquette Railroad and intended to construct a rail line to Pere Marquette and then build a terminus for cross-lake shipping to move his bounty. James Ludington from Wisconsin took controlling interest of George W. Ford's sawmill and 400 acres after Ford was unable to pay his note with Ludington. Remaining in Wisconsin, James Ludington was primarily an absentee landlord, but it was he who intended to build a permanent community. His efforts laid the groundwork for our community, insuring that Ludington would thrive long after the timber was harvested.

Another early lumber baron was Charles Mears out of Chicago, Illinois. He had a grand plan of controlling every port north of White River to Hamlin. He secured an interest in lands from Oceana County north. Originally, he founded the villages of Big Sable (Hamlin), located in the current Ludington State Park, and Little Sable (Lincoln Village), near where the current Lincoln River empties into Lake Michigan. Mears built dams at both locations to move his timber and run his mills, and he successfully had the county seat in Mason County moved to Little Sable. In 1861, he changed the names of those two villages to Hamlin and Lincoln in honor of his choice for president and vice president after attending the convention at which Lincoln and Hamlin were nominated. Mears also provided the pine boughs to decorate the wigwam in Chicago where the Republicans held their convention. It was about this time that James Ludington was looking for someone to manage his mill at Pere Marquette, and Mears jumped at the chance to control another harbor. Part of the agreement Mears signed was that he was to move and enlarge the harbor channel within two years. His success in changing the harbor channel was the key to his demise and diminished influence in the area.

When Mears changed the channel, he shifted the line of power to James Ludington. A better channel and harbor development meant that more ships, more people, and more freight came through Pere Marquette (Ludington) than Lincoln. In 1867, James Ludington platted the village, and the post office was named Ludington. In 1873, when the village was incorporated as Ludington, a vote was held by the county commissioners to move the county seat to the newly incorporated municipality. The village of Lincoln's influence was waning, and Mears soon sold his interests in Mason County and moved his operations south to Oceana County.

The political power was shifting, and it would shift yet again. In 1873, James Ludington must have certainly felt that his star was rising; it was a short-lived dream, as the winds would soon shift against his ambitions. During this time, Eber Ward was moving his empire ever closer to Ludington in the form of a steam locomotive and all of the power and influence that bringing in a railroad could harness. Ward had a dream, too, of a railhead and cross-lake service from Ludington, a place where he could build his sawmills, harvest his timber, and have a means to ship the timber to market. Ward was Detroit's first millionaire, and he was a shrewd and demanding businessman of the 19th century. He was a rags-to-riches story come to life, as if noted author of the time Horatio Alger had penned Ward's life story himself, but Ward was not a person that people said no to, as James Ludington soon discovered.

Ward attempted to buy lands and frontage on Pere Marquette Lake for his operations and railroad, and James Ludington mistakenly thought he was taking part in a negotiation. Ward knew that Ludington's crews were cutting round 40s (cutting timber outside of property lines and into another parcel), which meant that they were stealing timber off of Ward's holdings. Rather than saying anything, Ward remained quiet until James Ludington came to Detroit, where he was promptly arrested and subsequently sued. The settlement that ensued gave Ward leverage to get the lands for his terminus at Ludington and land for his mills on the Pere Marquette Lake. James Ludington's health suffered as a result, and this time it was his influence that was diminished. Ludington withdrew to Wisconsin and allowed his agents and partners to operate through the Pere Marquette Lumber Company.

Mason County has a rich past, and its communities have survived the changes over the decades as the area transitioned from lumbering to agriculture, maritime industries, manufacturing, and tourism. The communities again face a time of decisions as local efforts attempt to define the historical and cultural attractions as a destination for travelers and visitors who love history.

As local communities strive to celebrate and capitalize on their heritage and culture, these assets offer new opportunities to enrich the quality of life and produce economic growth and community prosperity. As a result, the community is developing a new maritime museum, a new sports-history museum, and several cultural-heritage trails. Mason County is unique in its embracing of history and determination to preserve and share the treasures of our past. We invite all lovers of history to come enjoy our heritage and history, relax on our beaches, and partake in all we have to offer as you step back in time.

It was a young man named Matthew "Mattie J.T." Stepanek who said, "Keep all special thoughts and memories for lifetimes to come. Share these keepsakes with others to inspire hope and build from the past, which can bridge to the future." These wise words are from a young soul wise beyond his years, and when Mattie passed away when he was 13, he left five volumes of poetry for our illumination and enjoyment. We can take a lesson from him in that we must build from the past if we are to create a bridge to a brighter future. Let *Mason County: 1850–1950* be that first bridge to share our memories and heritage.

One

Early History

Ludington as a city arrived in 1873 when it was incorporated. At this time, eight years after the end of the Civil War, Ludington was poised to grow and expand its influence in the area. The old guard of original lumber barons had withdrawn from the area after 1875, but nature of course abhors a void, and others soon moved in to take their place. Pine was still king, and pine was still making kings out of those who had the tenacity and foresight to climb over those who had come before them. Lumbering brought immigrants who would remove the last vestiges of the denuded forests and till the lands. The area south of Ludington was perfect for planting fruit trees, and fruit farms prospered. Merchants began to arrive and build stores to serve the needs of the new settlers coming into the area.

Advertisements were run in newspapers and journals throughout Europe, and waves of immigrants began pouring into the area: Germans, Lithuanians, Swedes, Finns, and Danes came in answer to the call of rich available farmland. The dream of owning one's own home and farming one's own land was a powerful draw for people who came from countries where all lands were controlled and owned by others.

The streets may not have been literally paved with gold, but the opportunity to build a new life, own property, and have a business was golden. The area around Ludington mill towns such as Buttersville, Taylorsville, and Seatonville came to life. The northernmost tip of the Buttersville Peninsula became known as Finn Town and was home to the local fishing community.

To the east, Amber Station, Sweetland (Scottville), Custer, Branch, Tallman, Walhalla, and Stearns Siding, just outside the county, were beginning. To the north there was Freesoil and Fountain. In those early days, however, there were dozens of small communities, many with their own post office such as Bird Settlement, whose stars rose and faded with the changing times. Mason County was coming to life.

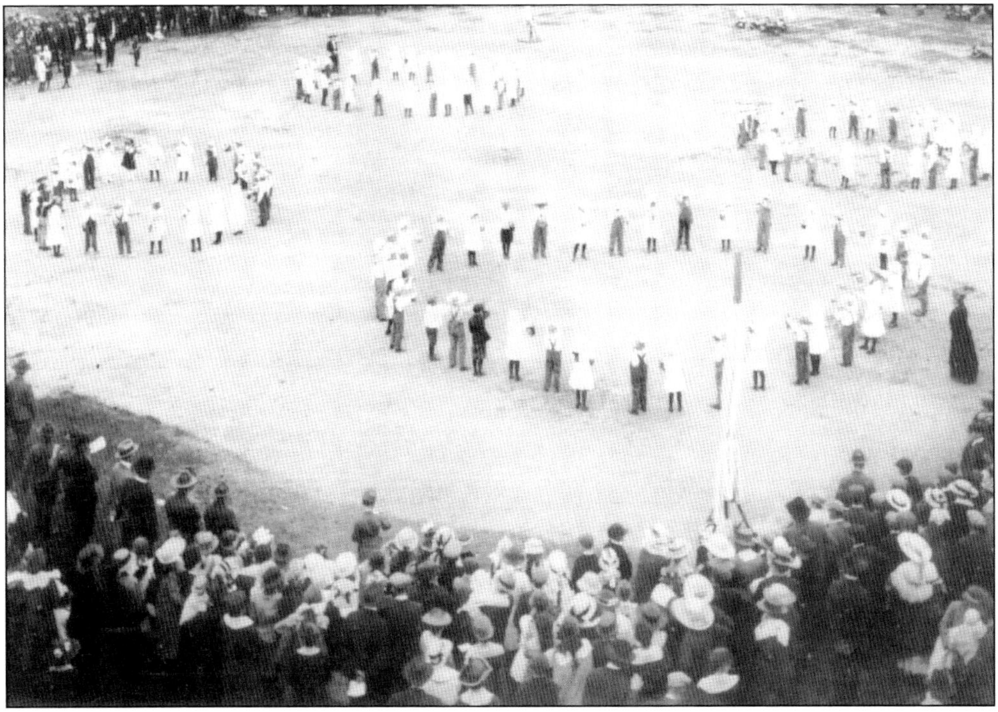

Fr. Jacques Marquette played a large role in the identity of the community that sprang up around the sandy knoll where he passed away in 1675. So much so, an annual Pere Marquette Pageant took place in the community, and hundreds of residents took part in the parade and reenactment of his final voyage and death. Schoolchildren are shown here at Culver field presenting their part to the community. (Courtesy of James F. Fay.)

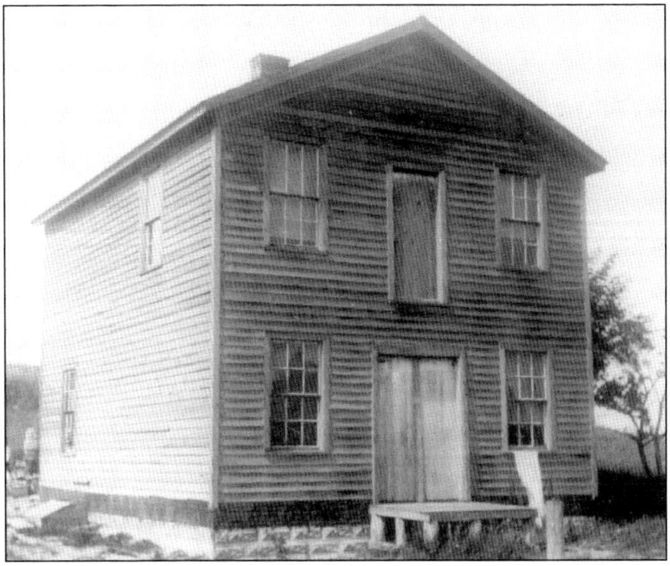

Burr Caswell was the first permanent settler of European descent to make his home in what would soon become known as Pere Marquette Township. Upon his arrival, the channel was too shallow for his schooner to enter, and Caswell and his family had to come ashore in the ship's yawl. The animals were pushed overboard and after swimming around the ship made their way to shore. His driftwood shack soon gave way to the first frame house in Mason County. (Author's collection.)

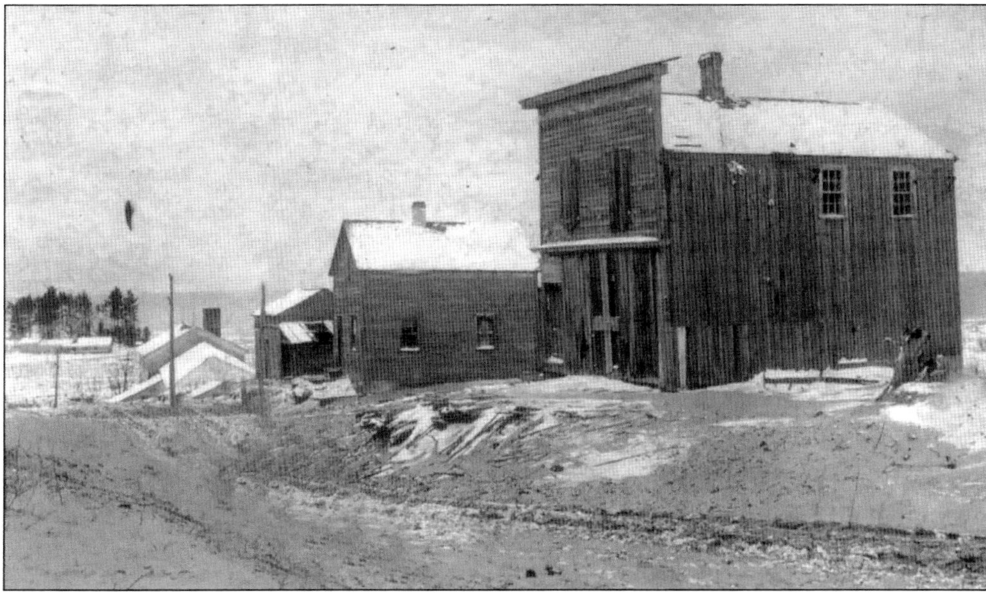

The county commissioners' first meeting was held at Little Sable on October 8, 1855, and the first order of business was to borrow $27 from Charles Mears. The treasury, however, was rapidly depleted, when at the second meeting $24 was paid out to Richard Hatfield as bounty for three wolves he had taken. The county seat was determined to be located at the Burr Caswell farm at a special meeting held on November 11, 1856. (Courtesy of the Epworth Museum.)

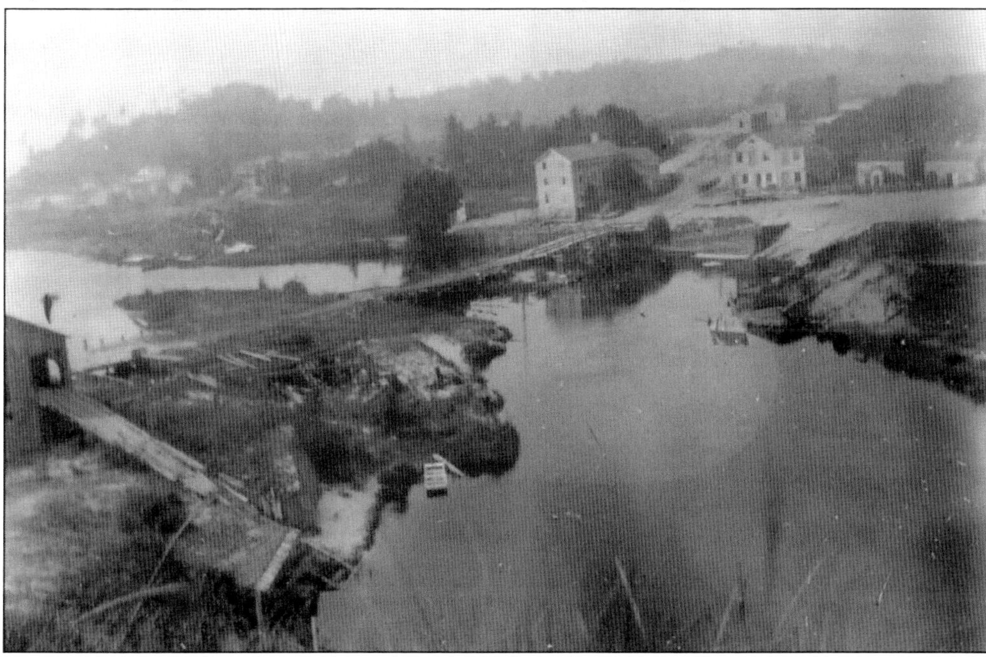

Charles Mears was busy planning, plotting, and building his communities for the day that he would claim the county seat for Little Sable (Lincoln) in 1861. Within 12 short years, he would see those dreams dashed against the rising influence of Pere Marquette (Ludington). He engineered his own defeat, and the villages of Lincoln and Hamlin disappeared into the mists of time. (Courtesy of the Epworth Museum.)

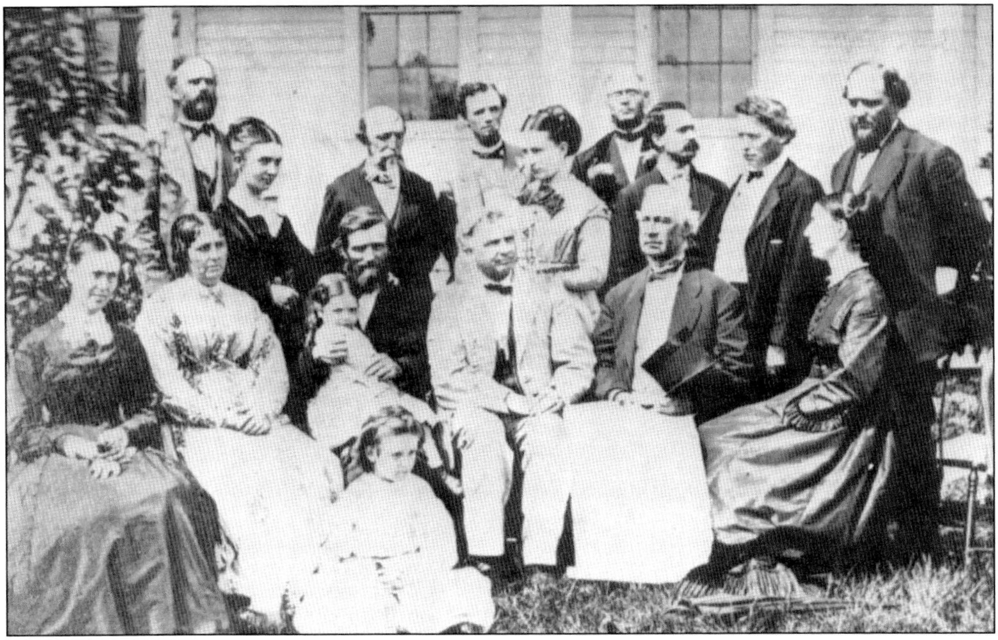

Eber Ward (seated, center) and James Ludington (standing, far right) are pictured here at the signing ceremony in which Ward received the property needed for a terminus to initiate cross-lake service for the Flint and Pere Marquette Railroad and lands to construct his sawmills. Ward passed away on January 1, 1875, just a few short months before the side-wheeler *Sherman* would make the first crossing from Ludington to Wisconsin. His death shifted the balance of power. (Courtesy of MCHS.)

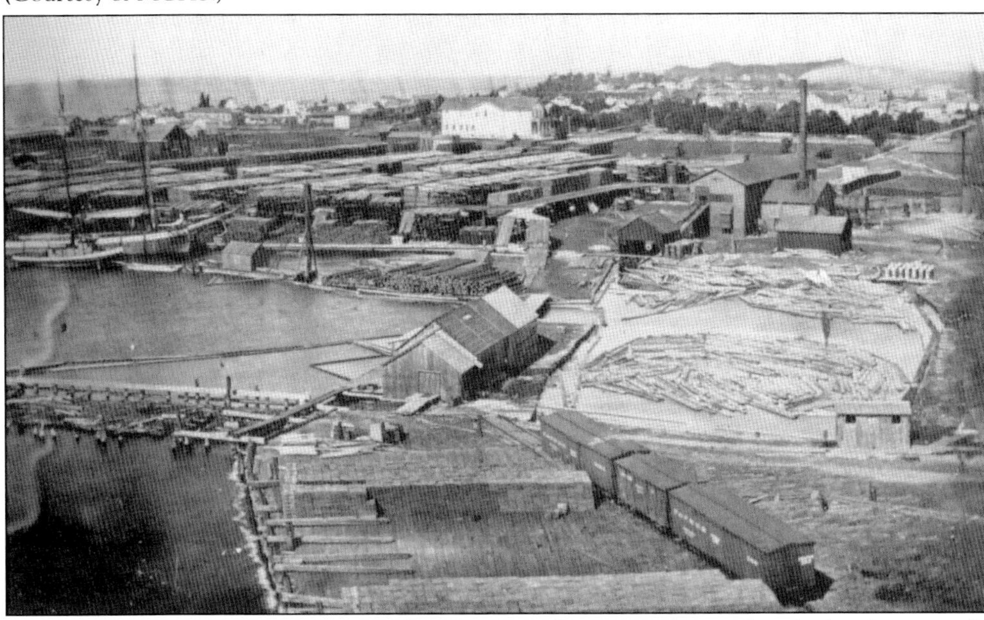

The Big Store, as it was called, was built by James Ludington and served as the headquarters for his operations at Pere Marquette. This early view shows the location of the store at the present-day corner of Gaylord and Ludington Avenues. Across the street, where the current city park is located, stood the Farrell House, a boardinghouse. (Courtesy of MCHS.)

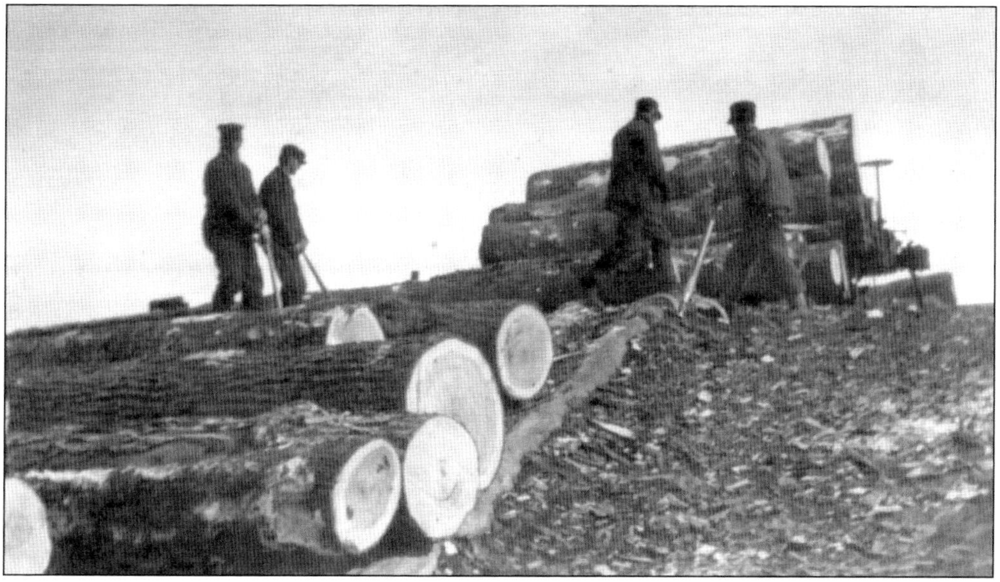

Logs were sent down the rollway to the river and on their way to the mills on the Pere Marquette. In the lumbering days, rivers were the only means of transporting logs, and A.E. "Joe" Cartier and his partner hired out to the lumber companies to move logs quickly downstream in the spring drive. If they could move 50 million feet in that short time, they could make good money. (Author's collection.)

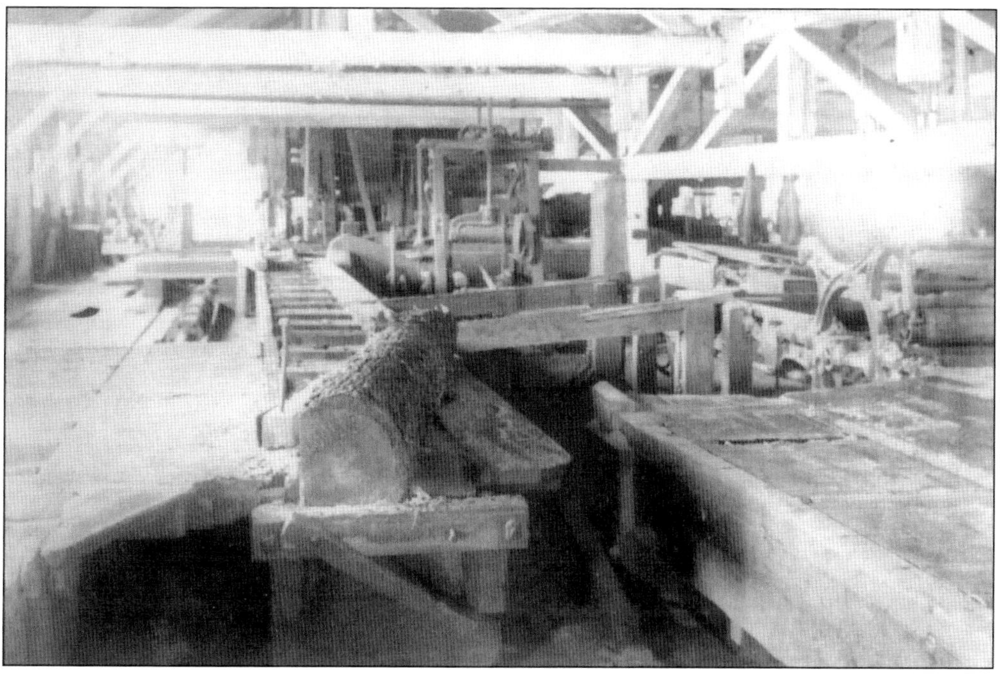

In 1882, Cartier purchased a mill from Allen Goodsell and Company at the foot of South James Street. This mill had a double circular saw and a capacity of 16 million feet per season. In a year or two, the infant business operated the entire Manistee River and tributaries. In 1871, the partners were able to buy a sawmill at Manistee. After a few years, Cartier was ready to strike out on his own. (Author's collection.)

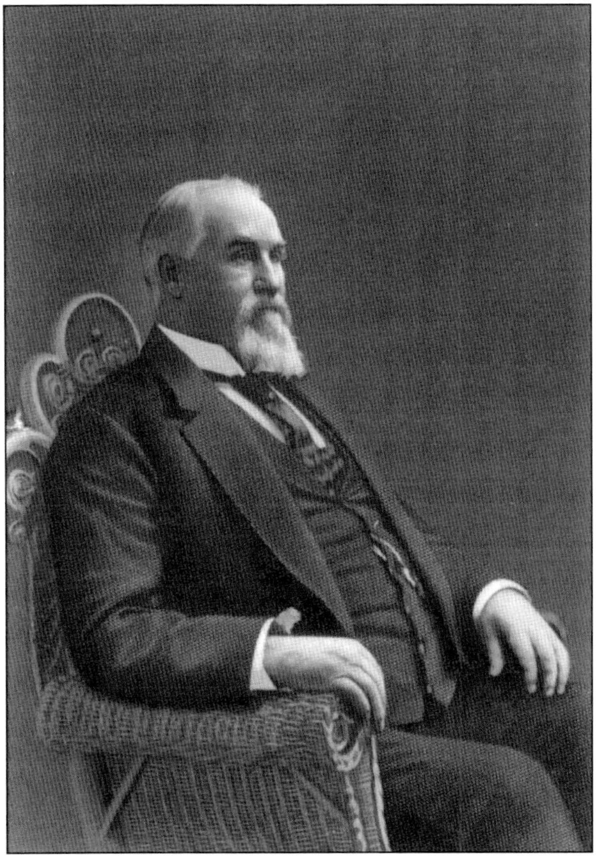

Horace Butters came to Michigan from Maine and settled in Manistee in 1851 and Mason County about 1877. He brought his family of eight children and moved into a home at 206 North Park Street. The operations of the Butters and Peters Lumber Company included Tallman and Buttersville, a narrow-gauge railroad with 30 miles of track known as the Mason & Oceana (but nicknamed the "Miserable and Ornery"), and the lumber hooker *Marshall F. Butters*. (Author's collection.)

In this 1890 image looking southwest from the Central (High) School, one has a good view of the grain elevator and the docks down at Pere Marquette Lake. Looking across the lake, the structures on Buttersville Peninsula can be seen, which was thriving in the 1890s. (Author's collection.)

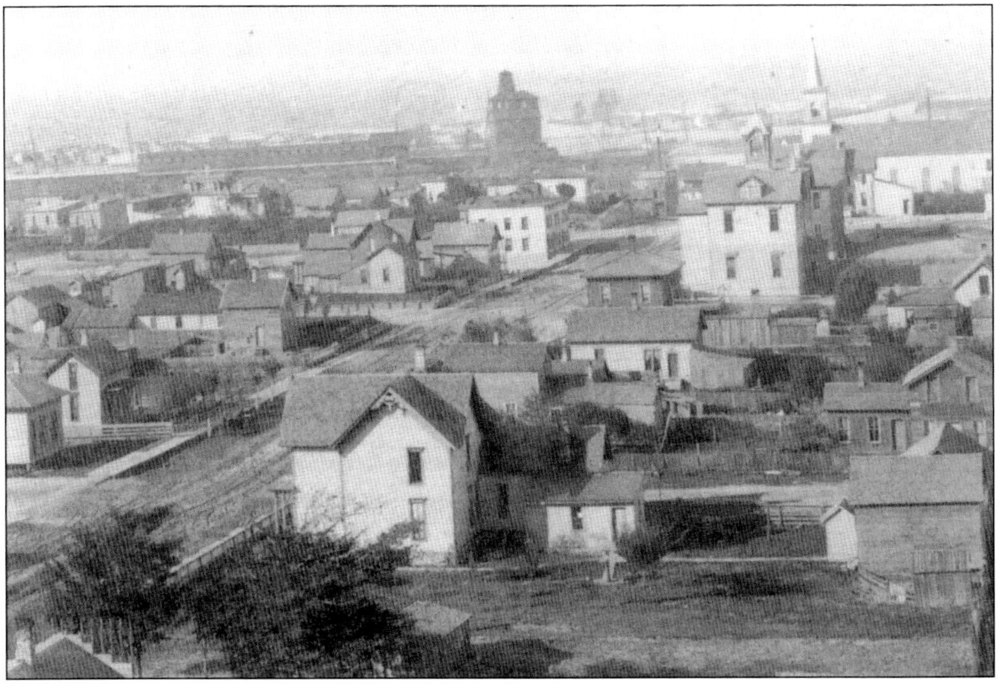

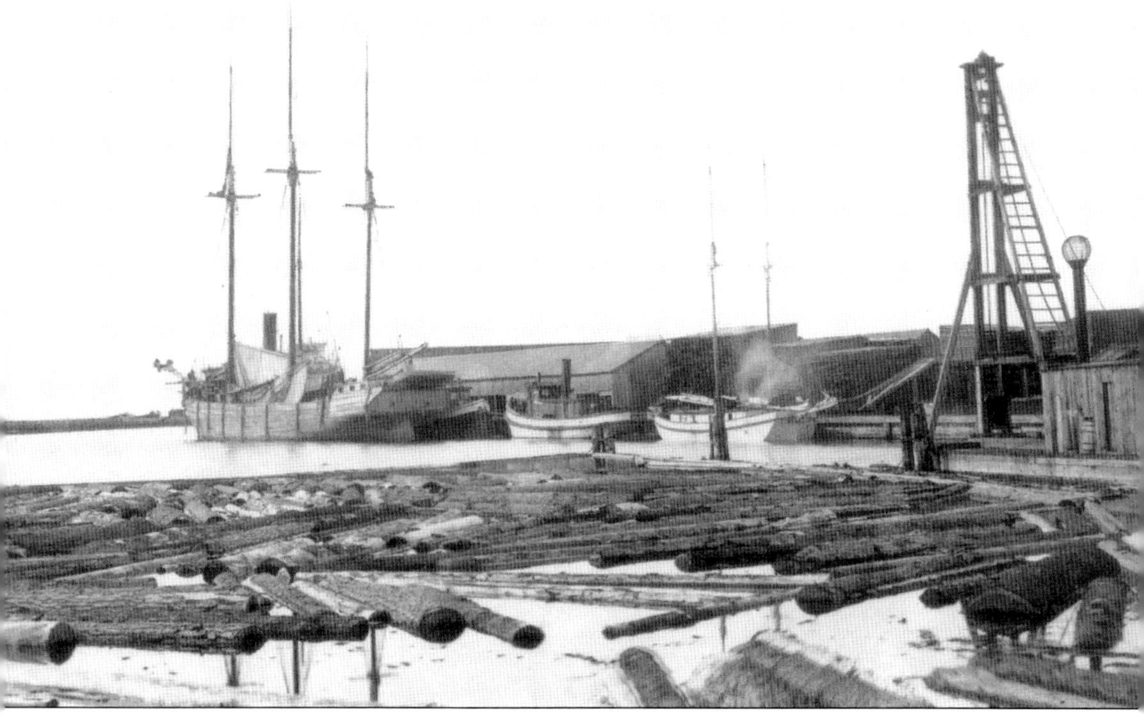

Travel was difficult overland, and for the most part roads and highways during the era consisted of rivers and lakes. Most of the commerce and settlements were directly connected to the waterways. A few blocks from this dock on the Pere Marquette River was the forest, sawdust trails studded with stumps, and swamps. In 1867, Ludington Avenue near Harrison Street still had old tree stumps that made passage difficult. (Author's collection.)

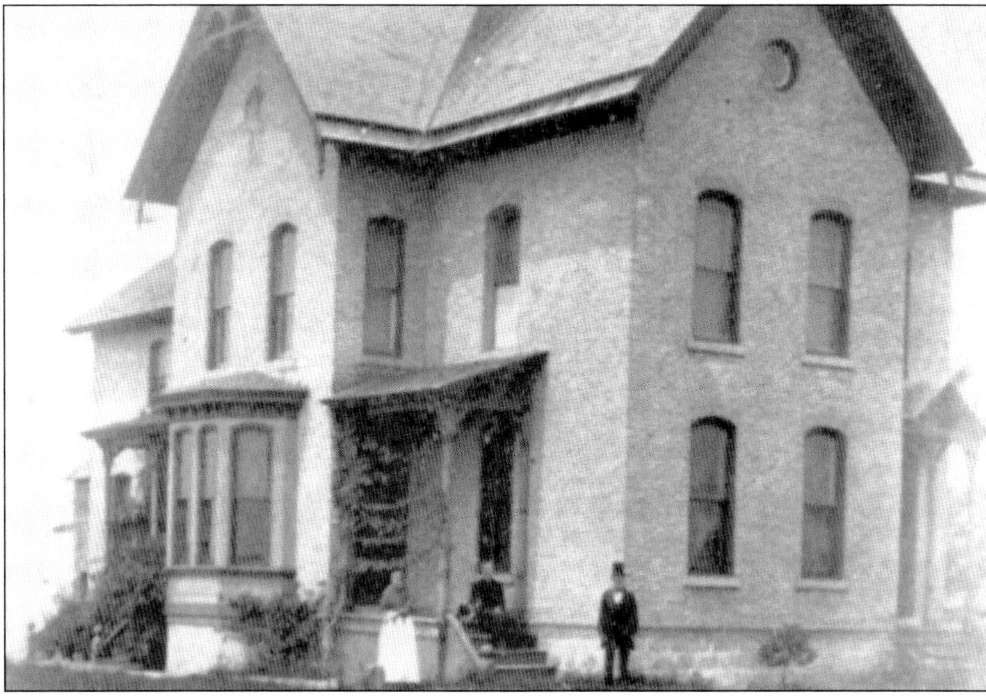

Attorney E.N. Fitch built his new home in 1879 with a $10,000 fee earned by the lawsuit filed by George Ford against James Ludington over 40 acres in the heart of Ludington he claimed still belonged to him. George W. Ford received a clear title to his 40 acres, which included Rath Avenue South from Ludington Avenue all the way down to Danaher Street and over to the courthouse. (Author's collection.)

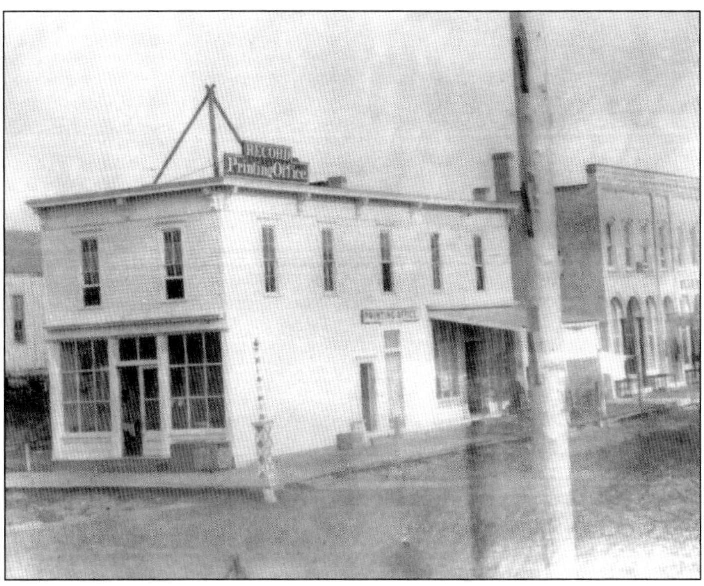

James Ludington was looking forward to how he could build his community and strengthen it for future growth. In 1867, he brought George Clayton to the village to start its first newspaper. This was part of Ludington's long-term plan to lay the groundwork for moving the county seat to Ludington, and he accomplished this in 1873 with the help of the *Ludington Record*. (Courtesy of Ron Lessard.)

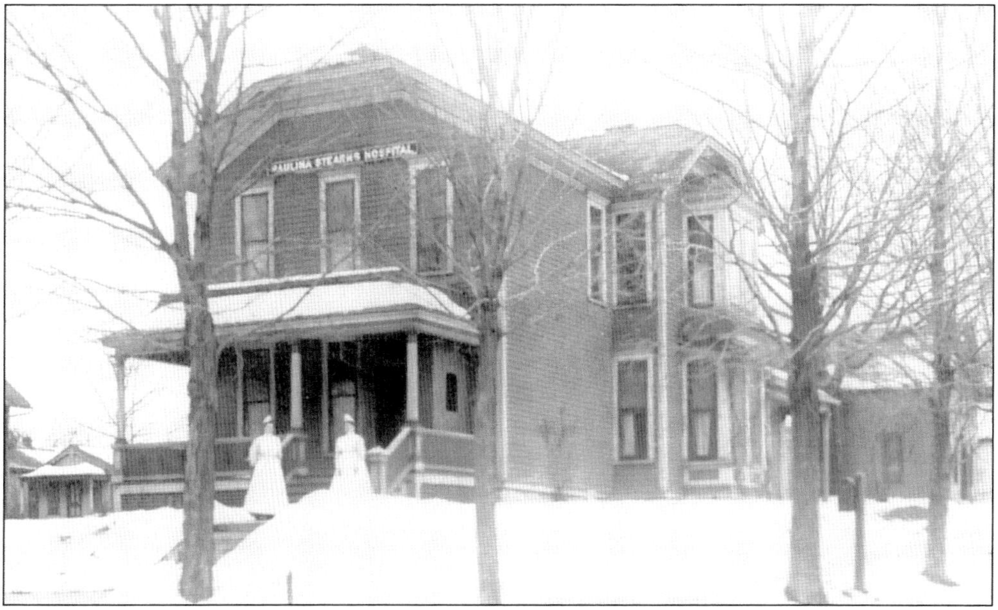

Justus Stearns was Eber Ward's brother-in law, and Ward's untimely passing allowed Stearns's star to rise. Justus was involved in logging, salt production, the Stearns Hotel, the Epworth Hotel, the Ludington and Northern Railroad, and many other concerns. Stearns lived in Ludington until his death and contributed greatly to the welfare of the community both in creating jobs, saving businesses, and promoting public works such as Paulina Stearns Hospital (pictured). (Author's collection.)

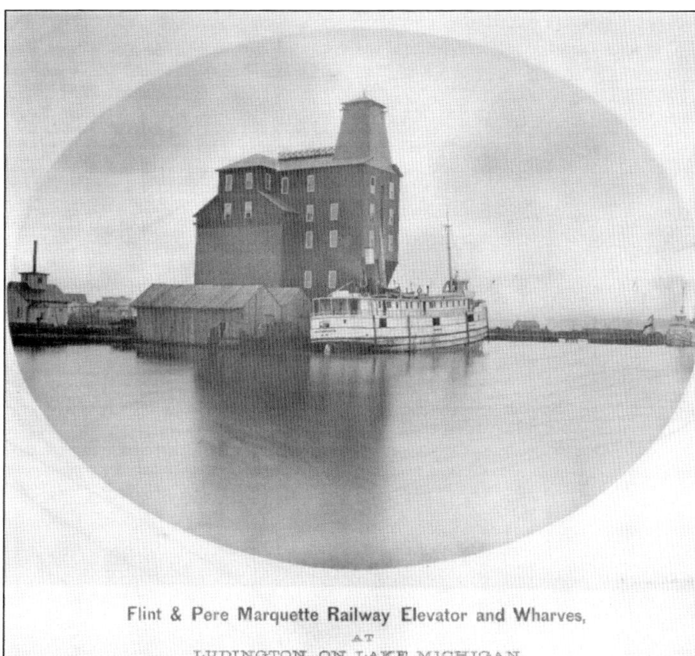

Cross-lake service was initiated in 1875, and a few years later the Pere Marquette Railway commissioned its first break-bulk steamships to carry freight across the lake. Prior to 1880, the railroad leased the ships that they needed, but this change ushered in a new era in which the company would develop the largest fleet of car ferries in the world. (Courtesy of the Charles Robertson Collection.)

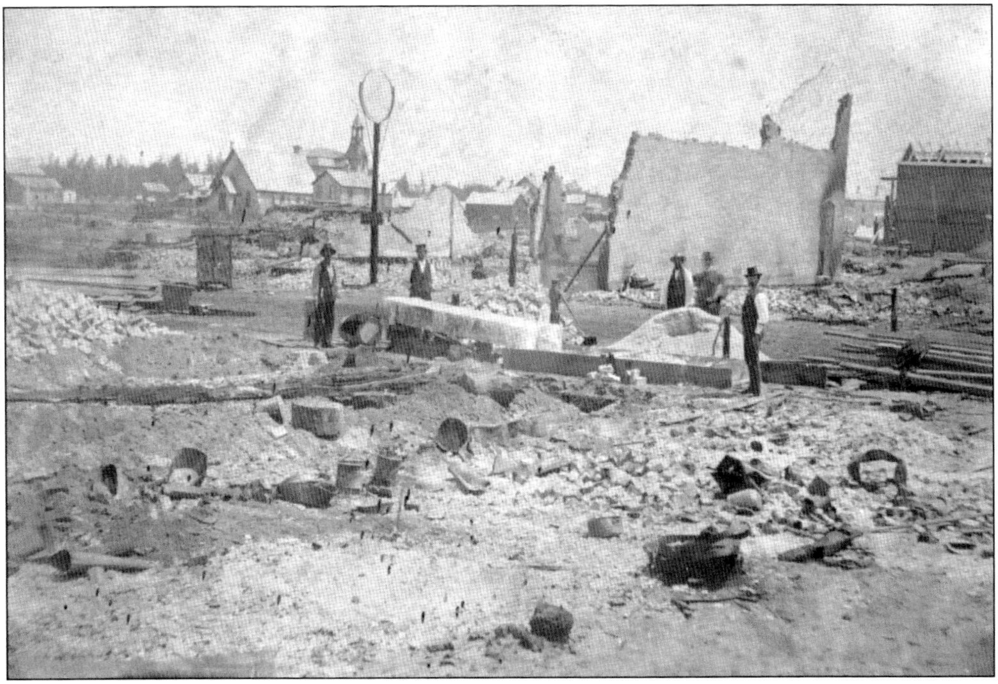

The Great Fire of 1881 left its mark on Ludington as it raged through and decimated almost 100 buildings around the central business district. The city was already in the grips of a diphtheria epidemic when the circus came to town on June 11, 1881. Children left the confines of their homes to watch their arrival as the fire began and within hours laid four blocks of the city to waste. (Courtesy of MCHS.)

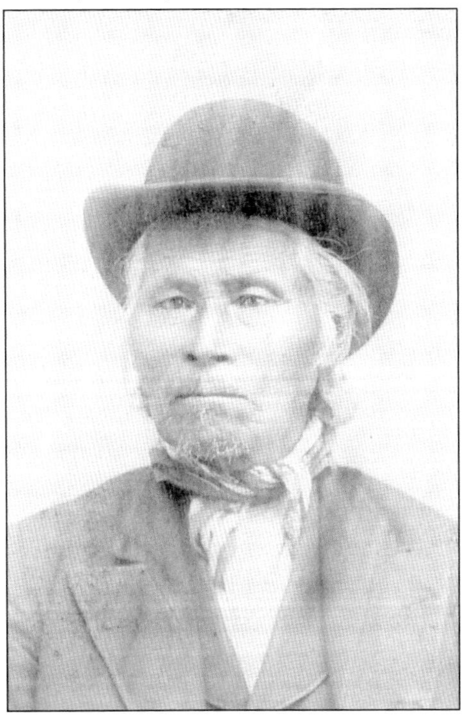

"Good John," as he was called by residents, was the last of the area natives who lived in Mason County; he was called Naw-gone-ko-ung, which meant "Leading Thunder." Good John converted to Christianity and led services throughout the area. He was highly regarded and respected by all who knew him. (Author's collection.)

Two

Township Histories

On January 3, 1855, Mason, Manistee, and Oceana Counties were set out of Ottawa County by the Michigan Legislature, and Mason County, consisting of three townships—Freesoil, Little Sable, and Pere Marquette—was officially organized on February 5, 1855. When Mason County was created, there were three original townships that stretched across the length of the county from east to west. As the population grew, townships were organized and carved out from those three original sections. There were 41 votes cast in the first county election, on April 2, 1855. Burr Caswell was elected both as judge of probate and fish inspector. The following were elected that day: Daniel Holmes (sheriff), George B. Roys (clerk and register), E.G. Farnum (treasurer), William Quevillion (coroner), and John Sedan (surveyor). Summit Township (1859) was organized next, out of the southern half of Pere Marquette Township, and is the smallest of the townships; it also takes in part of Bass Lake near the Oceana County border.

In 1860, Little Sable Township and village was renamed Lincoln to represent Charles Mears's choice for president, Big Sable was renamed Hamlin, and Hamlin Township was established in 1860. Lincoln Township was eventually absorbed by surrounding townships after the village slipped into obscurity. There were six townships named to celebrate victory in the Civil War: Victory (1867), Grant (1867), Sherman (1867), Sheridan (1867), Custer (1871), and Meade (1910). There were a large number of veterans who settled in Mason County after the end of the war, which contributed to the names of the new townships. Amber Township (1867) may have been named after a resident's daughter or possibly after the town of Amber, Indiana. Riverton Township (1868) was so named because the Pere Marquette River bordered the area. Branch Township (1871) was thought to be named after Branch County, Michigan, where several early residents had previously lived. Eden Township (1878) was previously part of Custer, and Logan Township (1903) was thought to be named after John E. Logan, the vice presidential nominee in 1884.

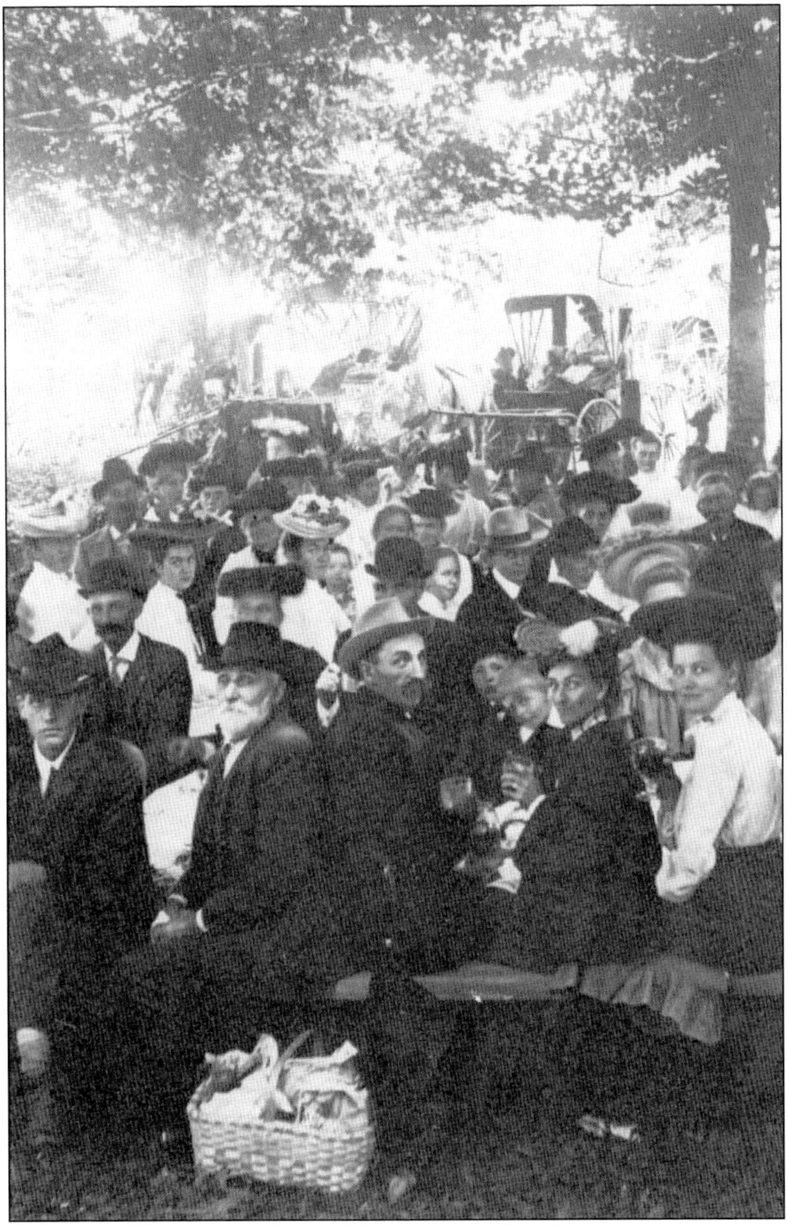

Amber was organized in 1867 and took in part of Sweetland (Scottville) until that city was incorporated. Amber was originally platted as a village located across from the present-day town hall. Early on, there was a general store, icehouse, and hardware store. It seemed that Scottville was better situated for development, possibly because two main roads intersected, there was a railroad station, and a bridge spanned the Pere Marquette River for easier access. The little village of Amber quietly faded away, and in 1915 a 40-acre plat, which included 16 village lots, was sold. The resulting fruit farm was named Amber Village Farm. The first town hall was not built in Amber until 1899, but early on the train depot was an important link to Scottville and Ludington, and residents gravitated to that locale. In 1905, the grove of trees to the south of the hall was purchased, and what was a favored picnic area became the home of the Amber Fair. (Courtesy of MCHS.)

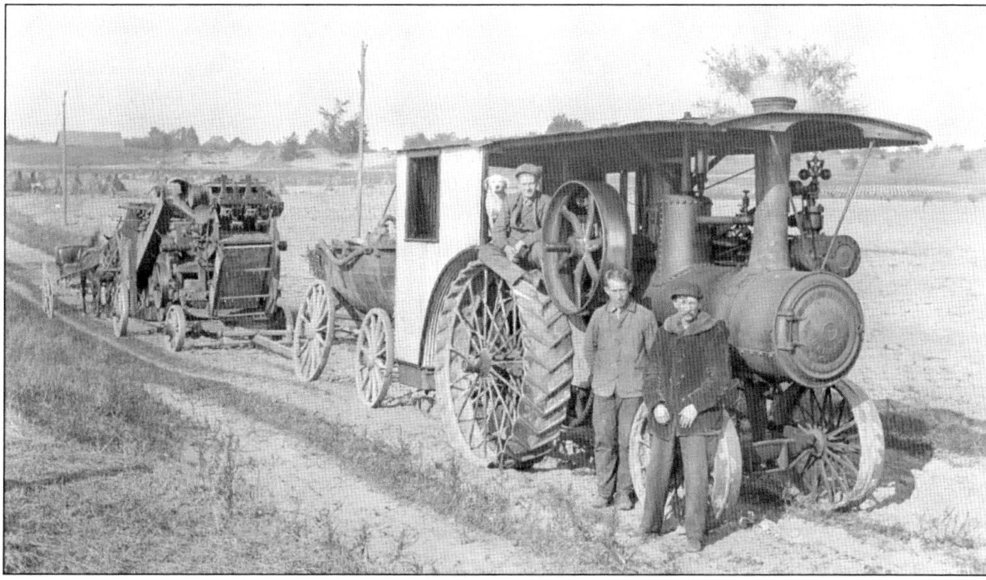

Bob and Ann Conrad raised four children—David, Barb, Pete, and Linnea—on a farm, and he had a lot of memories and stories. When interviewed for the barn tour in 2008, Bob said, "I remember when I was 12 years old and used a team of four horses to plow the fields here, then in the fall the threshing crews would come for the harvest, the meals were served on a large wooden table [that we still have]." (Author's collection.)

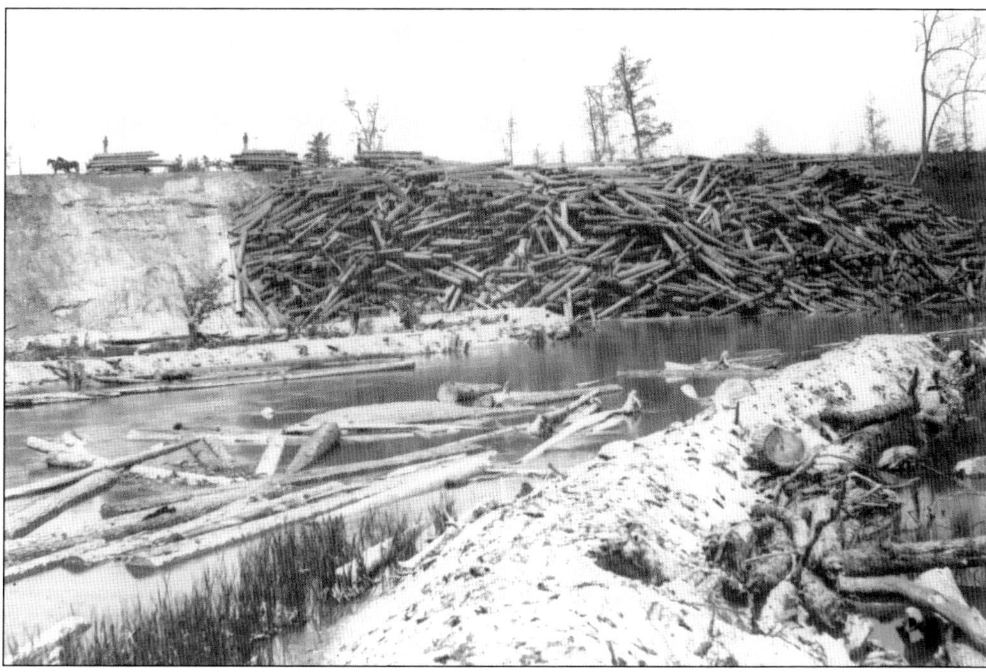

The Conrad farm consists of 180 acres and includes Chinnery's Rollway, a steep bluff over the Pere Marquette River that was used by loggers to roll logs down to the river. They were then pushed downstream by the currents and men who literally herded the logs to sawmills on Pere Marquette Lake. Ann Conrad said that everyone tries to put in an "*a*" to make "rollaway," but "rollway" is the correct term. (Courtesy of MCHS.)

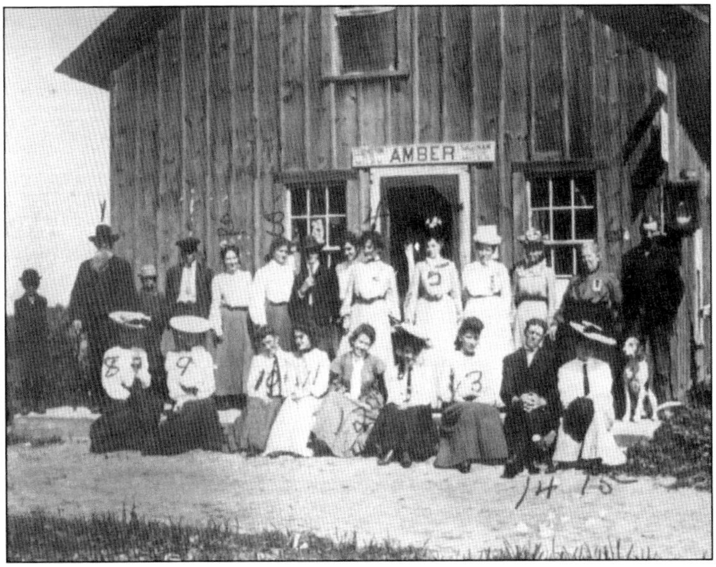

Standing in front of the Amber Station in numbered order are Grandpa Michel Moore (1), May Parmalee Taylor (2), Maggie Matthews (3), Lizzie Baily (4), Ida Hackert (5), Vill and Fay Parmalee (6), Louise Pittard (8), Alice Pittard (9), Lizzie Matthews Foster (10), Dora Baily (11), Mable Parmalee (12), Ella Parmalee (13), Steve Pelter (14), Tina Ewold Johnson (15), and Old Pilot (dog). (Courtesy of MCHS.)

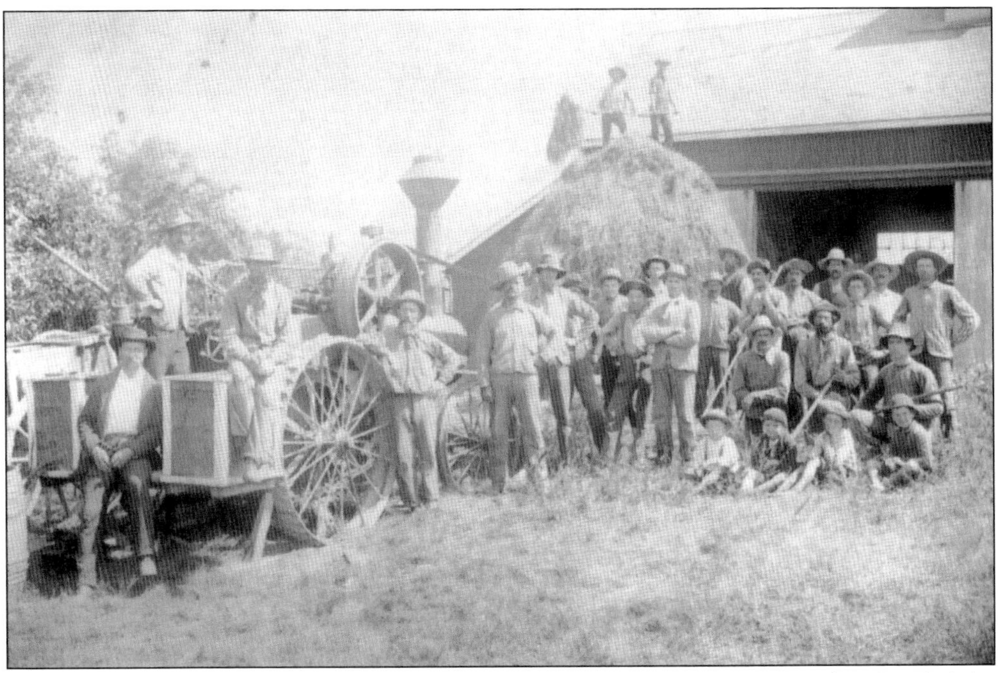

Charles Hackert was born in Prise, Germany, and came to America as a young boy. In 1848, he married Sarah Ann Williams, and 11 children were born to the union. In 1861, the family traveled north and stayed temporarily at Crystal (Hackert) Lake while their log homes were being built; they intended to homestead on South Stiles Road. This image shows the crews and local farmers working on bringing in the harvest. (Courtesy of Lois Dumas.)

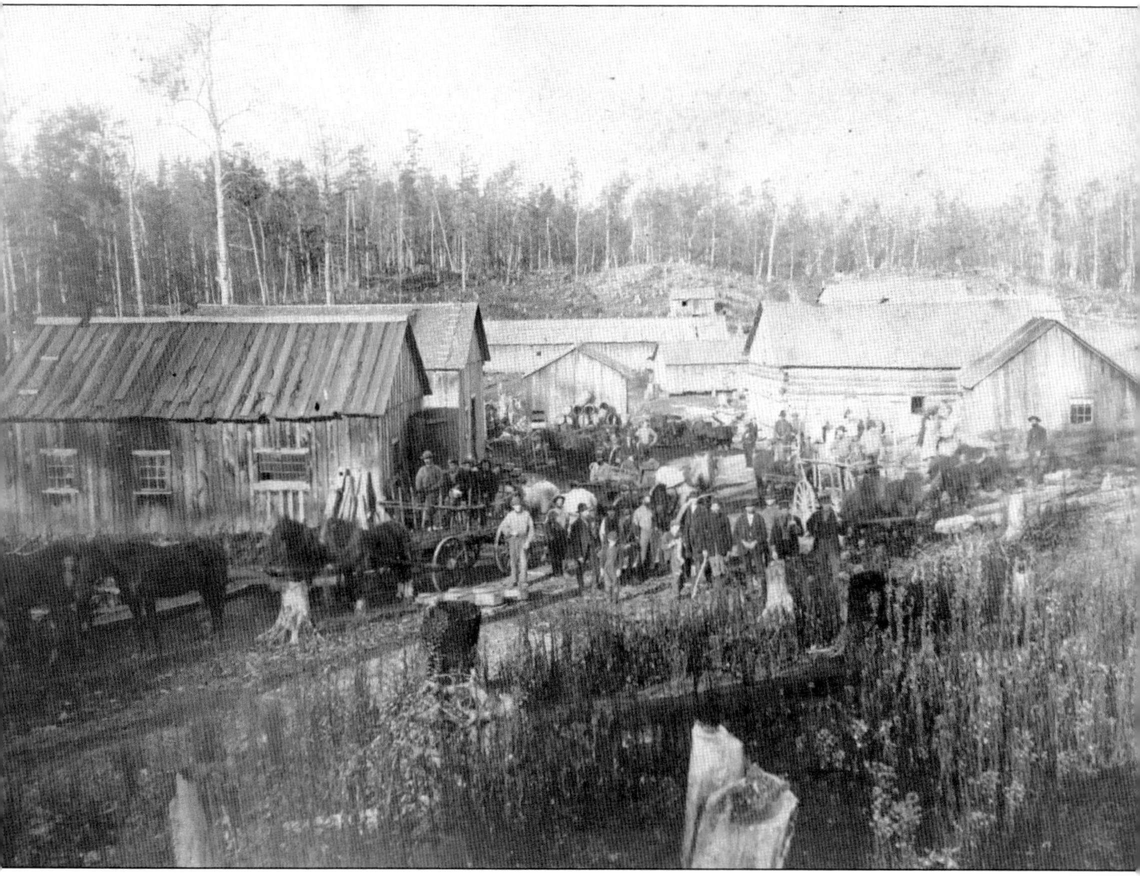

Branch Township originally included Logan Township when organized in 1871; it was divided in 1903 to create Logan Township. Branch Township is thought to have been named so as a result of several families there who had come from Branch County in Southern Michigan; others say it was due to being near the north branch of the Pere Marquette River. There were few settlers in the area in 1871, although several lumber camps were in operation, such as J. Loucks's lumber camp on the Pere Marquette River. In fact, the population was so sparse, only 43 votes were cast in the first election in 1873. Travel was difficult in those days, and supplies were brought by riverboat to the camp docks, as seen in this image. Logging was the primary occupation in the area and driving force behind the settlement of the region. Small villages and places such as Wever (Tallman), Butters Junction (Walhalla), Swedish Settlement, and Grass Lake came about because of the influx of loggers as well as Civil War veterans who settled in the area after the war. (Author's collection.)

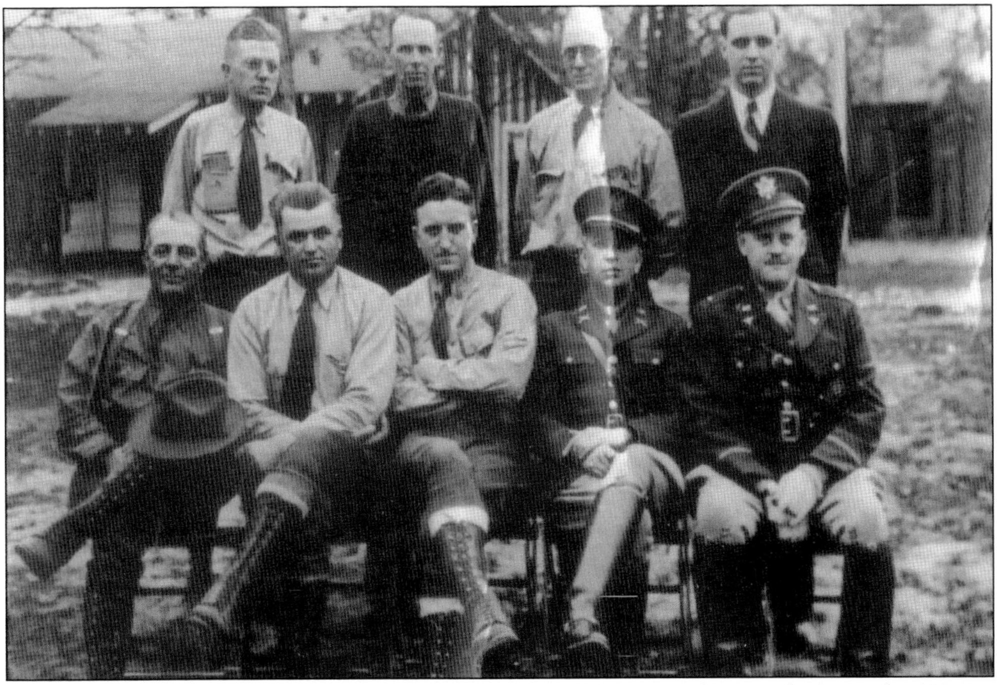

These Civilian Conservation Corps (CCC) officers ran the camp that was built south of Kinny Road in 1934. The camps were started by Pres. Franklin Delano Roosevelt as a means to give young men a purpose and a job. Most of what they earned was sent home to their families, which provided the additional support so they could stay in their homes. (Author's collection.)

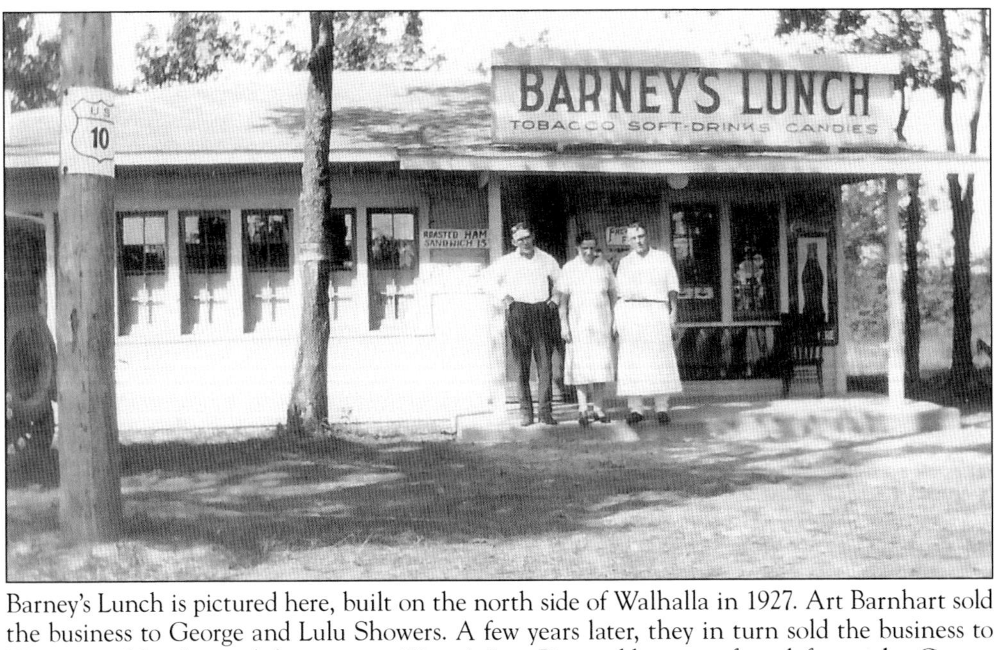

Barney's Lunch is pictured here, built on the north side of Walhalla in 1927. Art Barnhart sold the business to George and Lulu Showers. A few years later, they in turn sold the business to Weaver, and he changed the name to Wever's Inn. Pictured here are, from left to right, George and Lulu Showers and Art Barnhart. (Courtesy of Wayne Johnston.)

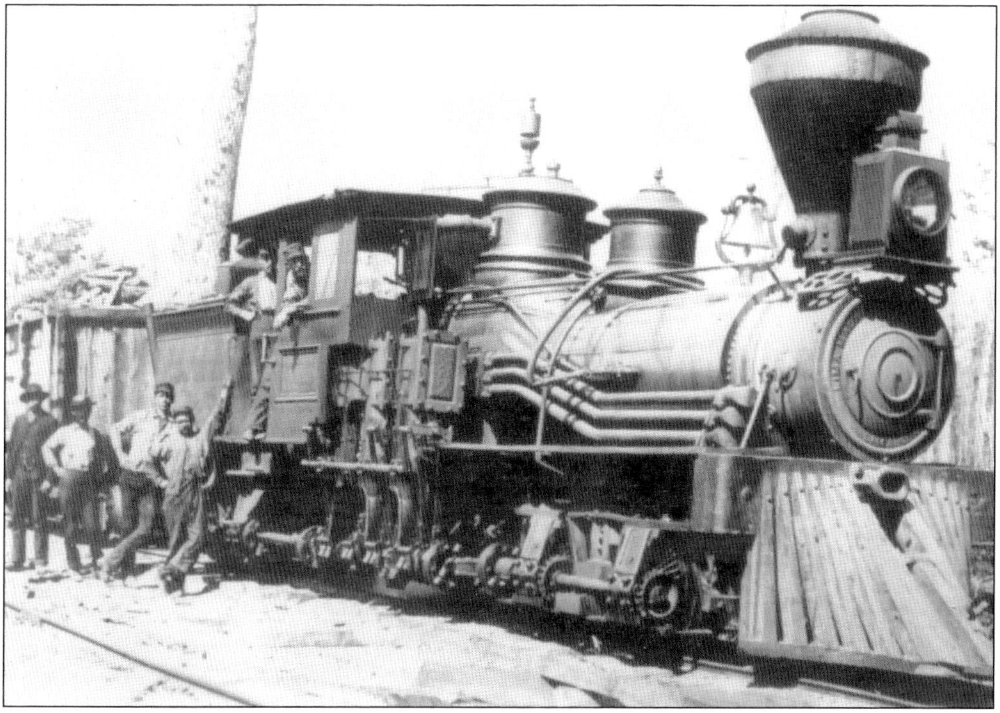

Originally named Merritt and Butters Junction, it was then Manistee Junction in 1882 due to the railroad spur (pictured) running north past Tallman, extending to Manistee. Dr. Arpad Barothy of Chicago discovered mineral springs on the south bank of the Pere Marquette River. He was instrumental in having the name changed to Walhalla ("haven of rest") in order to promote the health spa he wished to build. (Author's collection.)

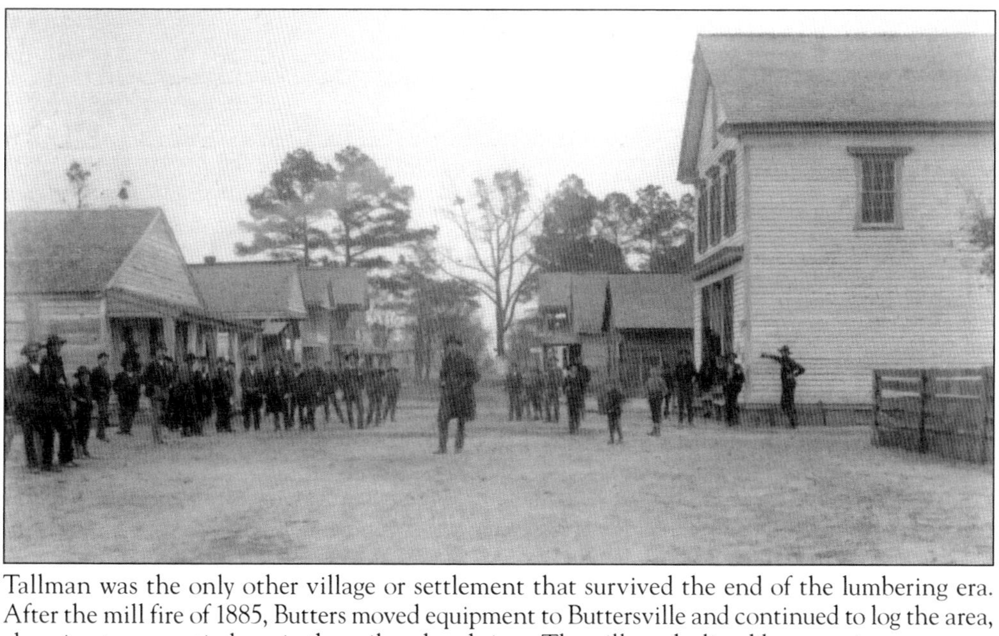

Tallman was the only other village or settlement that survived the end of the lumbering era. After the mill fire of 1885, Butters moved equipment to Buttersville and continued to log the area, choosing to move timber via the railroad and river. The village declined but remains as a resort area with many beautiful lakes and recreational opportunities. (Author's collection.)

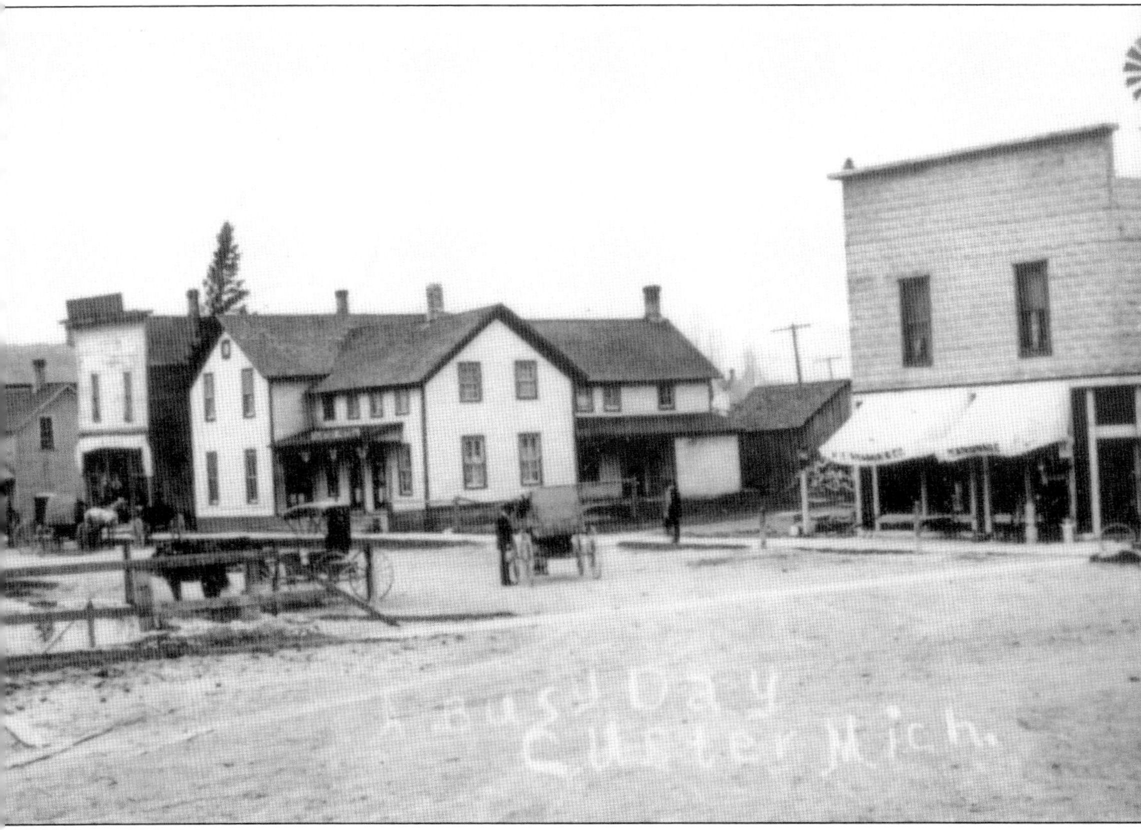

Custer Township was originally a part of Eden Township but separated with the first elections in April 1879. Originally rich in white pine, the area was lumbered off by the end of the 19th century, and agriculture took hold in those parts of the township that could support farming. Custer Township shared an Indian reservation with Eden Township, which was established in 1855. The last native village in Mason County was located there, just south of Custer in an area referred to a Herrickville. Interestingly enough, the original settlement south of present-day Custer was originally called Black Creek after its first resident and located on the Pere Marquette River. The area was also known as Ferryville in 1875 and renamed Custer in 1878 after Gen. George Armstrong Custer. Early in its history, residents settled near the river, but the community moved north as the Pere Marquette Railway came through the area in 1874. The main center of business moved again after the post office was built on present-day US 10 Highway in 1950. (Courtesy of MCHS.)

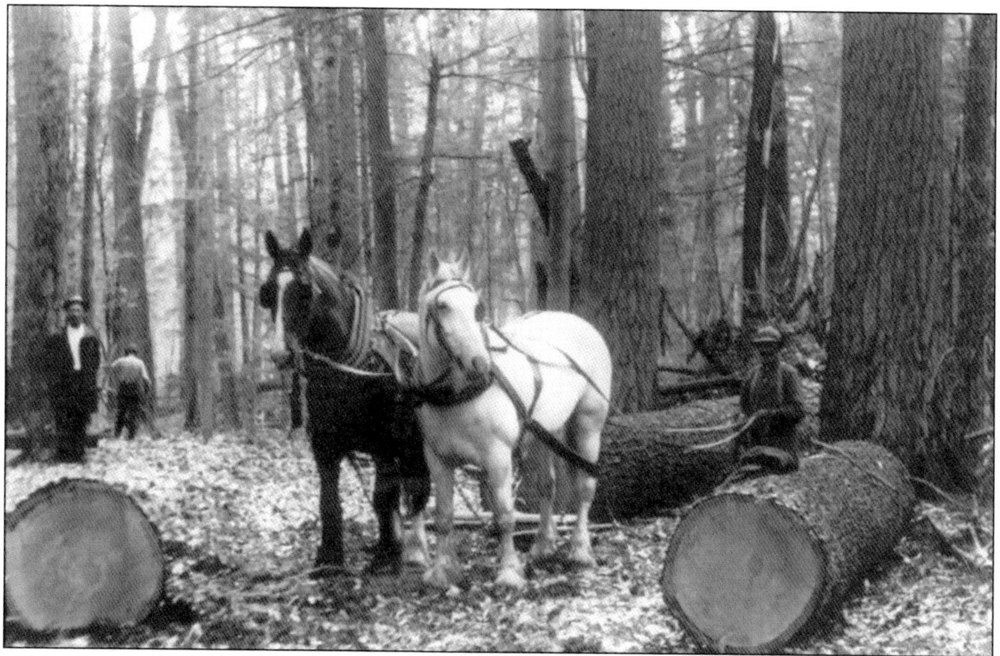

Extensive logging revealed that portions of southern Custer Township were not well suited to farming, as the lands there were quite sandy, unlike the areas in the northern part of the township. Years after the area was logged, the CCC came in and planted thousands of seedlings to reclaim the area. (Author's collection.)

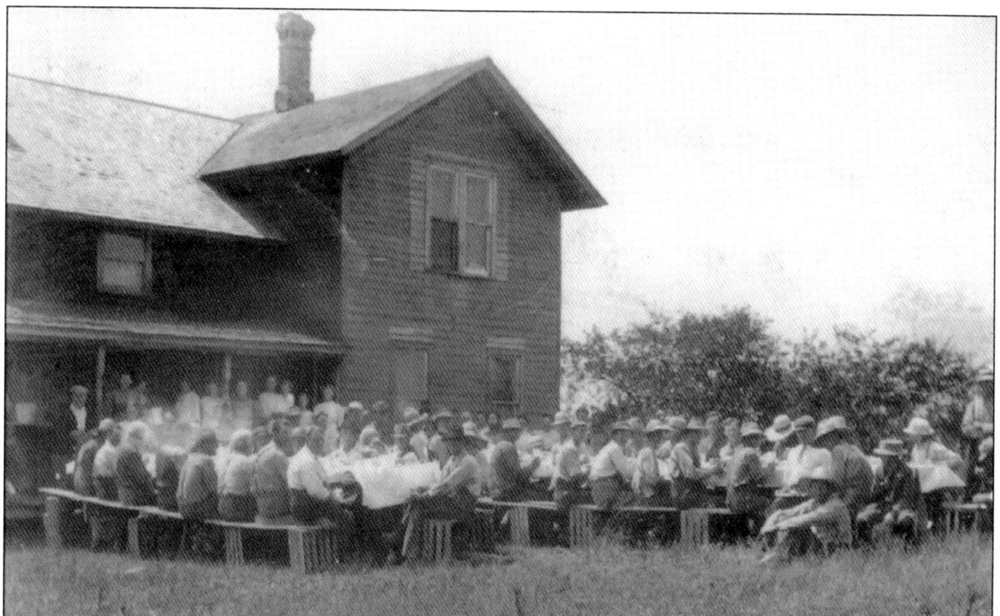

In years past, the humble barn played an important role in the community for its people and their work, livelihood, and entertainment. Often the barn was built before the house, and the family bunked in with the livestock and machinery until the house was completed. This image was taken in 1913 at the barn-raising dinner for Robert Johnson in Section 32 of Custer Township on Wilson Road. (Courtesy of Eric Blocher.)

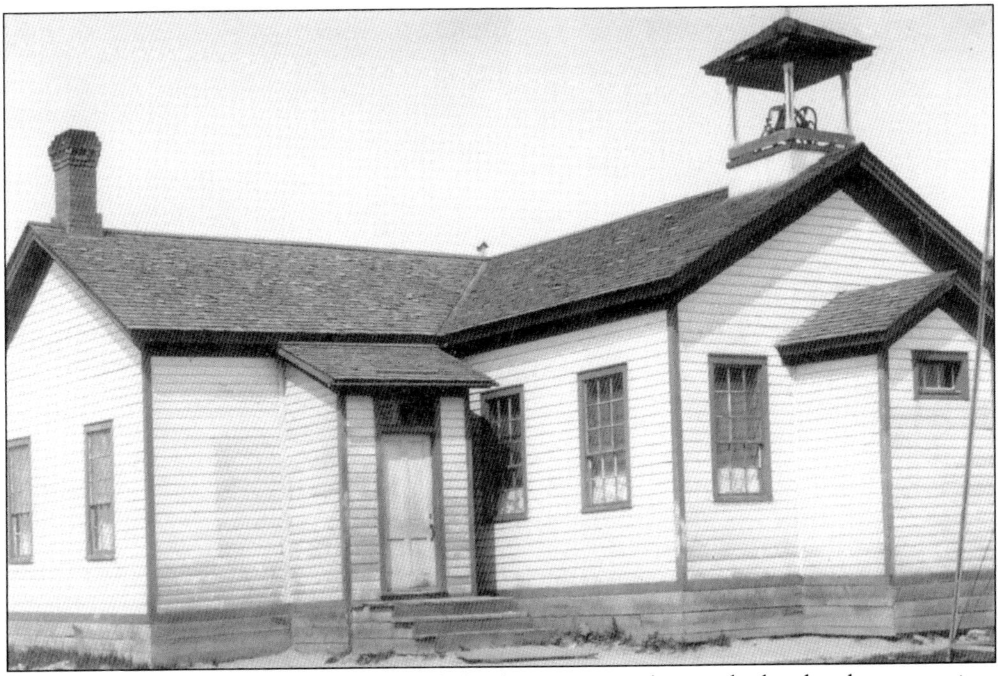

Resseguie School was built in 1859 to provide for the native population who lived at the reservation. The original school board was entirely made up of Native Americans, including Good John. The first school was built of logs, the second shown here was a framed building, and the third was built of blocks. Other one-room schools in the Custer system were Weldon Creek, McClellan, Wilson, Riverside, and Menninger. (Courtesy of the Iva Resseguie collection.)

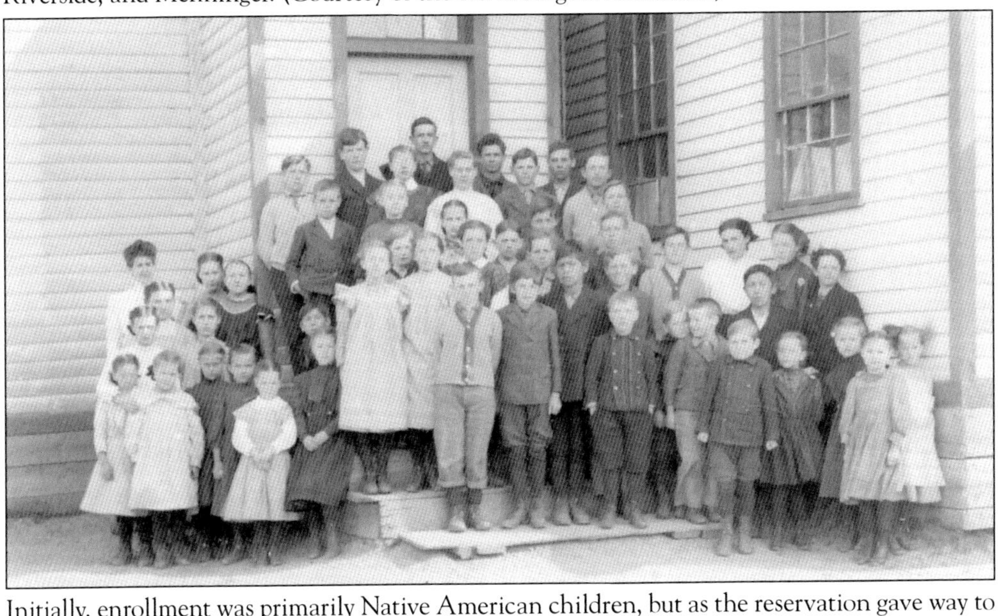

Initially, enrollment was primarily Native American children, but as the reservation gave way to farms and new settlers, the makeup of the school's students began to change. By 1900, there were upward of 60 students enrolled, and the frame schoolhouse was replaced by a new concrete-block building in 1911. Schools were consolidated in the late 1950s, and the rural schools were closed. (Courtesy of the Iva Resseguie collection.)

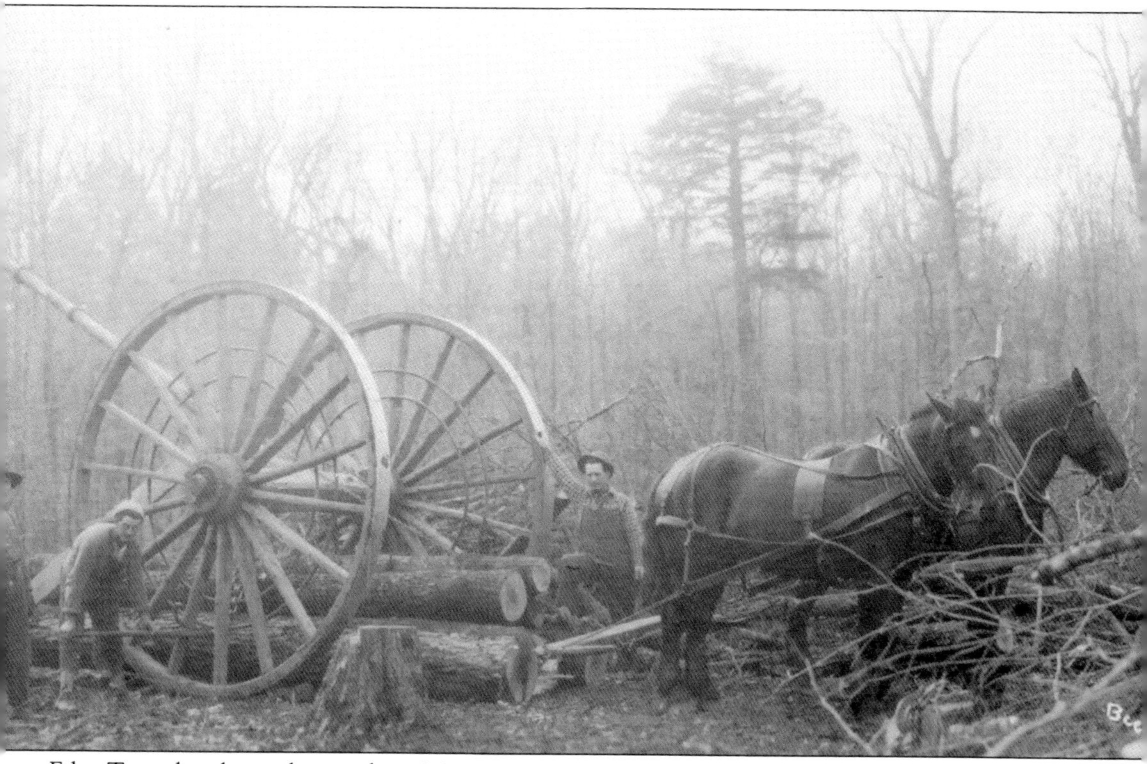

Eden Township, located in southern Mason County, was established in 1878 and originally part of the lands set aside for an Indian reservation in 1855. The reservation took in part of northern Oceana County as well as what would be Eden and Custer Townships in Mason County. Communities in Eden included Fern and Wiley. Originally, Fern was called Adamsville, but the name was later changed in recognition of the ferns that grew in great numbers in the vicinity. Wiley was named for Lemuel Wiley and his wife, Sarah, who arrived in 1869. The Murphy Brothers Lumber Camp in Eden Township illustrates work in the pinery using big wheels developed by Silas Overpack of Manistee. Eden Township was established in 1878 after being divided from Custer Township. Eden's primary product was the lumber that was taken from its forests. The Mason & Oceana Railroad transported logs from as far south as Walkerville to Buttersville. The township remains a rural area with large sections of land in the Manistee National Forest. (Courtesy of MCHS.)

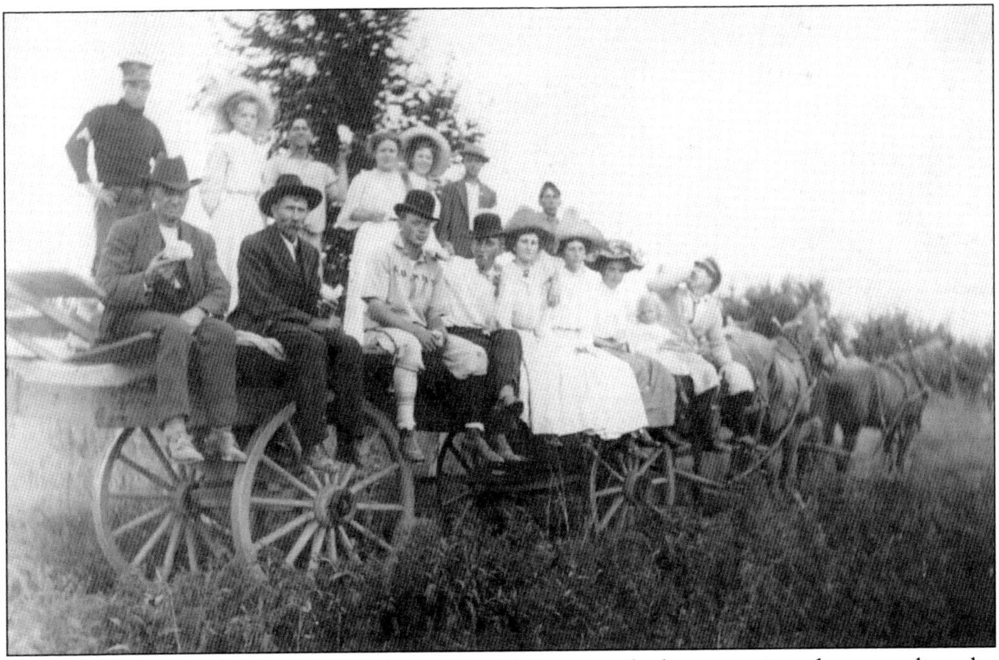

Going to a ball game in 1906 took a little more planning and a lot more time than traveling the same distance today. The inscription on the back of this image states, "We got so hungry on the way home that we stopped and luckily the lady sold us 2 loaves of bread and it was delicious." (Courtesy of MCHS.)

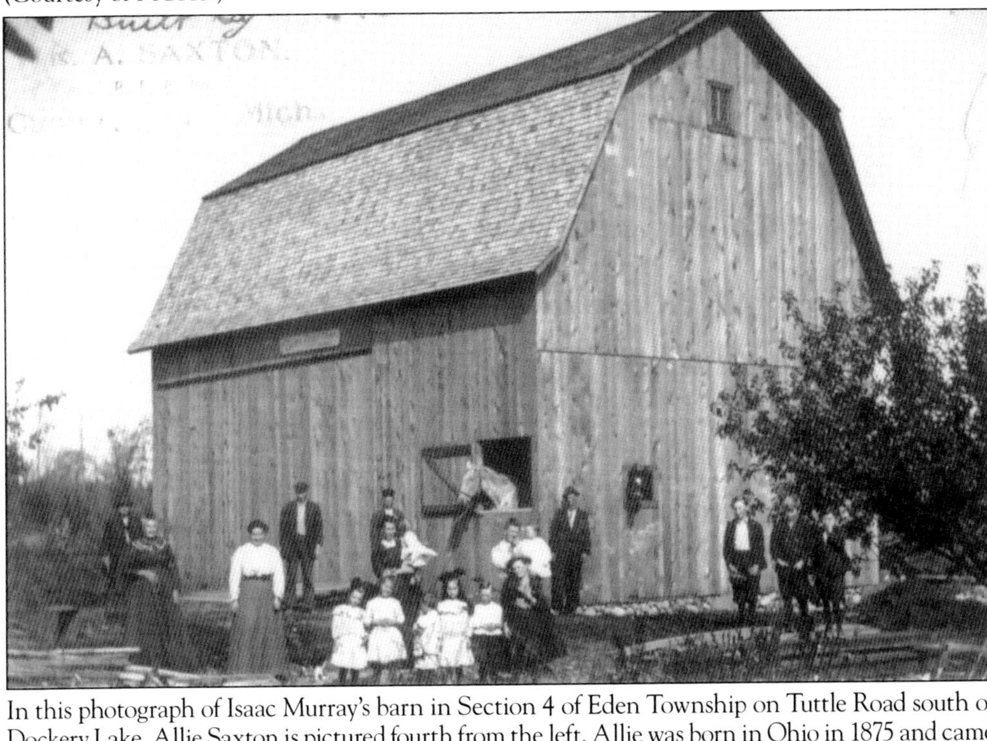

In this photograph of Isaac Murray's barn in Section 4 of Eden Township on Tuttle Road south of Dockery Lake, Allie Saxton is pictured fourth from the left. Allie was born in Ohio in 1875 and came to Eden Township about 1895 after his marriage to Laura Brovont. (Courtesy of Eric Blocher.)

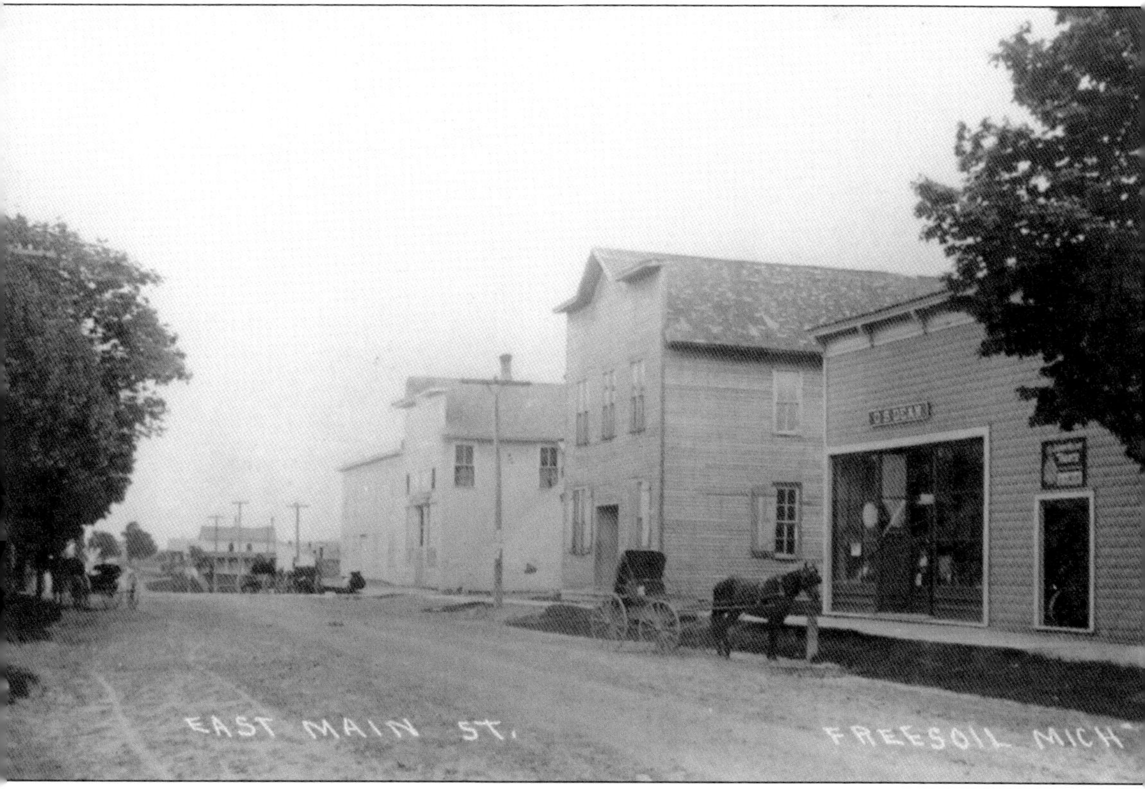

Freesoil Township was one of three original townships in Mason County. Grant and Mead Townships were later carved from Freesoil Township, which spanned the top third of the county. The first township meeting was held at the home of Charles Freeman in the spring of 1855. The isolation of a veritable wilderness experienced in the outer reaches of the county at that time must have certainly put the hardiest pioneer to the test. In an article in the August 27, 1941, issue of the *Daily News*, the beginnings of Freesoil are discussed, and the reader is asked to imagine what it would be like to be in a small, cleared space in the forest, living in a crude log cabin, with a team of oxen and the barest of necessities to survive in the wilderness. For pioneers to purchase or trade supplies, even for those close to the rivers and the villages of Lincoln or Pere Marquette, it was a journey of two days to make the round-trip to a store or the gristmill at Lincoln. (Courtesy of MCHS.)

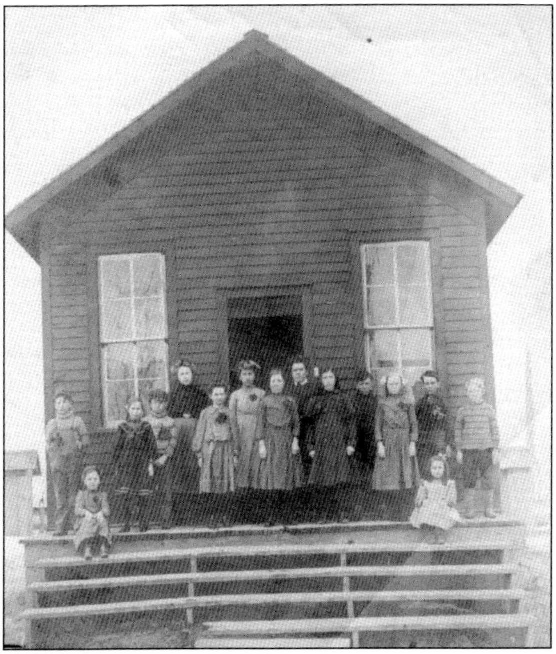

Old Freesoil was located at the mouth of Guerney Creek, now part of Grant Township. The village of Freesoil came about after early resident Philip Ritter built his home and was joined by many other loggers of the region north of Freesoil toward Manistee. In 1870, a log building constructed on the Ritter farm housed the first school (School District No. 2). (Courtesy of Benita Eddy Hurd.)

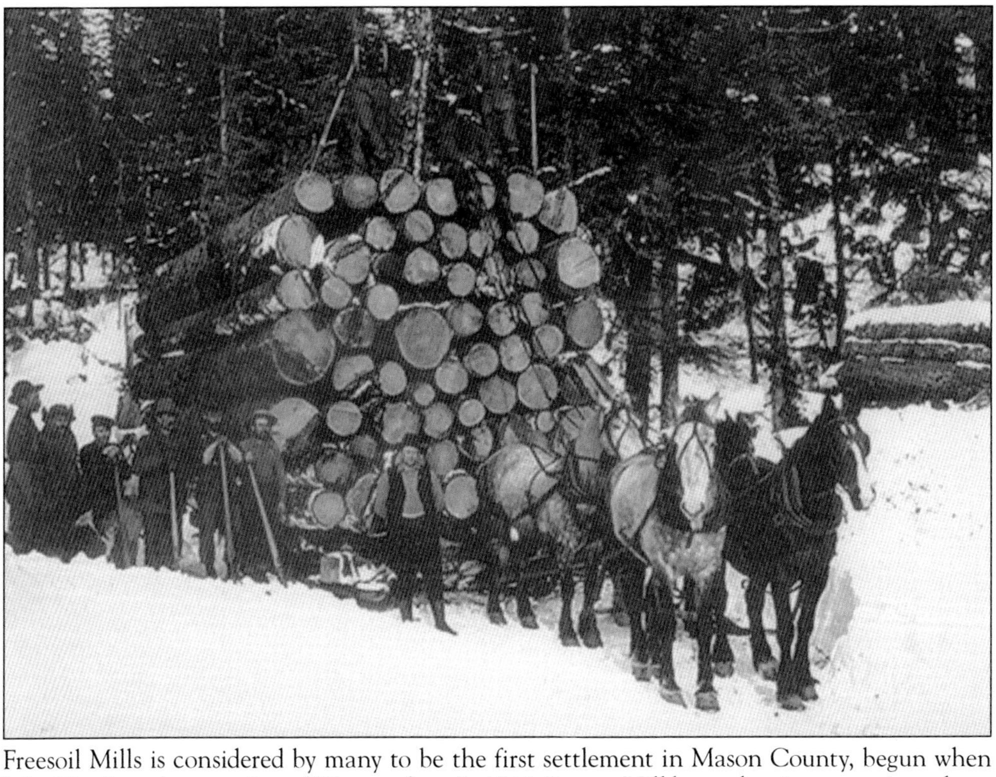

Freesoil Mills is considered by many to be the first settlement in Mason County, begun when John Harris took possession of 37 acres there in 1844. Porters Mill began logging operations about 1845, but after the mill burned, it was not rebuilt until 1855 by Freeman and Hopkins. As a result, the distinction of the first permanent settler of European descent in Mason County went to Burr Caswell in 1847. (Author's collection.)

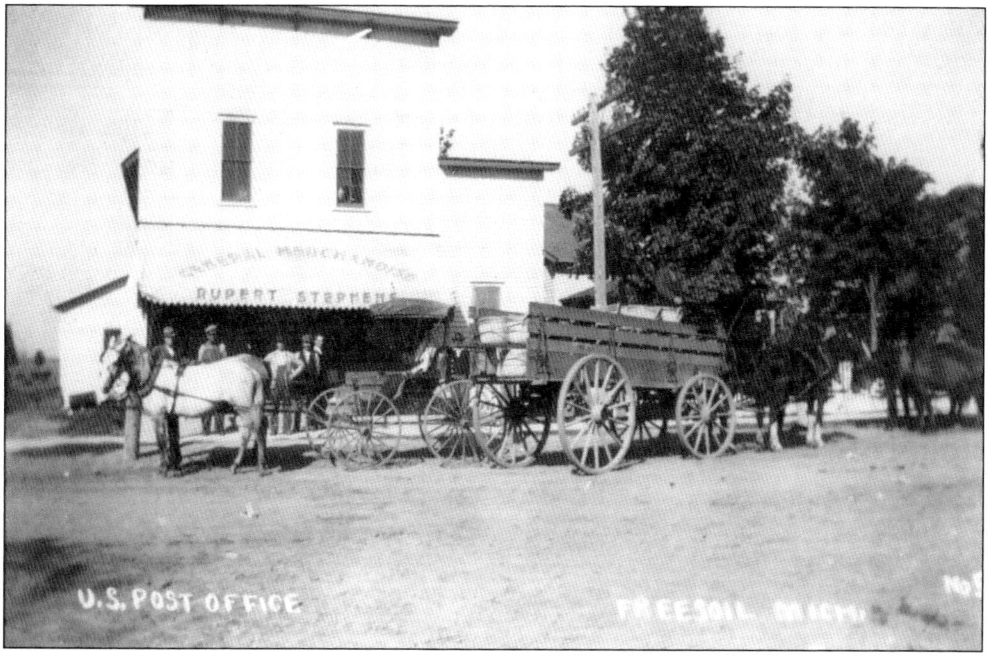

The village of Freesoil began in the early 1860s, and logging was the principal economy, followed by agriculture. The population of the village had grown to as much as 400 at one time. In 1880, Freesoil Township had 318 residents, which was during the reign of "King Pine," and it developed into a successful farming community after logging went bust. (Courtesy MCHS.)

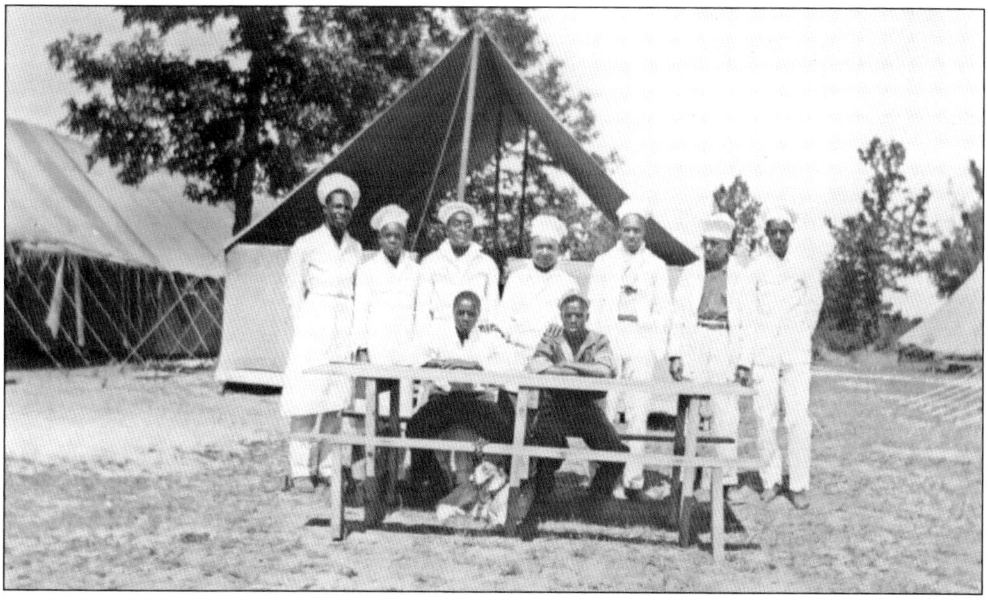

The CCC camp was located east of Freesoil and Freesoil Road, a quarter of a mile east of Campbell Road on the north side. It was later moved northwest of Freesoil, closer to the Manistee and the Mason County line, and called Camp Stronach. Other CCC camps were located near Walhalla and at the new Ludington State Park. (Courtesy of Benita Eddy Hurd.)

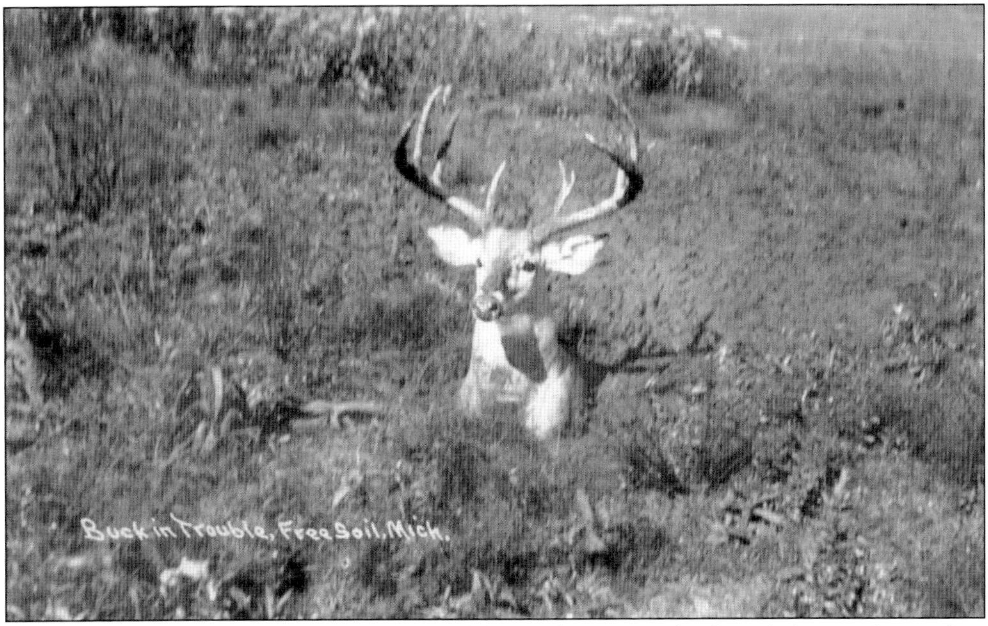

On Tuesday, September 22, 1936, Adolph Bialek found a 13-point buck neck deep in the muck at Gun Lake (above). He quickly found a group of local men, William Hunt, Frank Eddy, Laurence Tobey, and Clare Tubbs (below, second from left), and two campers from Indiana, Chester Jacobs and Virgil Cover, to help him save the animal from certain death. By working together and laying planks across the muck so that they could get close enough to place a rope around the buck's antlers, they were able to slowly pull the 200-pound animal from his dire situation. After removing the rope, it was reported that the buck slowly loped off into the nearby woods. (Both courtesy of Benita Eddy Hurd.)

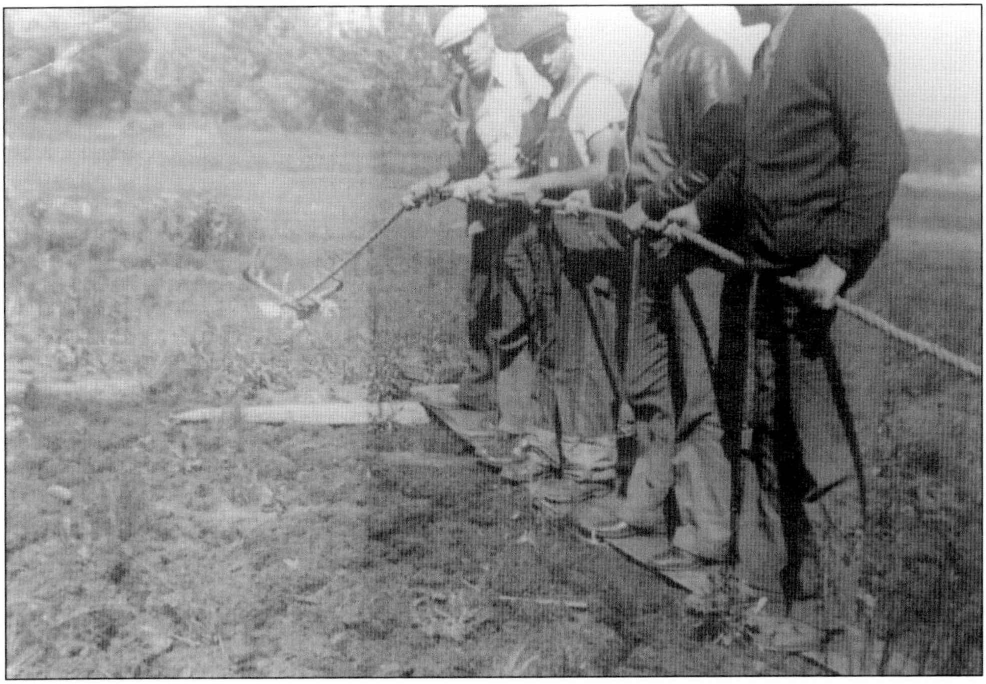

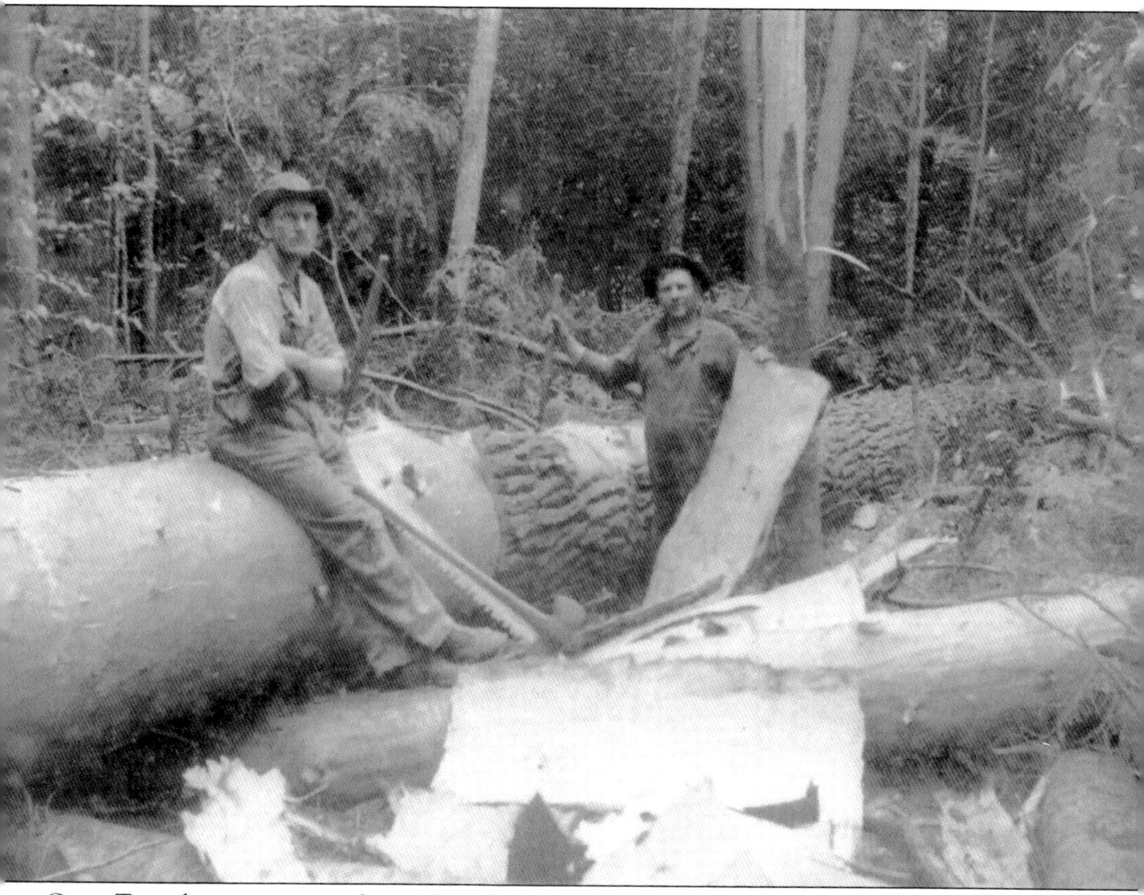

Grant Township was organized in 1867 and set out from Freesoil Township. At the first meeting, on April 6, 1868, only 19 votes were cast. Logging was the primary occupation and business of the area, with the earliest records indicating a mill at Old Freesoil located near where Guerney Creek empties into Lake Michigan. Old plat maps of the area show sections belonging to Charles Mears, Antoine Cartier, and other lumber barons who logged the area. The Huron Manistee National Forest takes in large sections of the township along with the Nordhouse Dunes Wilderness Area. The Big Sable River cuts through the southeastern corner of the township before emptying into Hamlin Lake, which is situated just to the south of the township's border with Hamlin Township. The small lake, named Nordhouse, is just to the north of Nurnberg Road and at various times dries up completely. Due to large tracts of land being included in the national park system, the population of the township in the 2000 census was only 850 people. (Author's collection.)

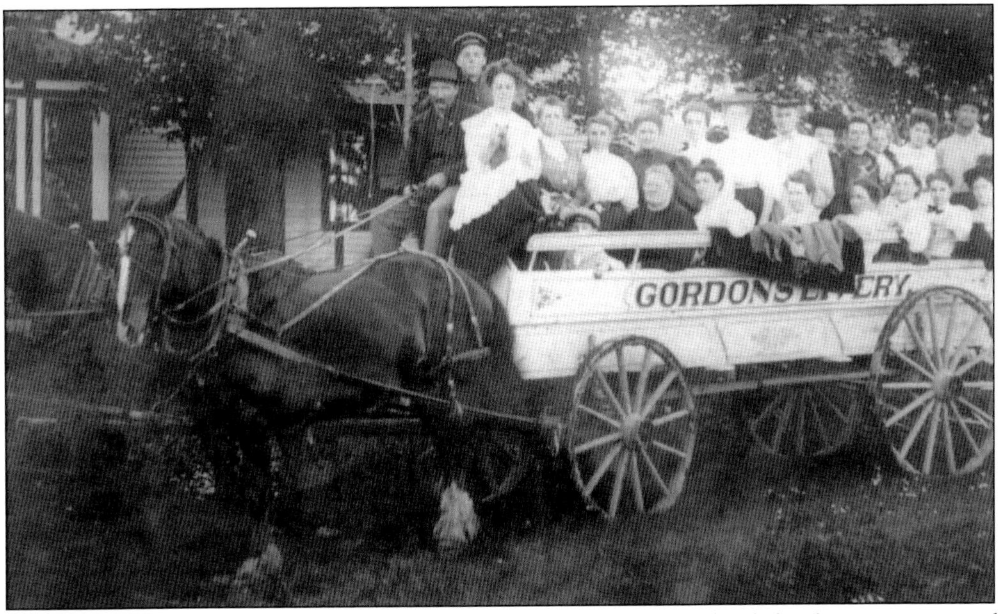

Newberry Gordon moved to Grant Township in 1871 with his family, his father being a veteran of the war. Gordon became known as one of the largest dealers of horses in Michigan. By 1900, he built a livery in the city of Scottville and by 1903 had moved to Scottville from Grant Township. (Courtesy of MCHS.)

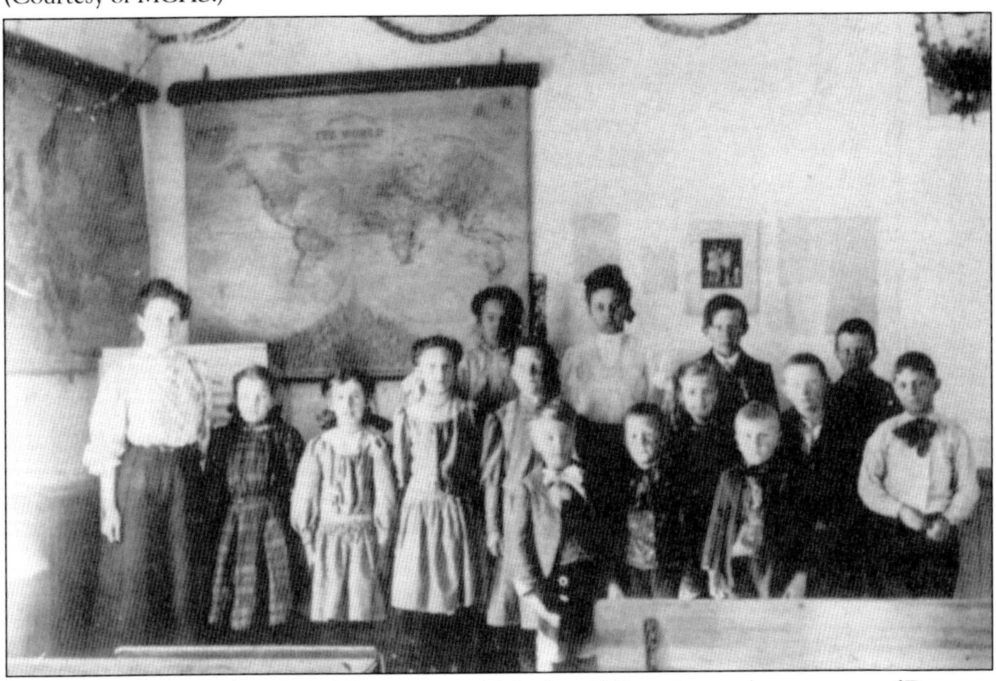

Grant Township schools included Freeman, established in 1870 on the southwest corner of Freeman and Quarterline Roads. Peltons School (pictured) was located on the west side of US 31 between Freeman and Freesoil Road and Lasalle on the corner of Lasalle and Hogue Roads. Old Freesoil was built in 1902 on the northeastern corner of Cass and Morton Roads and Center School on the east side of Quarterline between Koenig and Treml Roads. (Courtesy of MCHS.)

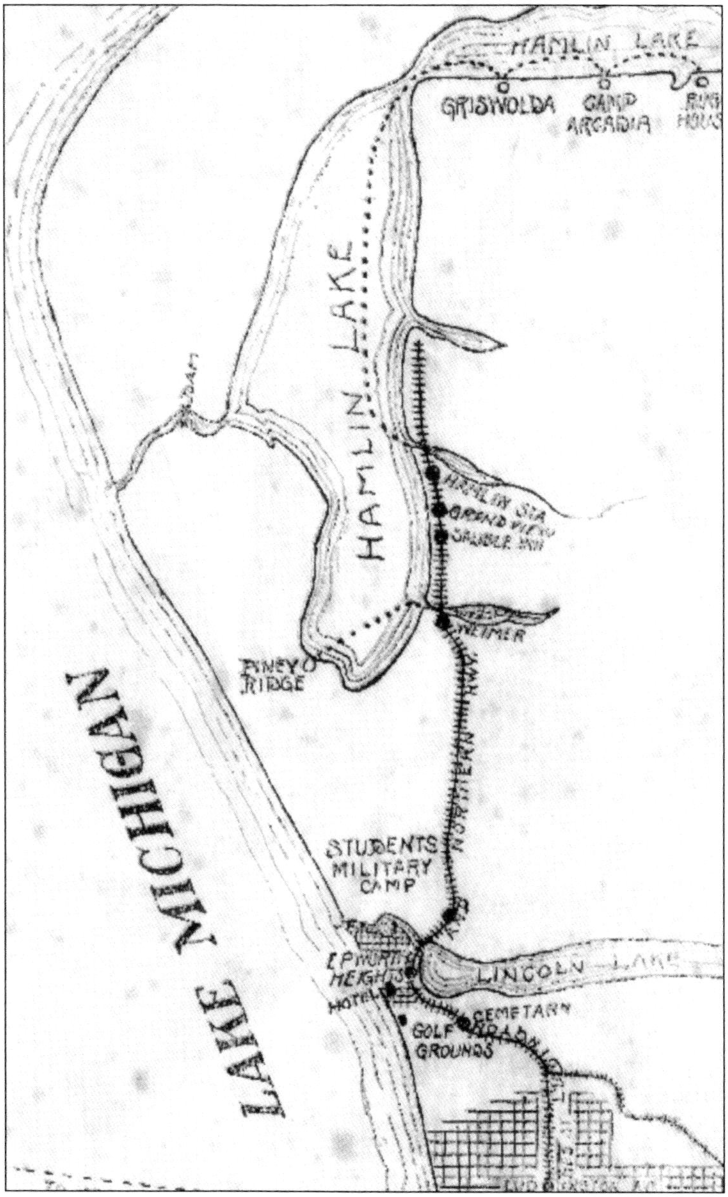

A brochure promoting Ludington on the lake as *the* vacation spot for weary city folk states, "Where you decide to go for your summer vacation should be selected with the same care and thought you might give an important investment, for your summer vacation is after all an investment in Health, Happiness, and Recreation." Hamlin Township, with its man-made lake, was the chief beneficiary of a campaign to move from lumbering to a tourism-based economy. Resorts appeared on the shores of the lake, and in 1913 many were accessible only by motor launch after taking a ride on the Ludington and Northern Railroad north to the middle bayou of Hamlin Lake. The dam at Hamlin (originally named Big Sable) has given way on several occasions since the first one was built in 1859 by Charles Mears. When it collapsed in 1887, the lumbering village of Hamlin was washed away. The dam collapsed again in 1888 and 1912. Originally built to aid Mears in moving timber to the mill at Hamlin, the resultant lake has been a boon to the local economy long past the days of lumbering. (Author's collection.)

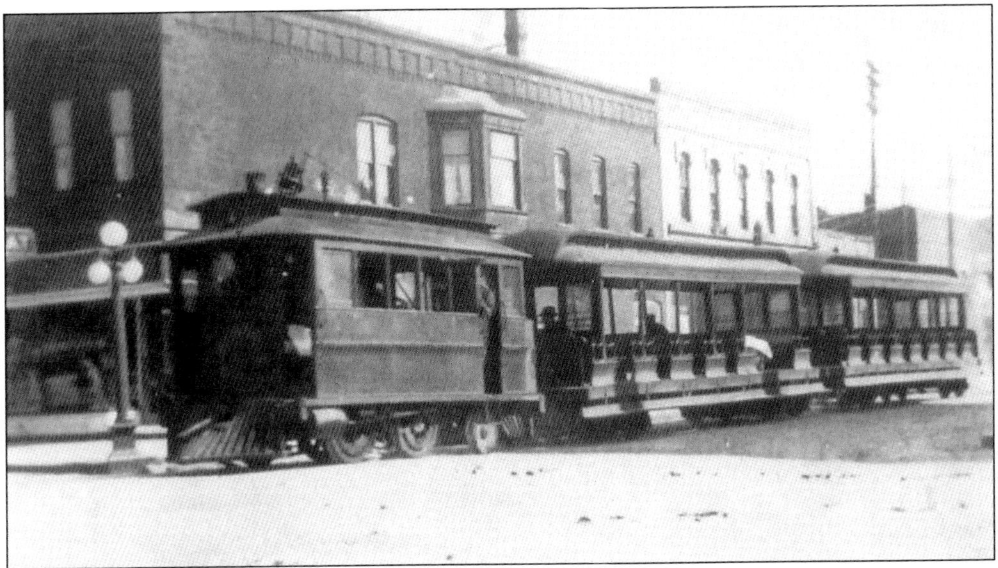

Many people are confused by the Ludington and Northern Railroad being called the "Dummy Train." The moniker has more to do with how the engine was constructed; a box for the engineer was literally constructed around the engine. It was a fake, not a real railroad engine, hence the name Dummy Train. Light, open-air cars were used to bring passengers to Epworth Heights and later to the stops and resorts on Hamlin Lake. (Author's collection.)

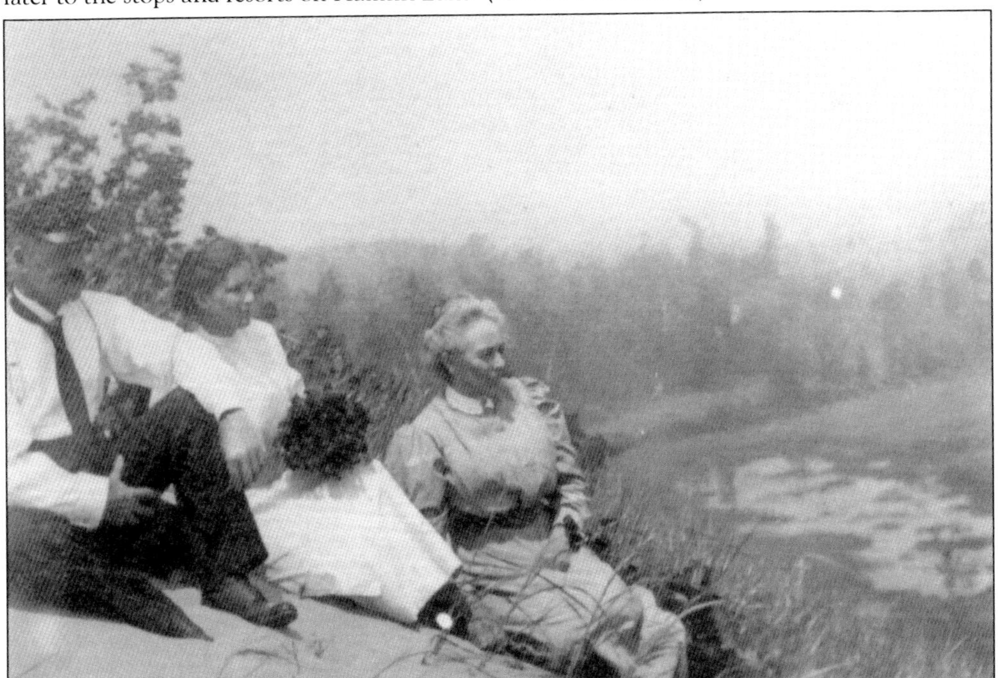

Mount Baldy was not really a mountain at all, but it was, however, the tallest dune north of Epworth Heights. It was the destination of picnickers and resorters, and people could not have said they took in all the local attractions unless they climbed Mount Baldy. The dune was a financial boon, for the sand was of great quality, and carload after carload was hauled off to the foundries until it was gone forever. (Author's collection.)

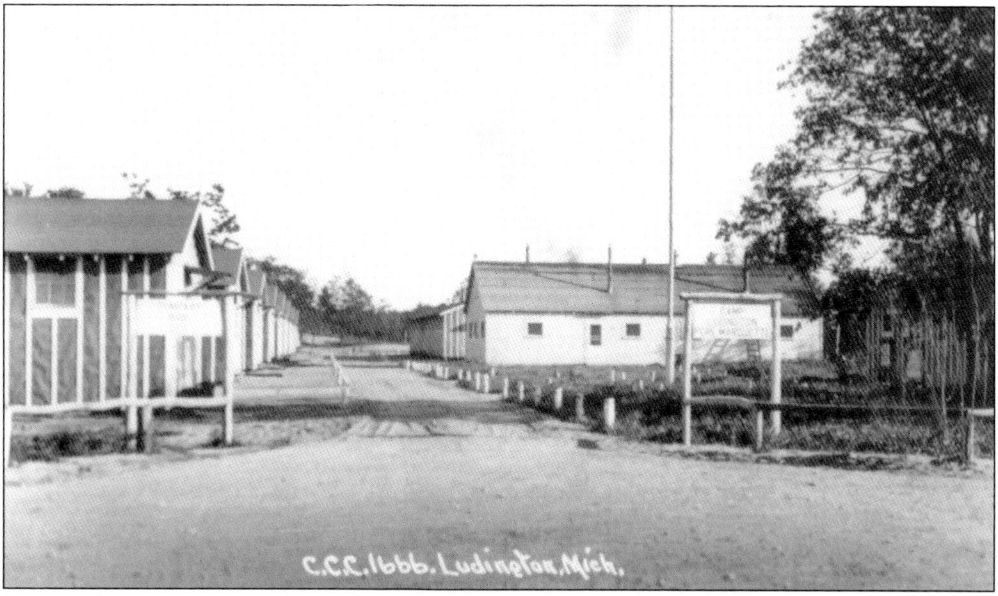

During the 1930s, Roosevelt's New Deal saw the creation of the Civilian Conservation Corps. Camps were filled with young men, many of whom had never been away from home, to take part in public-works projects all over the country. One such camp was located at the newly created Ludington State Park, where residents undertook the building of trails and shelters, many of which are still in use today in what has become "the queen of Michigan state parks." (Courtesy of Carol Elve.)

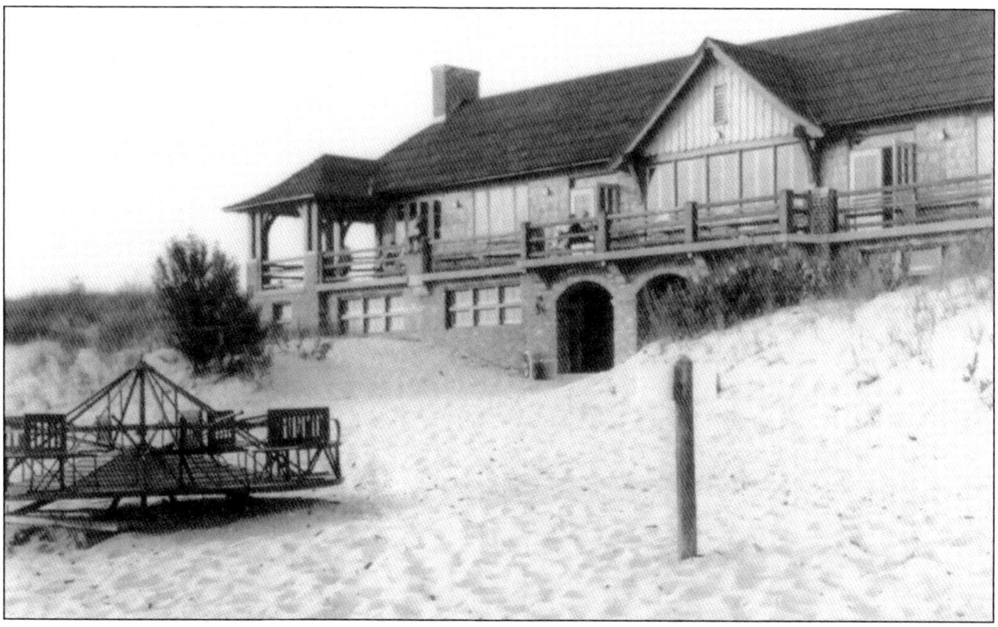

The "CCC Boys," as they were called, built the beach house, shelters, and trails at the Ludington State Park. During the Depression, the CCC Boys cleared the trails and made general improvements. It gave a purpose to young men to create something that benefited everyone, and the park continues to be a beacon calling out to those weary of a busy life to come and enjoy the lakes and woods. (Courtesy of Carol Elve.)

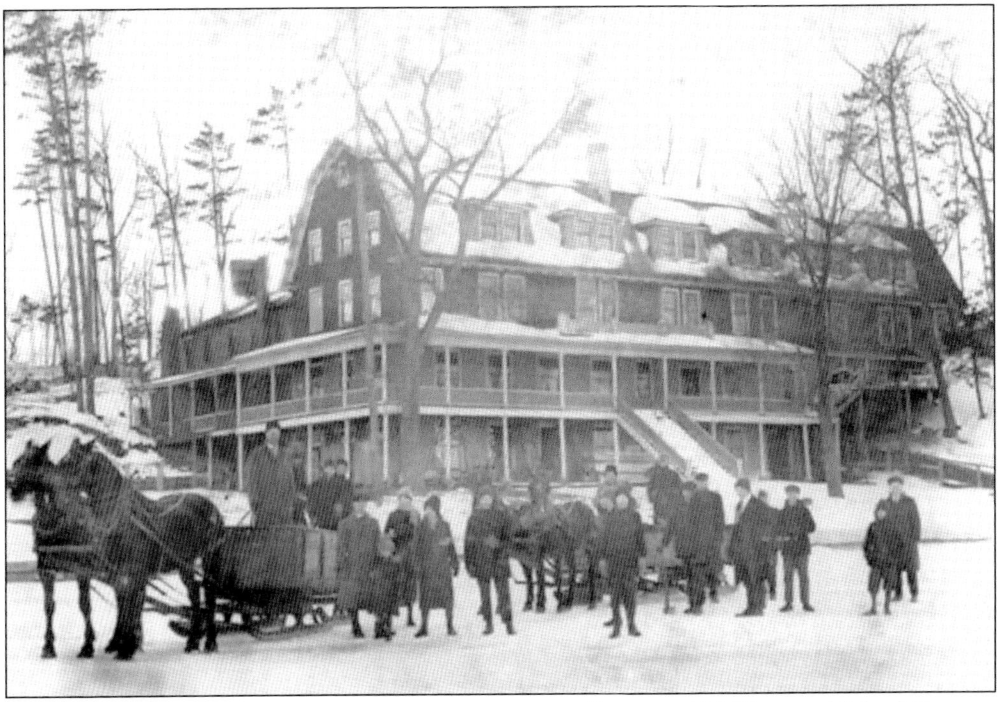

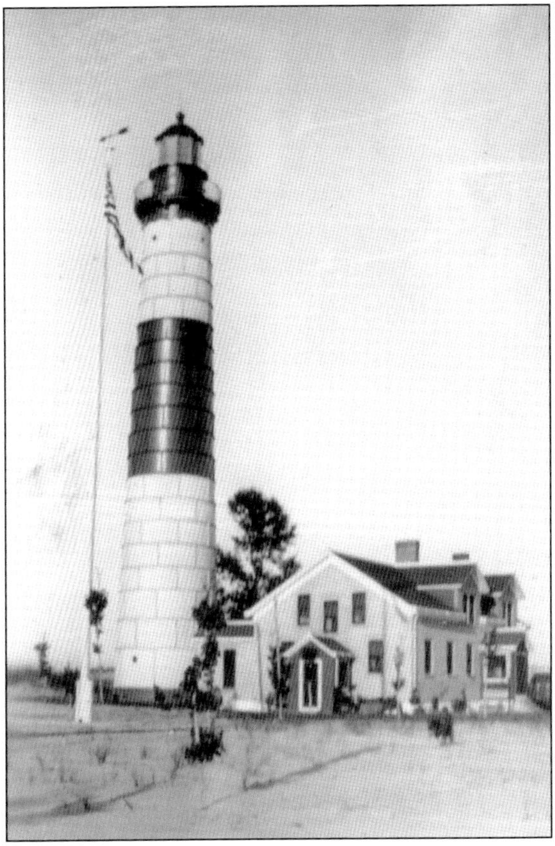

Carter and Helling established Piney Ridge Resort in 1901 at a cost of $10,000. The 40-room hotel did not celebrate its formal opening until July 4, 1902. The hotel was constructed just to the front of the old Hudson Bay Lodge, and at 40 feet by 60 feet and three stories high, it dwarfed the old structure completely. The Hudson Bay Lodge was built in 1894 by William Hudson, a Civil War veteran and one-time Ludington postmaster. (Courtesy of Sylvia Nickelson.)

The Big Sable Lighthouse was built in 1867 at a cost of $35,000. Originally, its brick exterior was difficult for mariners to identify; to improve visibility and reinforce the structure, the steel casing was painted white and black around 1900. This made it a better aid to navigation and transformed the structure to the familiar one seen today. (Author's collection.)

Margaret Petersen is sitting near the dock of one of the more popular haunts around Ludington until it burned. Scotty's Wrens Roost was built on the shore of the middle bayou and was a favorite among residents who could enjoy a perch dinner at their table with the water lapping literally at their feet under the deck. (Author's collection.)

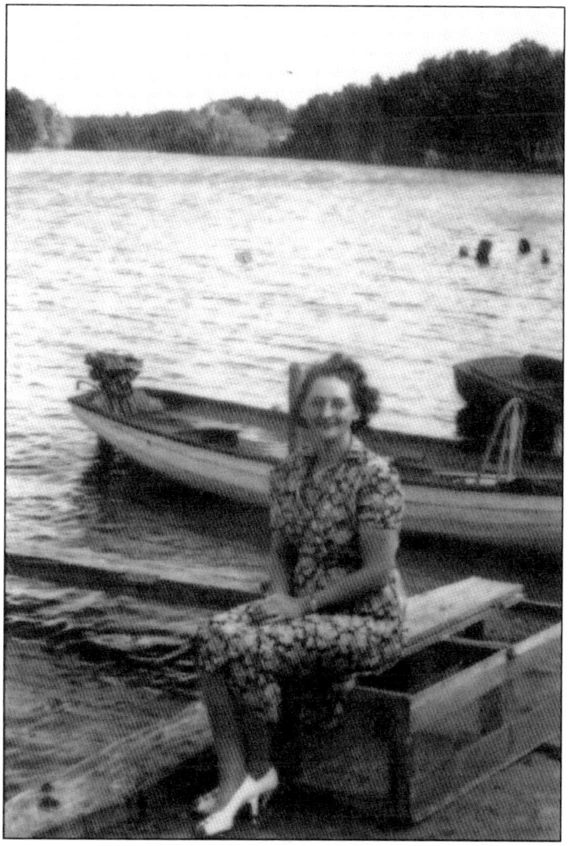

The Sable Inn Resort was serviced by the Ludington and Northern Railway, and during the resort season, one could expect the train to make a round-trip every half hour as it ferried resorters back and forth for the price of 25¢. As roads were improved and more families bought automobiles, passenger use declined, and the railway was discontinued in 1919. (Author's collection.)

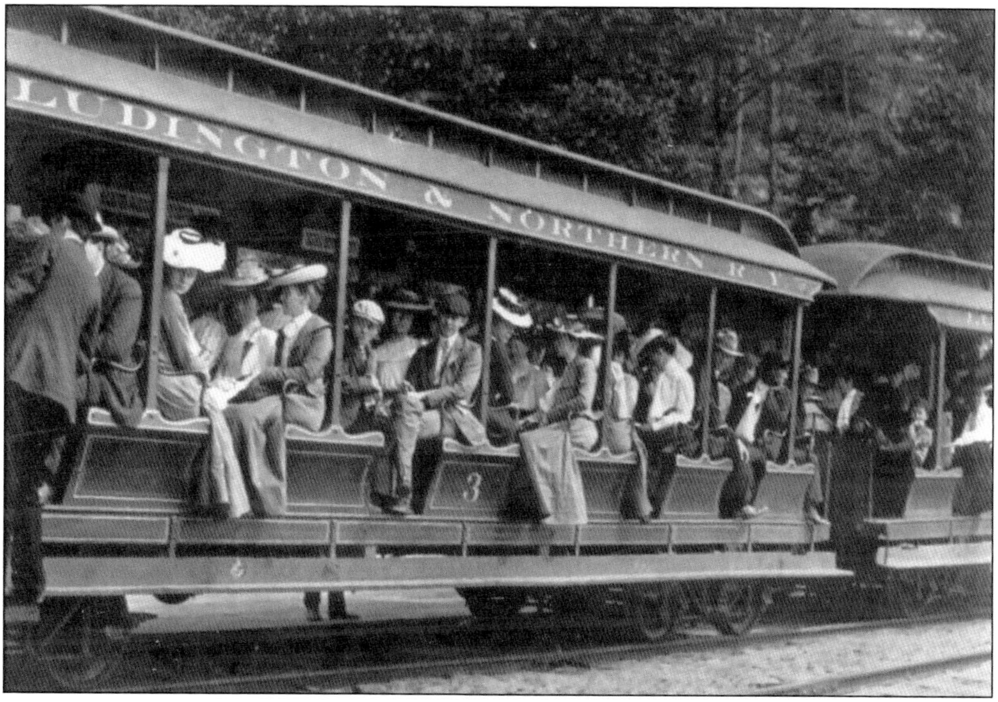

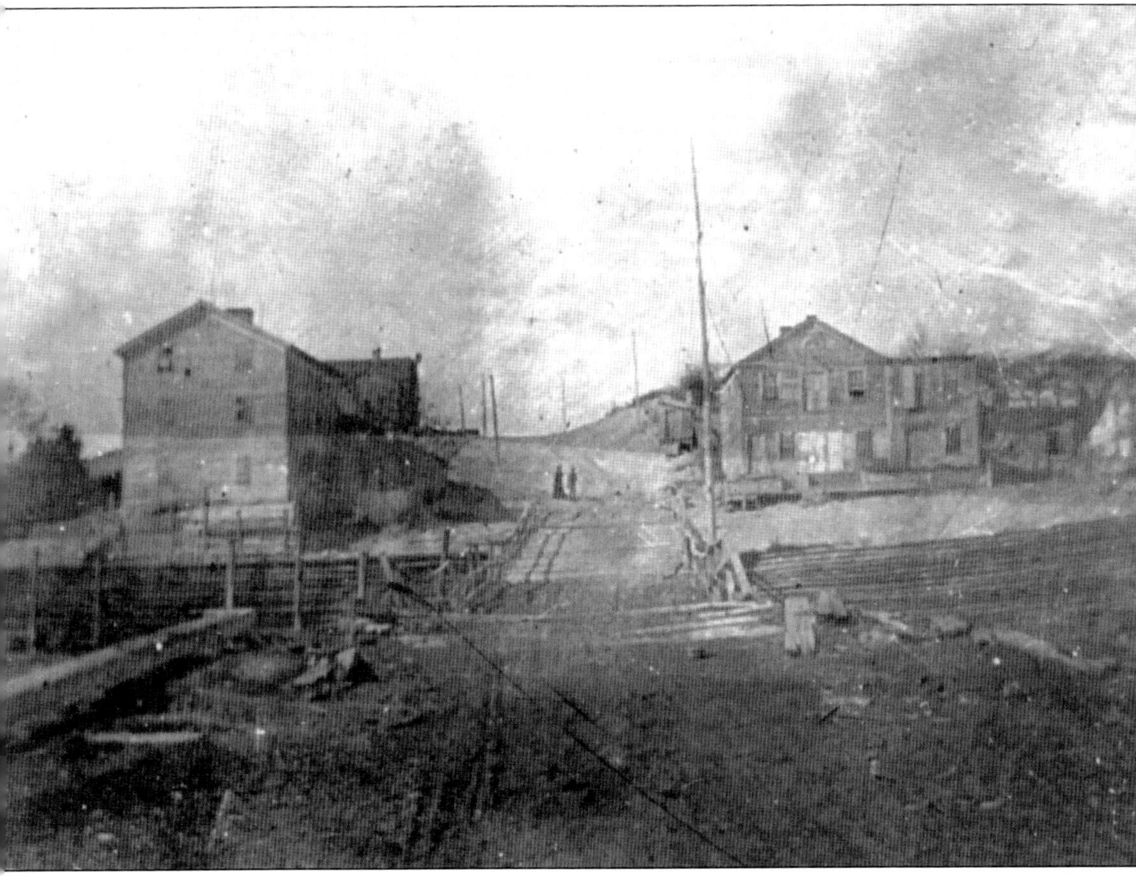

Charles Mears succeeded in having the county seat moved to Lincoln Village in 1861. After being elected to the Michigan Senate, he used his influence to change the names of Little Sable to Lincoln (his choice for president) and Big Sable to Hamlin (his choice for vice president). The year 1861 saw the formation of Lincoln Township squeezed in between Hamlin, Amber, and Pere Marquette. The lands that comprised the village were owned by Charles Mears. It was built primarily on the north side of what was originally called Little Sable River. The village boasted a three-story boardinghouse, grist and sawmills, a big store, docks for lumber schooners, and a post office in 1855. The area boasted a spacious, well-stocked store building, and a boardinghouse towered above the cottages of the workmen. White picket fences protected the gardens that ornamented the village yards. Mills, stores, houses, and fences were refurbished each spring with a fresh coat of whitewash. Big Sable was four years younger than its sister village but differed little except in size. (Courtesy of Epworth Museum.)

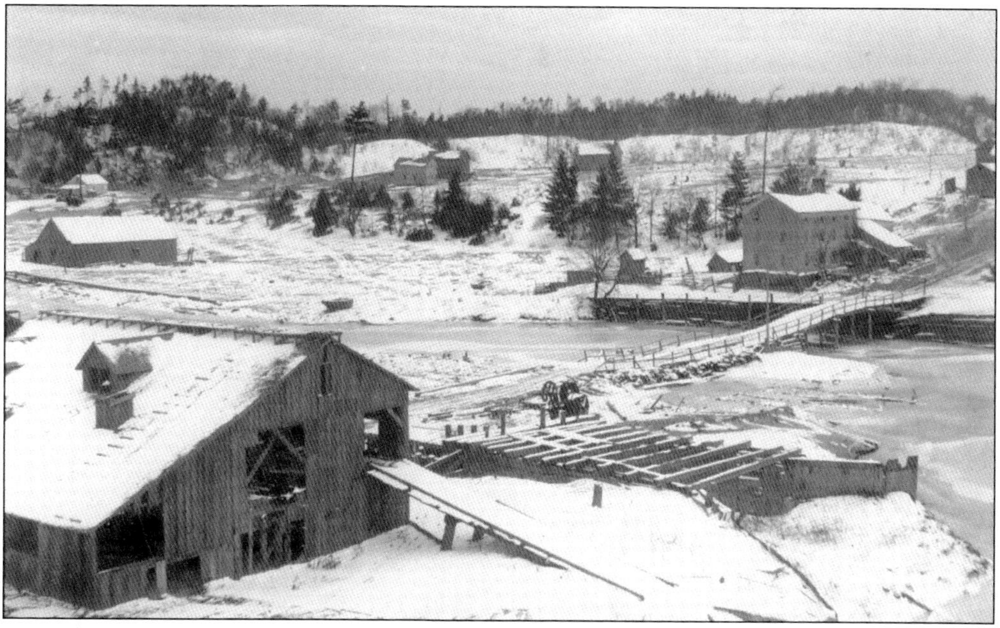

According to *Sand, Sawdust, and Saw Logs* by Frances Caswell Hanna, "By the late fifties Little Sable which had been born in 1851 was growing healthily. A wooden was dam built where the lake narrowed to form a channel into Lake Michigan which now generated sufficient power to run the mills. The Lincoln Dam washed out and in 1884 Pardee and Cook closed the mills. Families moved out and moved on to find work." (Author's collection.)

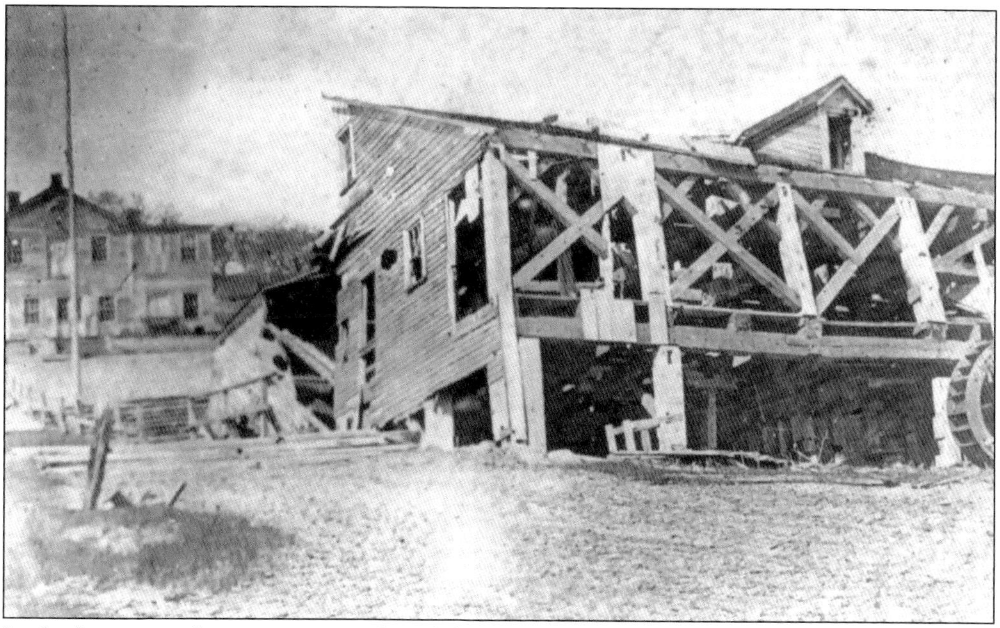

In the beginning, business was good, and the gristmill was a center of commerce. The *Charles Mears*, built in 1856, and the lumber schooner *Blackhawk* were two of the vessels that made regular trips to carry mill workers, settlers, and their families and goods. By 1870, Charles Mears certainly must have seen the writing on the wall and sold his lands and interests in Hamlin and Lincoln to Pardee and Cook in order to consolidate his business in Oceana County. (Author's collection.)

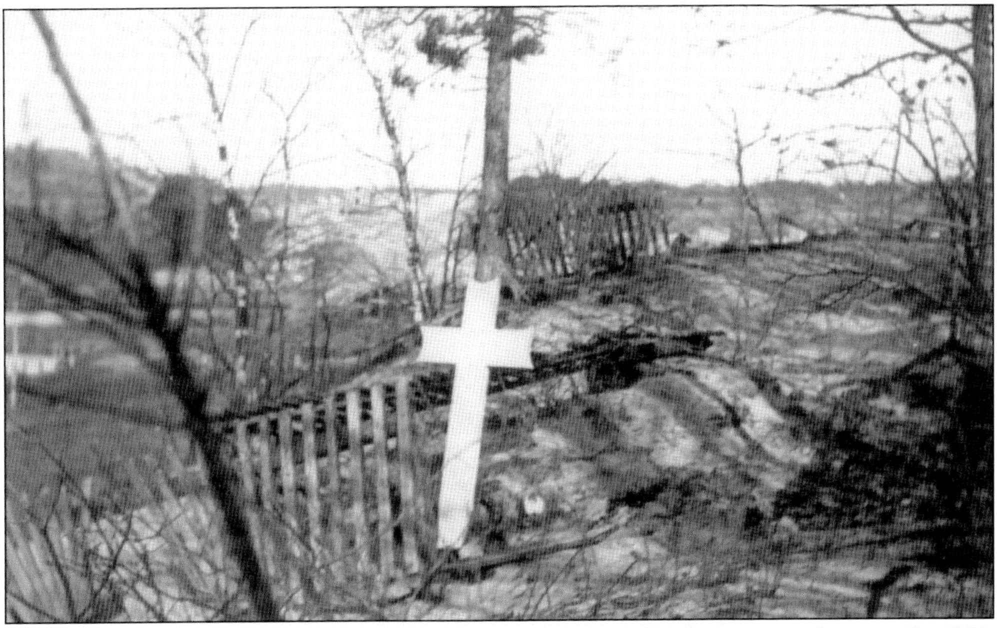

From the cemetery hill, the remains of the old courthouse in the distance can be seen. By 1884, the town was deserted, and in 1891 the township was absorbed into adjoining townships. When Epworth was formed in 1894, Lincoln Village had passed into the dubious distinction of ghost town. Lumber was scavenged from the remaining buildings, and what was left of a once-promising village became summer cottages. (Author's collection.)

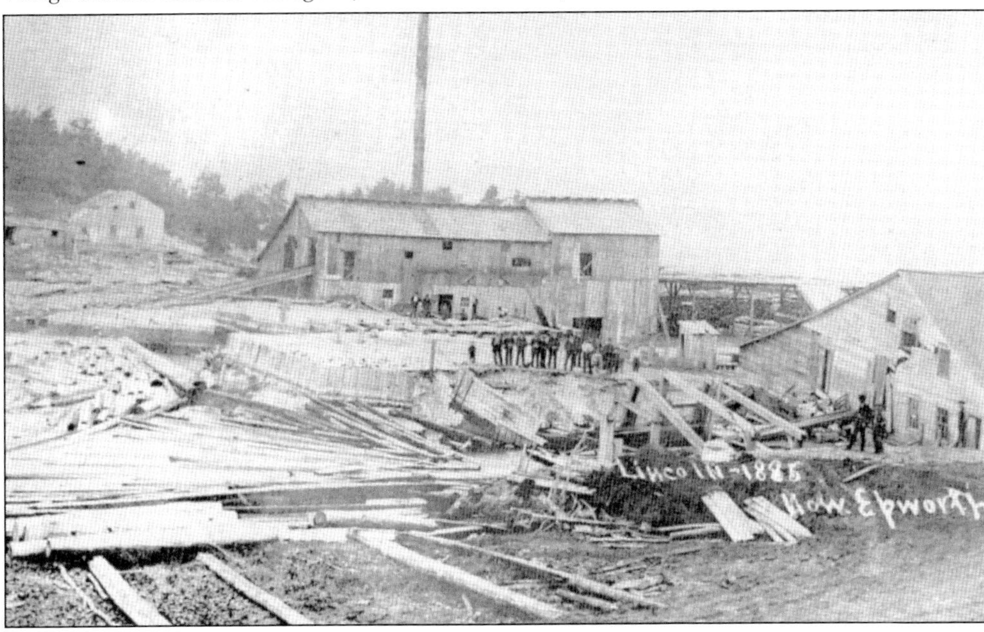

Mears originally claimed the lands surrounding the Big and Little Sable Rivers because the land at Pere Marquette was taken by Joseph Boyden, and the lands at Freesoil were taken by Wheeler and Harris. Trade was good, as ships brought a variety of goods from Chicago for residents and employees of Mears's mills at both Big and Little Sable. When the ships left, they were loaded with furs, maple sugar, and lumber products. (Author's collection.)

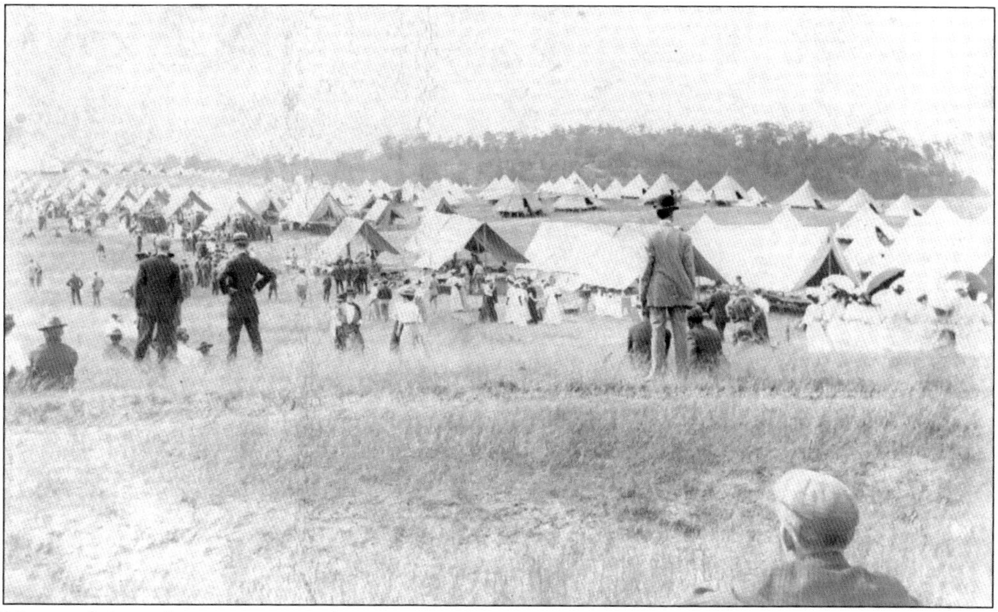

National Guard encampments began in Ludington after the guard was offered use of Lincoln fields for summer exercises. Thousands of men descended on Ludington, arriving in their troop train and disembarking to set up at their new camp. Exercises took place for several weeks over the summer until the Michigan National Guard secured land in Northern Michigan and moved operations to the Gaylord area. (Author's collection.)

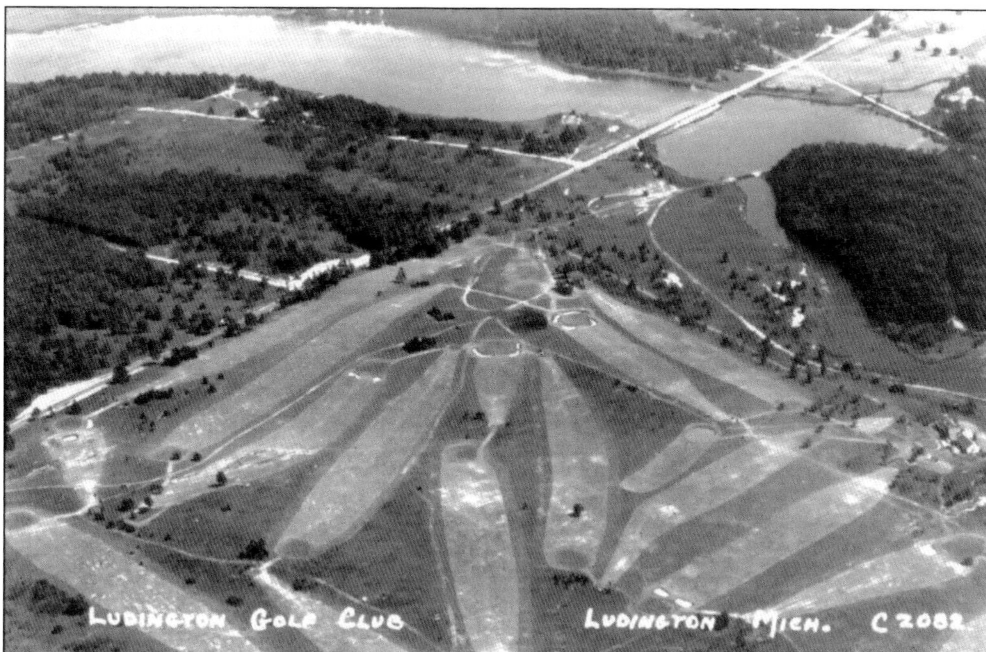

This aerial photograph illustrates the layout of the Lincoln Hills Golf Course, built over what was once the practice grounds for the Michigan National Guard. In 1904, Bert Olney and George Cartier arranged at no cost for the Michigan National Guard to hold its annual summer training session at Camp Lincoln, located at what was described as the "historic Lincoln Fields." (Author's collection.)

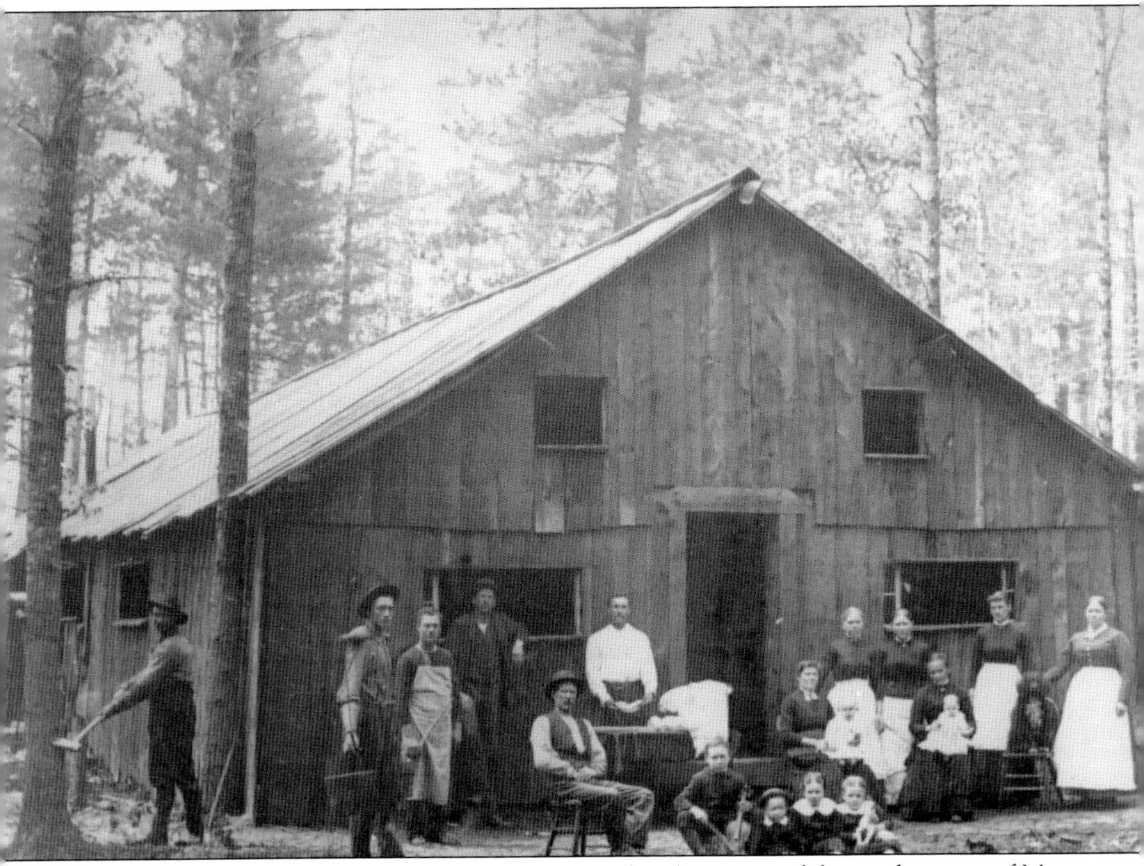

Initially, Logan was a part of Riverton in 1868 and took in most of the southern tier of Mason County. It was included in Branch Township when Branch formed in 1884. "Black Jack" John E. Logan was the vice presidential candidate in 1884 and is thought to be the source of the name when the township was divided in 1903. Logan is in the southeastern corner of Mason County and shares much of the same history as its neighbors in the region. Logging played an important role in its development, but it remains to this day rural, one of the most sparsely populated areas in the county. Carr Settlement, which is discussed further in the next chapter, was the primary settlement. When the first settlers arrived, there were no roads or residents and barely more than a couple of pathways through the woods. The south branch of the Pere Marquette River runs the full length of the township. (Author's collection.)

Early pioneers in this section included Carrs, McCumbers, Mastens, Burkes, Tyndalls, Potters, and Lakes. Much of Logan Township is not suitable for farming, but there are some areas around Carr Settlement with enough quality soil to support farming. In Logan, the Pere Marquette River was used to move millions of board feet of white pine to mills. (Courtesy of Mary Mitchell.)

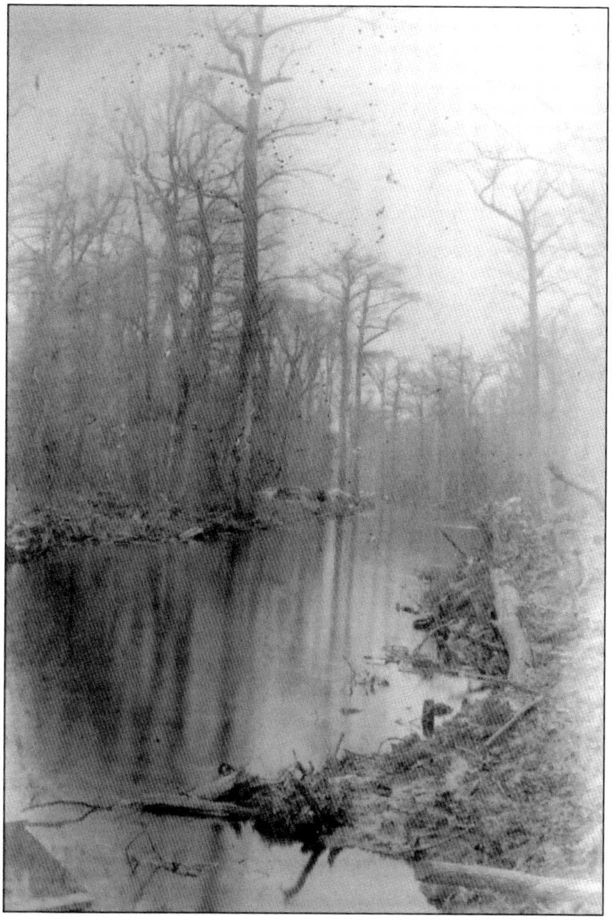

Locke School was originally built on the corner of Hawley and Tyndall Roads. In 1908, the new Locke School was constructed of concrete blocks at the intersection Masten and Hawley Roads. This two-story building housed kindergarten through 10th grade. Another school in Logan Township was McCumber School, built near Anthony and Masten Roads. Both schools were named after local families. (Courtesy MCHS.)

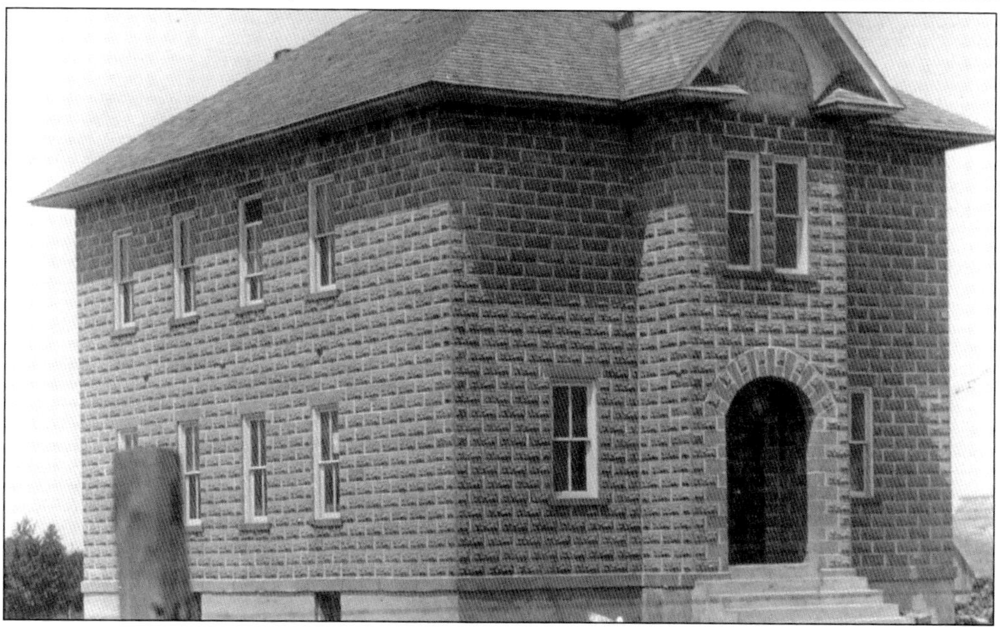

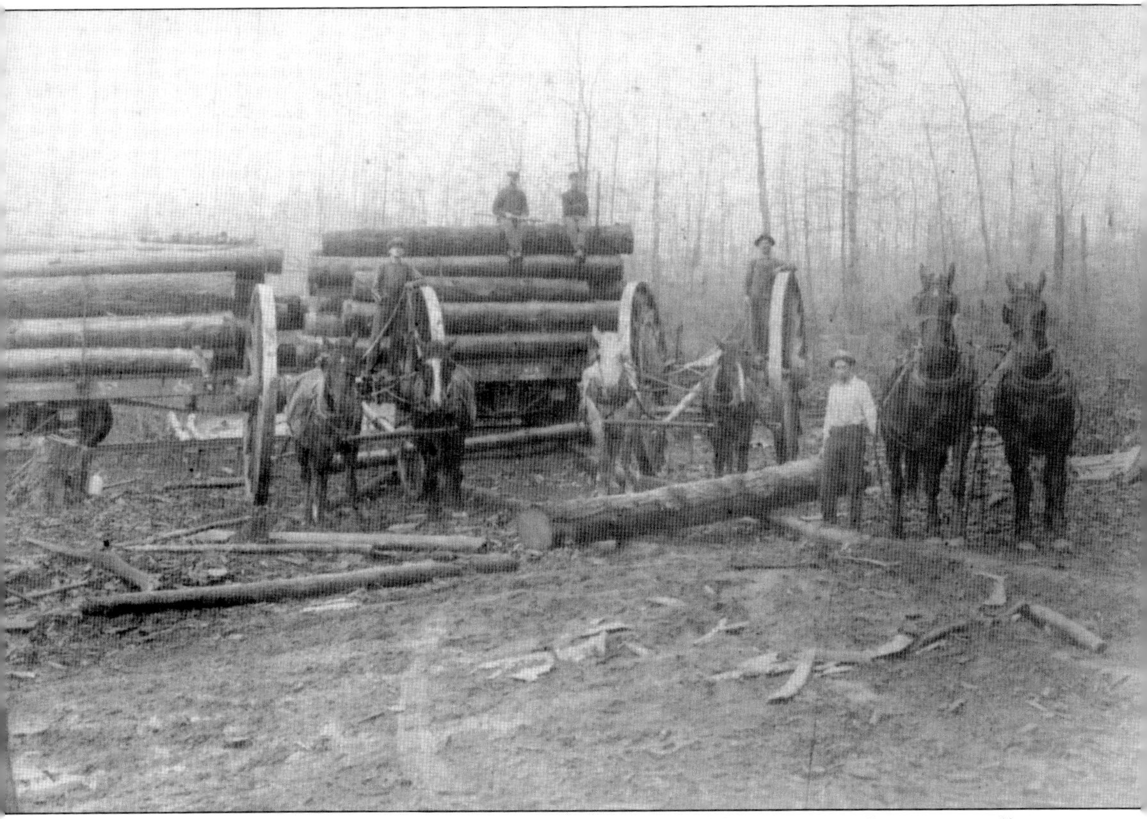

Meade Township is located in the northeastern section of the county and was originally a part of Freesoil Township until it was organized in 1910. It is primarily a wooded area without towns, villages, or settlements, and much of the township is also included in the Manistee National Forest. Logging was the primary source of income and employment for early settlers of the region, with Charles Mears being a primary landowner. The Big Sable River runs through the southwest portion of the township. There were two railroad stops: Elmton and Meadville. Originally, the railroad transported logs to mills in Manistee, but it was closer and more economical to transport them north on the Grand Rapids East and West Line (previously the Manistee and Grand Rapids Railroad). The second growth of pine in the area was suitable for bolts and provided an additional source of income and livelihood when the Filer City Fiber Plant opened. The township population has been historically low and is sparsely populated, with only 287 people being recorded in the 2000 census. (Courtesy of Benita Eddy Hurd.)

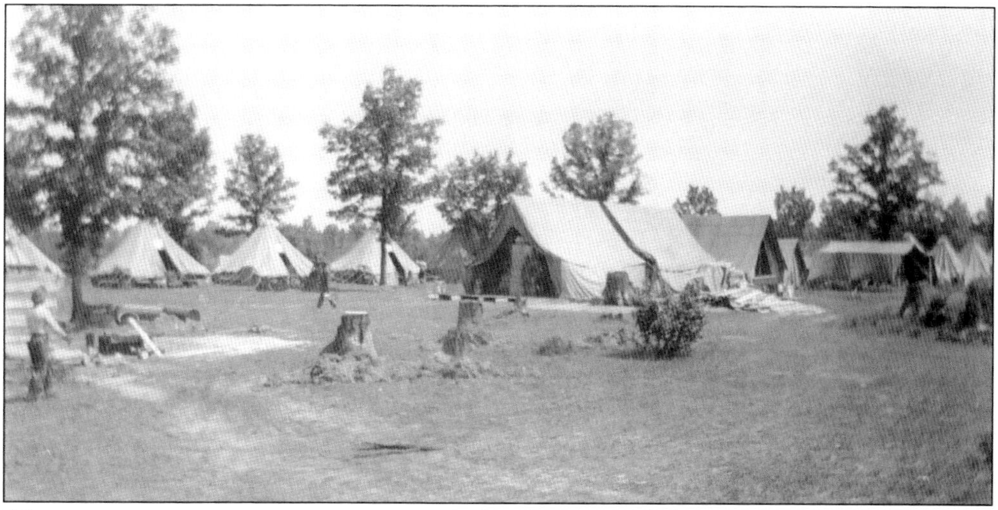

Often it was necessary to start a new camp with only tents as shelter against the weather. As the CCC camp settled in and began work, materials for barracks would arrive and the camps would begin to take the form of a more established community. (Courtesy of Benita Eddy Hurd.)

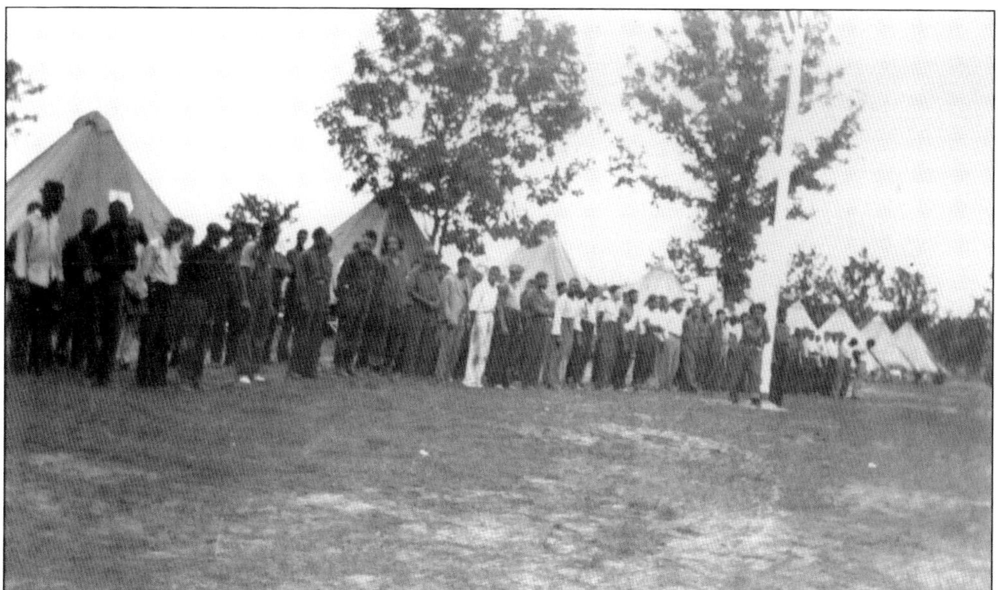

The CCC had a camp in Meade Township, established in 1935 and located north of Freesoil Road and east of Campbell Road. The men in this camp built fire roads and truck trails and planted millions of pine seedlings in the lands that had been cutover by previous logging concerns. (Courtesy of Benita Eddy Hurd.)

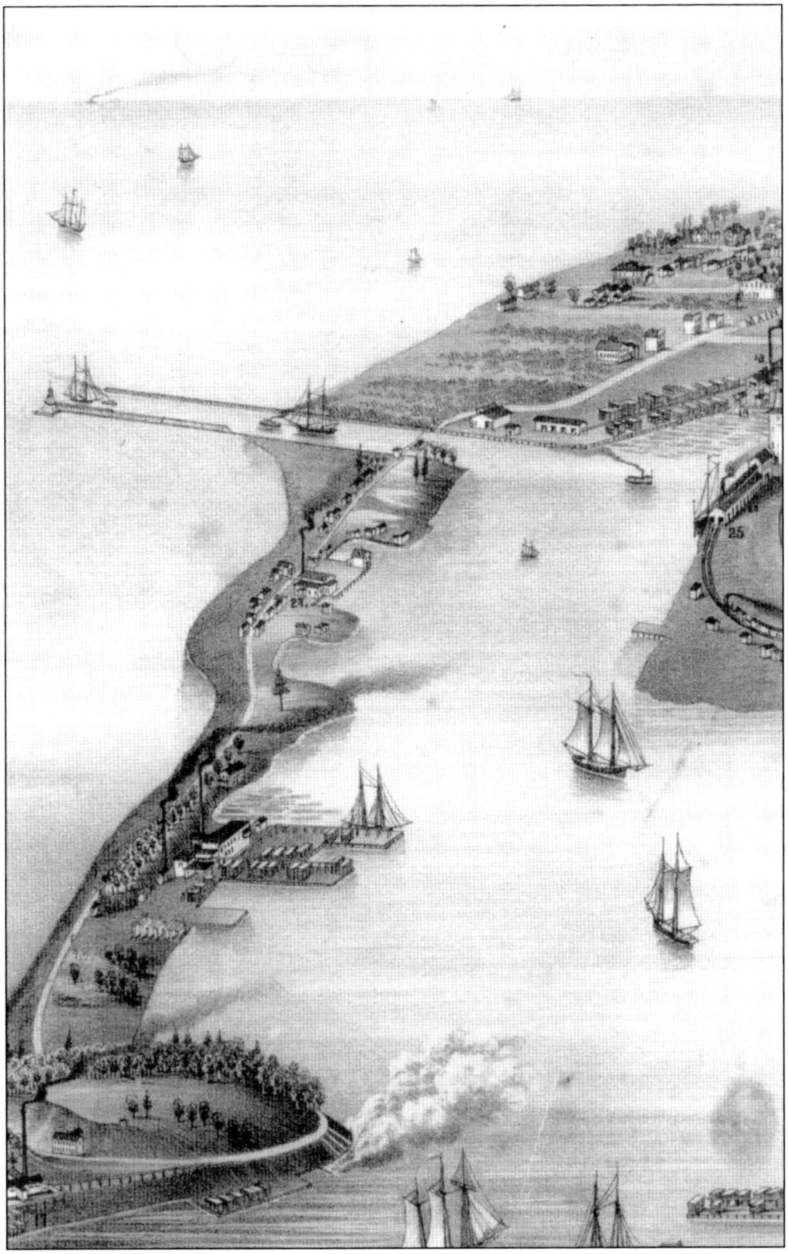

Early records indicate that Joseph Wheeler purchased land on Pere Marquette Lake in 1840, John Harris 37 acres in Freesoil Mills in 1844, and Joseph Boyden and Burr Caswell (Pere Marquette Lake) and Charles Mears (Big and Little Sable Rivers) in 1847. Even though there were white residents working in the area earlier than 1847 trapping, fishing, lumbering, and making shingles, Burr Caswell is recognized as the first permanent white settler. Caswell had been there in 1845 and returned in 1847 aboard the schooner *Eagle* with his wife, Hannah, and their four children. Frances Caswell Hanna wrote, "The cattle were dropped overboard and swam to shore while the family was rowed to land in a small boat." Here, Burr Caswell built his small home out of driftwood and two years later built the first frame house in Mason County (now preserved at White Pine Village). (Author's collection.)

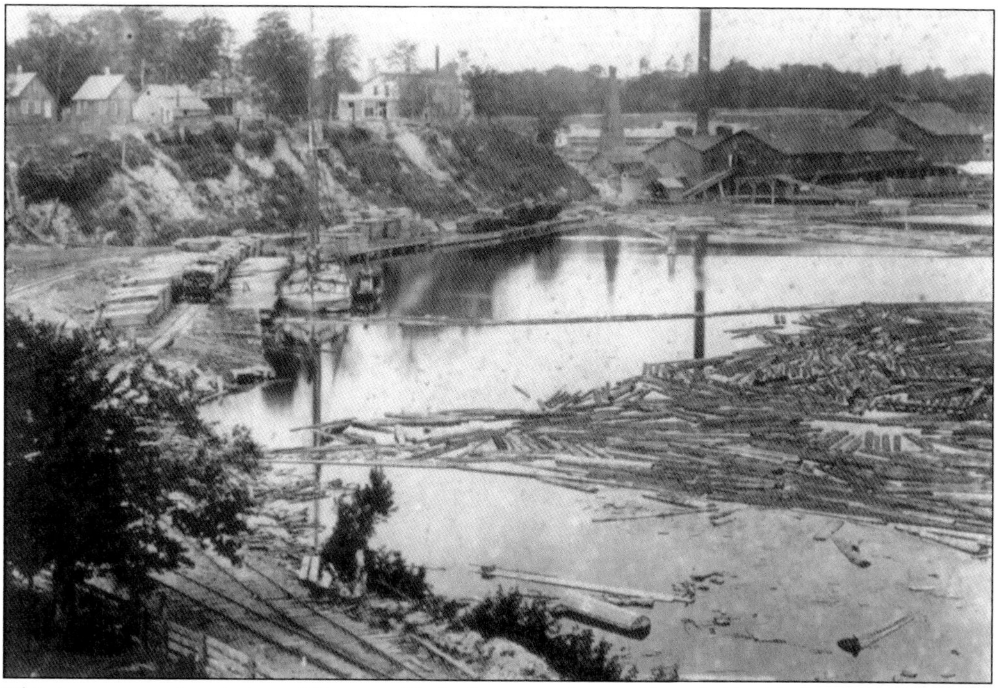

This is an exceptional view of Buttersville looking northwest. Founded by Horace U. Butters and managed along with his son Marshall F. Butters, Buttersville was the largest community on the peninsula. Seaton and Taylor's Mills were to the north, and Finn Town occupied the northernmost tip of the sandy spike. (Author's collection.)

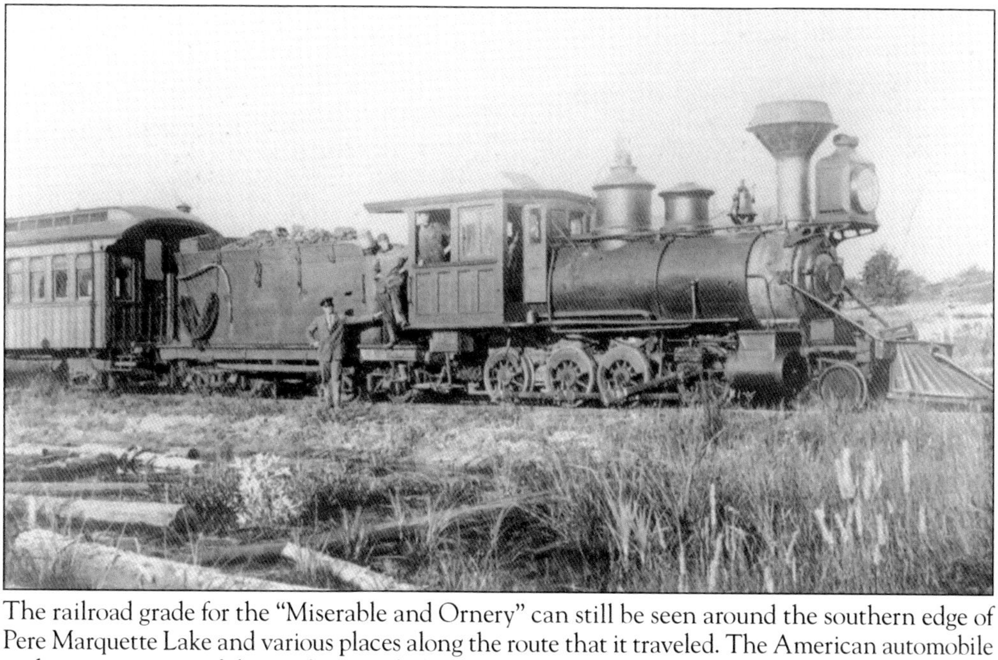

The railroad grade for the "Miserable and Ornery" can still be seen around the southern edge of Pere Marquette Lake and various places along the route that it traveled. The American automobile and improvements of the road system helped bring about the decline and end of small railroads. There were no passengers and no freight or logs to haul to the mills as people took to the roads. (Author's collection.)

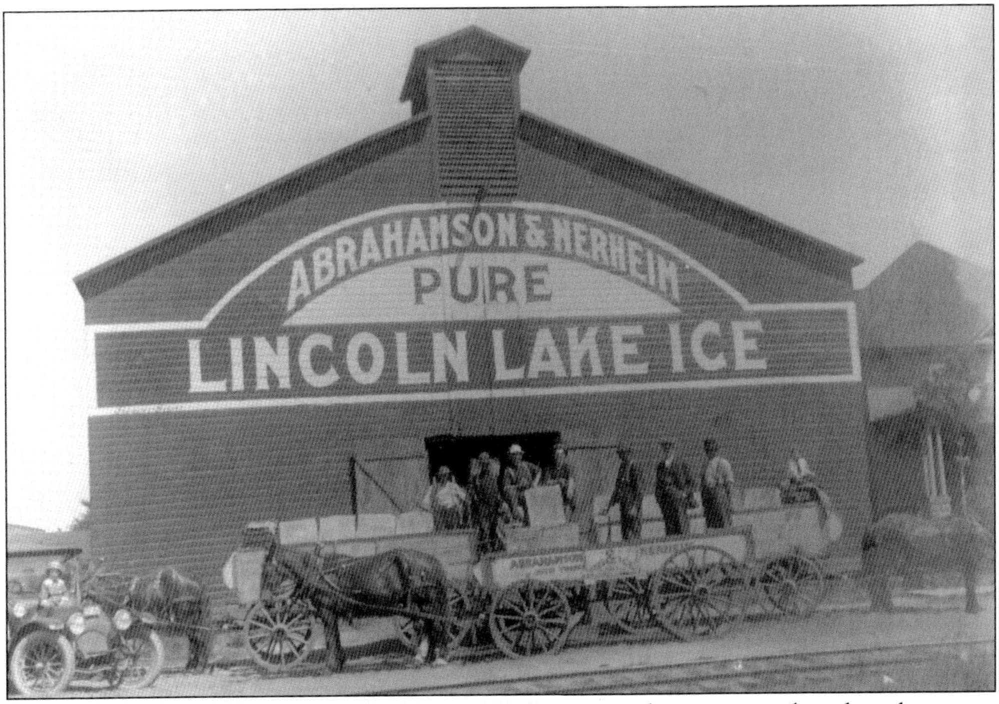

An icehouse thrived on Lincoln Lake, but in 1892 the surrounding area was thought to be a great location for what was hoped to be *the* Midwest tourist mecca called Lincoln Heights. Its virtues were extolled during the 1892 Ludington the Beautiful Campaign. The interest in developing it at that time did not materialize, nor did the power plants and factories that were to line the banks of Lincoln Lake. (Courtesy of Warren Abrahamson.)

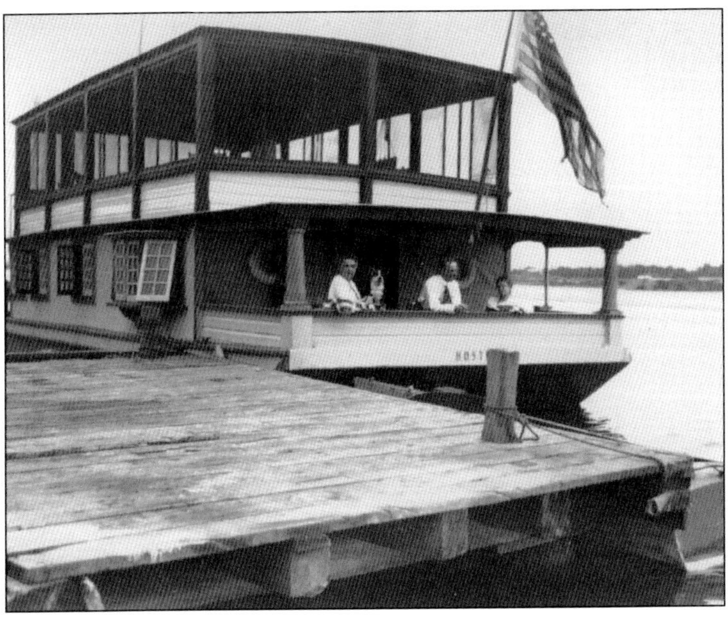

Linlook Park is located on the west side of North Lakeshore Drive across from the cemetery. It is a small community of cottages and summer homes, some of which have been winterized. The cottage pictured here was at one time a houseboat called *The Hostess*, owned by the Butters family. When it no longer was useable as a boat, they dragged it to the top of the hill and made it into a cottage. (Author's collection.)

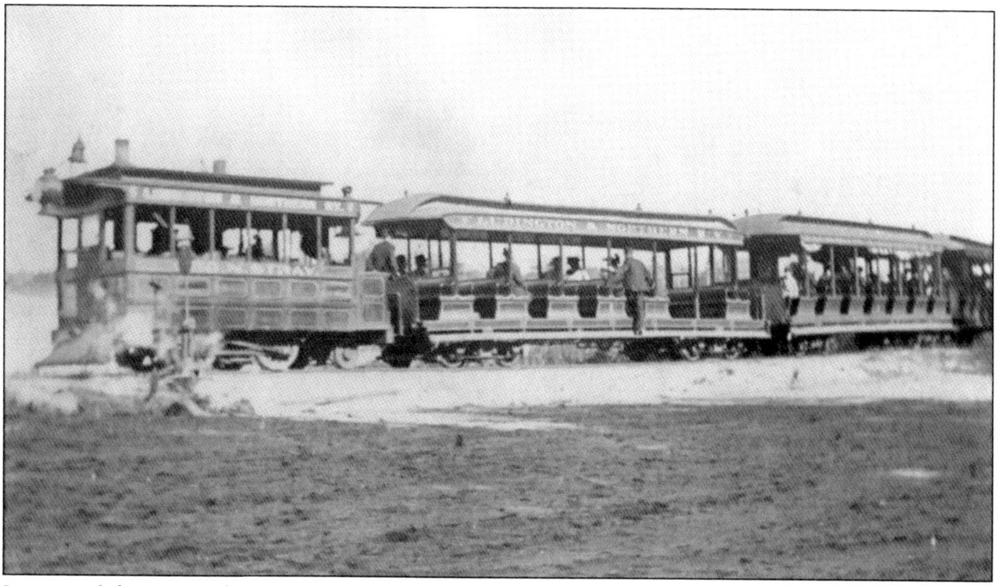

Images of the original Dummy Train are always a treat when discovered. The Epworth Railway became known as the Ludington and Northern Railway, a narrow-gauge line that ran out to Hamlin's middle bayou. The train was so ingrained into community history that long after it closed in 1919 the sand train and the bridge were still referred to as "the Dummy." (Author's collection.)

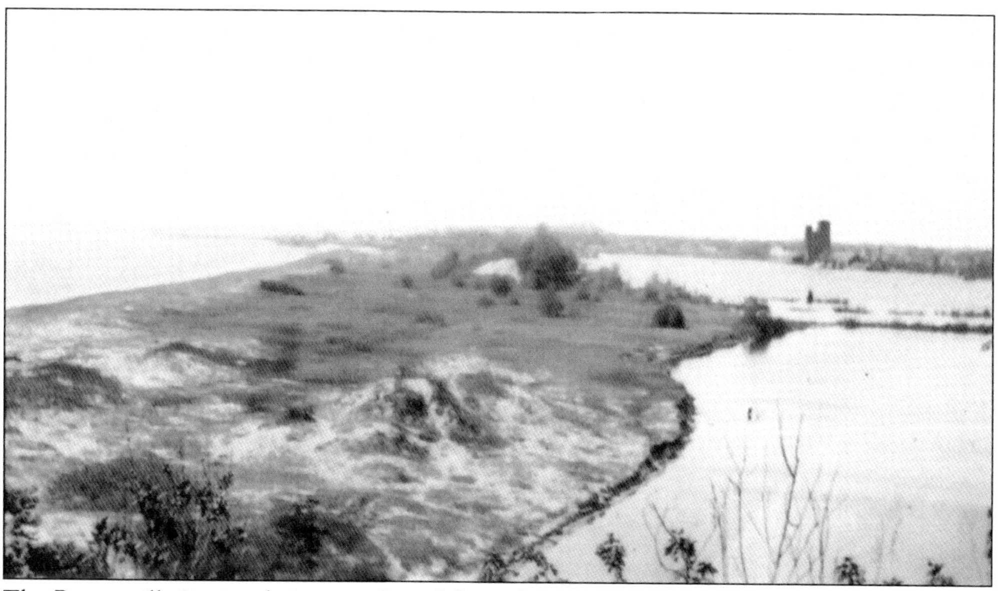

The Buttersville Peninsula juts northward from the top of the hill near the campground. The remnants of the lives, hopes, and dreams of those who lived and worked there have been all but stripped clean. The shadowy remains of the Taylorsville docks and the hilltop knoll where Father Marquette passed away can be seen, but the homes and businesses have all disappeared. (Author's collection.)

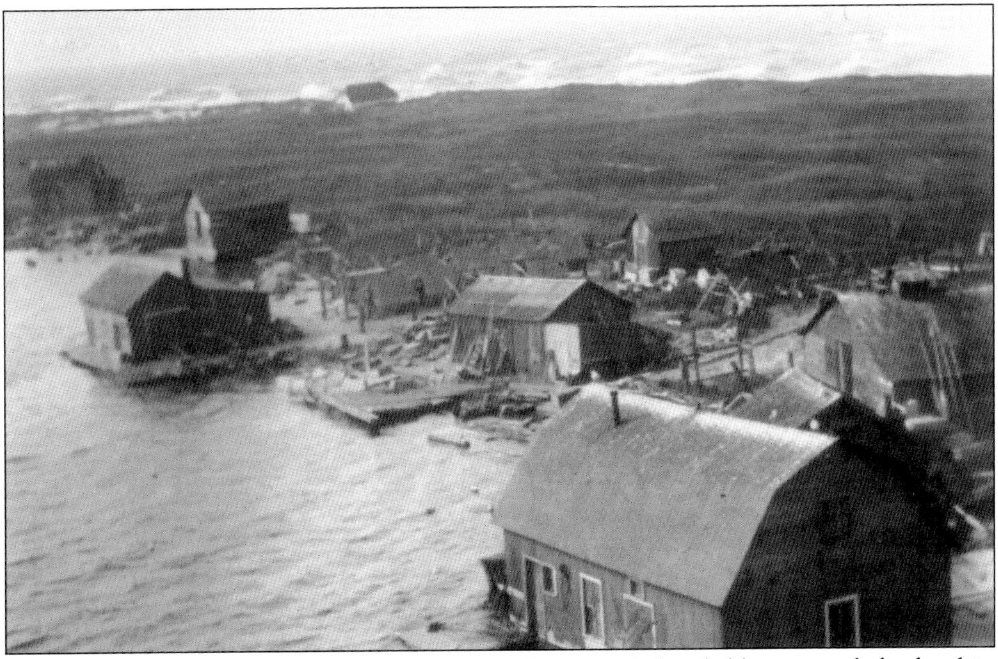

A grocery firm made weekly deliveries to Finn Town, and the children attended school in Buttersville or rowed across the lake to Ludington's First Ward School. From early spring until late autumn, Finn Town was astir long before dawn, as fishing boats started early for the long trip out into Lake Michigan to haul in the day's catch and set new nets. Often the sun disappeared below the western horizon before the day's work was done. (Author's collection.)

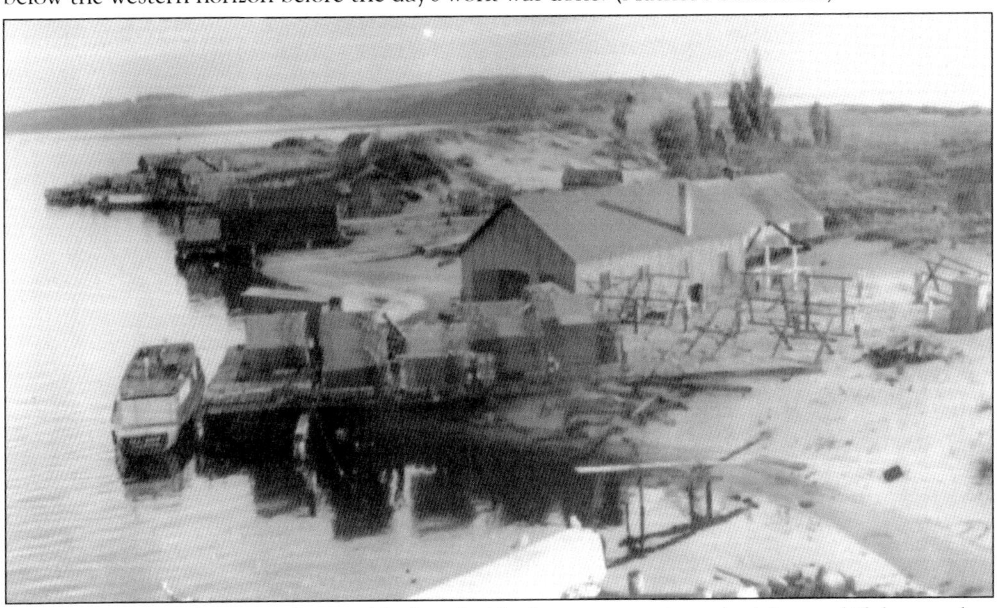

Many had only sailboats, and it would take a half a day to get out into the lake, and if the weather was calm, they had to row out and back. Most of the fishing was for lake trout, and the nets would be set 5 to 10 miles out in the lake. An average catch of fish was about 200 to 300 pounds, and they were sold for 5¢ to 6¢ a pound. The fish were iced in barrels and shipped by boat to Milwaukee and Chicago. (Author's collection.)

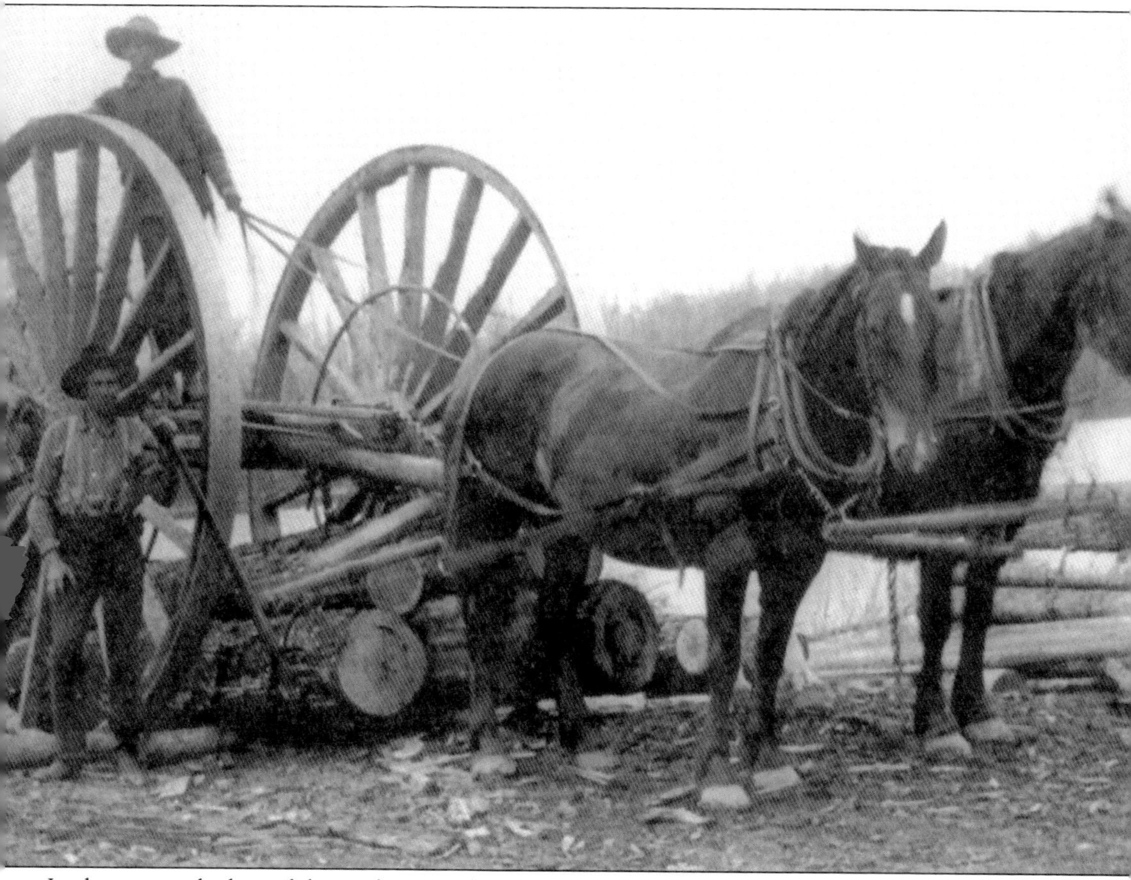

In the very early days of the settlement of Riverton Township, travel was difficult, as there were no roads but rather trails running through the forest from cabin to cabin and communities such as Lincoln, where many residents conducted their business. Because of the difficulty in moving goods and supplies, they had to rely on baskets to carry their goods. The Pere Marquette River runs the full length of the township's northern border with Amber Township and is the basis for the name of the township. The original petition requested that it be named either Rivertown or Riverton, and it was approved as Riverton in 1868. Logging was the initial industry in the township, with Horace Butters establishing the first lumber camp there. Logging cleared the lands and laid the groundwork for a very prosperous and profitable fruit-farming community to become established. (Author's collection.)

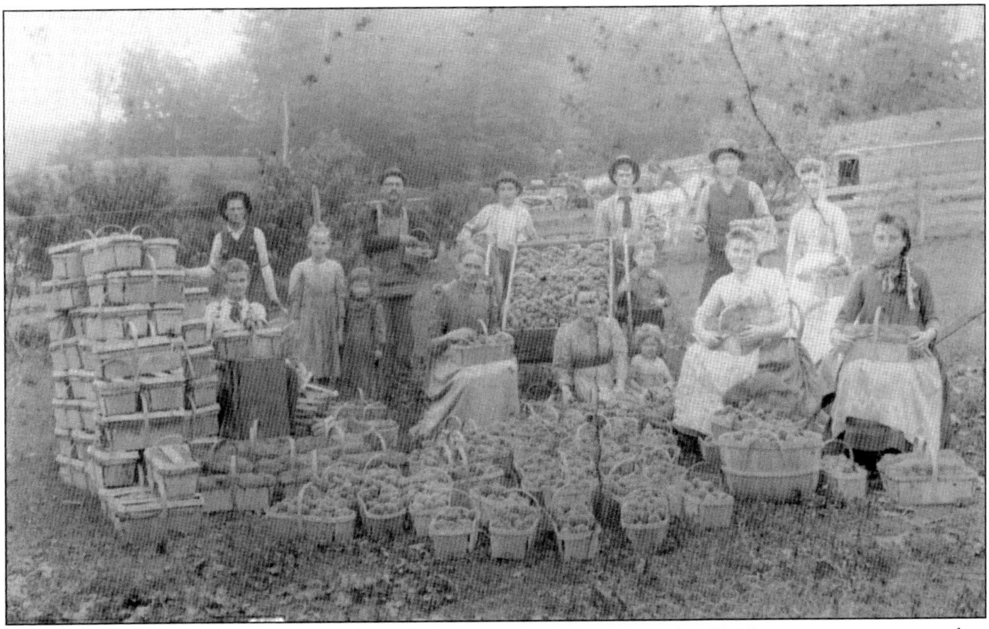

During the 1892 Ludington the Beautiful Campaign, the region south of Ludington was promoted as having some of the best orchard lands in the state. Once the area had been logged and the lumber barons moved out to the eastern sections of the county, farmers began clearing and tilling the land. They discovered it to be rich and well suited to growing fruit of all types. (Courtesy of MCHS.)

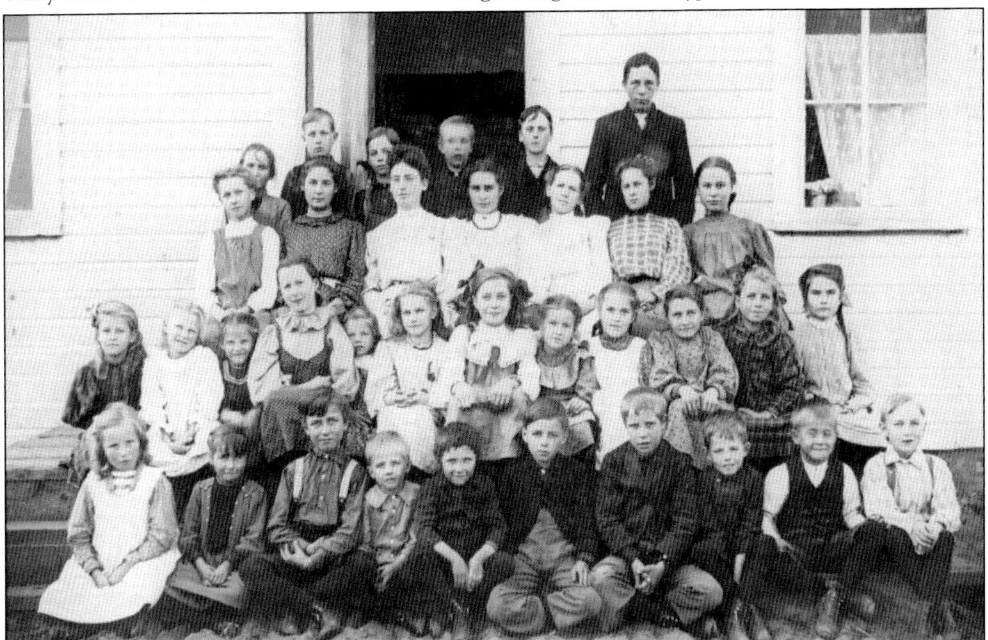

Early pioneers were somewhat isolated, and it was a true test of faith and perseverance living in this new land. Circuit riders, ministers with a horse and a Bible, made the rounds from farmhouse to house to preach the good word. There were a total of seven churches established in the township. (Courtesy of MCHS.)

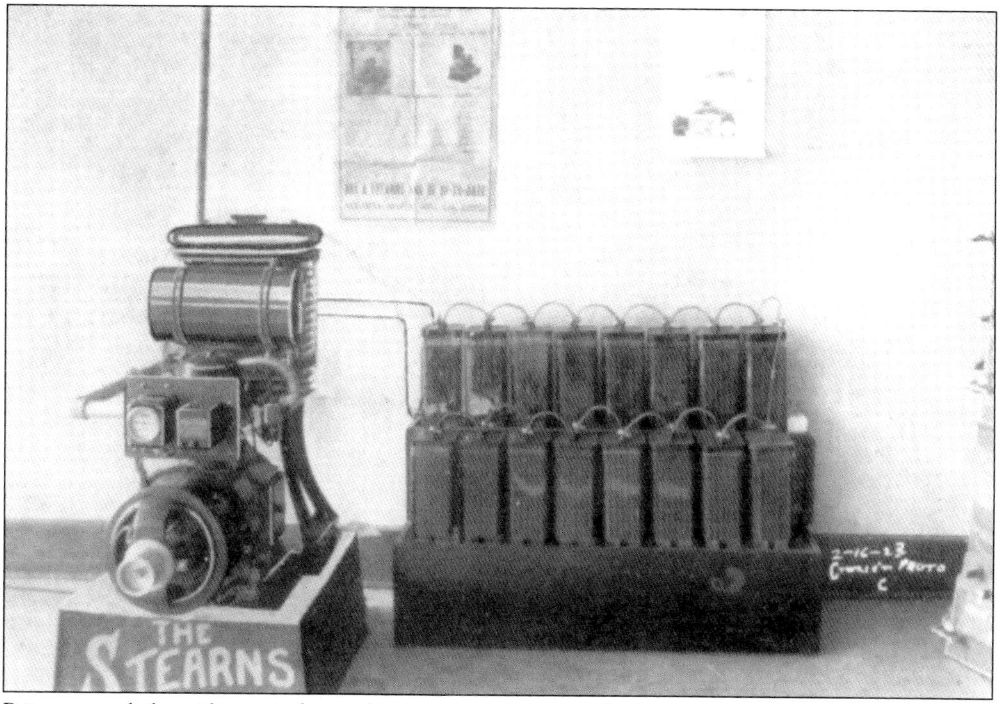

Prior to rural electrification, farms that required electricity had to generate their own. There were a number of different home power units that could be purchased nationally, and one was available locally. Justus Stearns of Stearns Power and Lights offered generators for such applications that were very popular until the Rural Electrification Administration extended power lines to outlying farms. (Author's collection.)

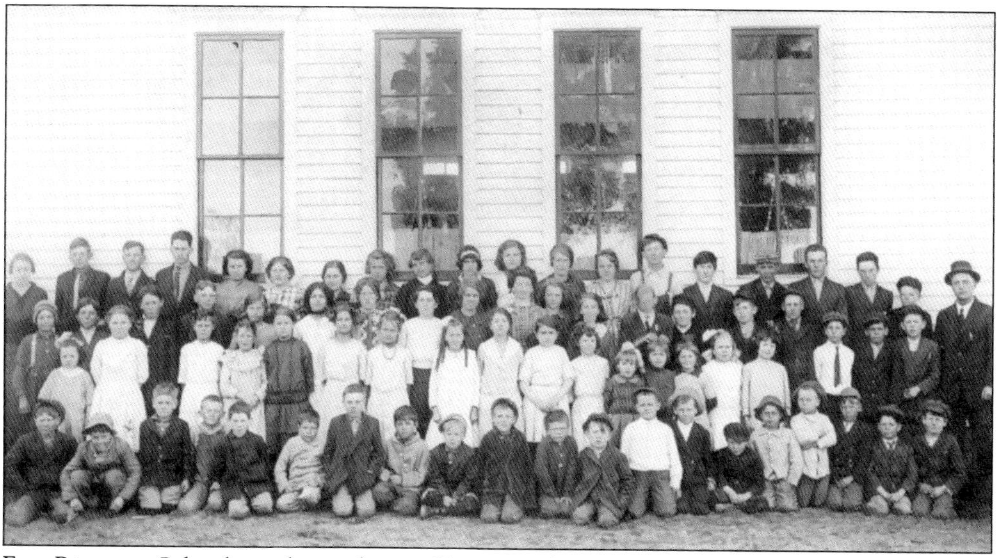

East Riverton School was located near Chavez and Riggle Roads, and there were four other districts in Riverton Township: Morton School on the corner of Morton and Deren Roads, Saint Mary's Lake at the corner of Marrison and Lasalle Roads, West Riverton at Morton and Gerbers Roads, and Center Riverton on the southwest corner of Haley and Schwass Roads. (Courtesy of Benita Eddy Hurd.)

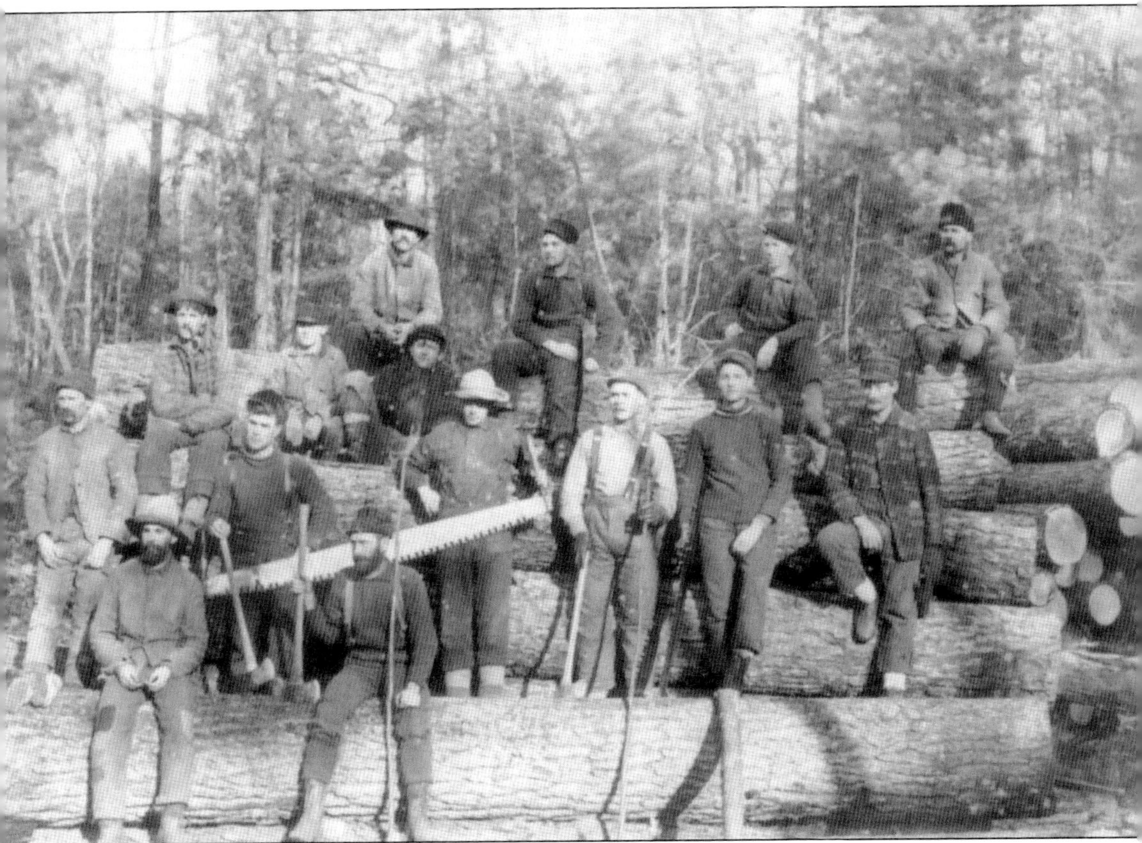

Sheridan Township was a part of Sherman Township until it was split apart in 1889. One of the first decisions reached for the new township was that hogs should not be able to run at large. As with other such separations, when new townships were created, steps had to be taken to divide the equipment owned by the parent township. Even library books were to be divided evenly, along with receipts from the dog tax. There were several communities: Tallman, also known as Weaver, was founded by Horace Butters and located on the southern side of Tallman Lake in Branch Township; Millerton was located where the Manistee and Grand Rapids Railroad crossed the Sable River; and Batcheller, also spelled Bachelor, sprang up around a sawmill built by Alden Batcheller and was a thriving lumber village until a fire in 1891 destroyed much of the area and many of the buildings. After logging ended, Sheridan Township became popular as a resort area because of the many lakes for fishing and woods for hunting camps. (Author's collection.)

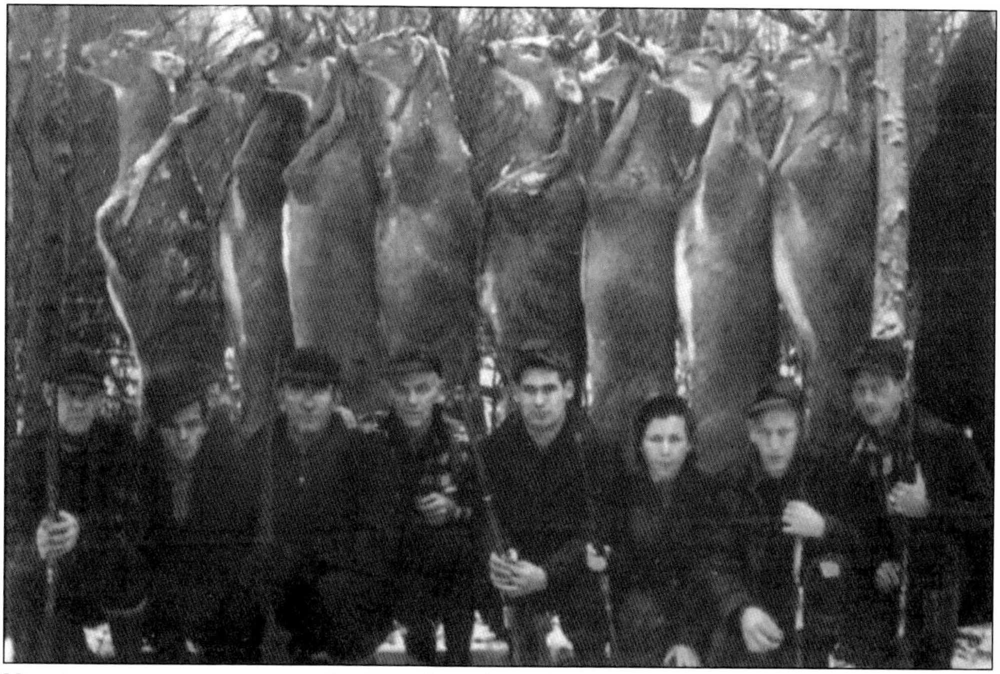

Hunting was not just a pastime for the rich in the early days of settlements in Mason County—it was one of necessity and need. Early residents relied on the game that was available and the fish in the lakes to provide basic needs and food for the supper table. The Curt Shoup family bagged eight bucks and a bear on one hunting trip to eastern Mason County to fill their needs. (Courtesy of Shirley Shoup.)

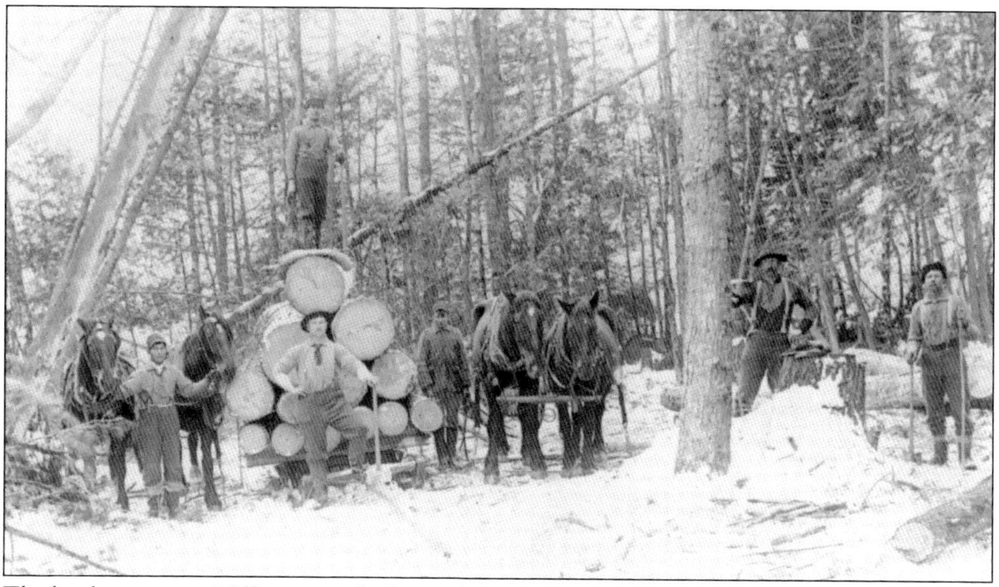

The lumber camp at Millerton sparked a settlement that existed past the turn of the 20th century in Sheridan Township, although there is little if anything remaining to suggest that it was so. It was named after John Miller, a local farmer. The sawmill burned in 1901 and was rebuilt, but the community continued to decline. After the train stopped coming to Millerton, it slowly disappeared. (Courtesy of MCHS.)

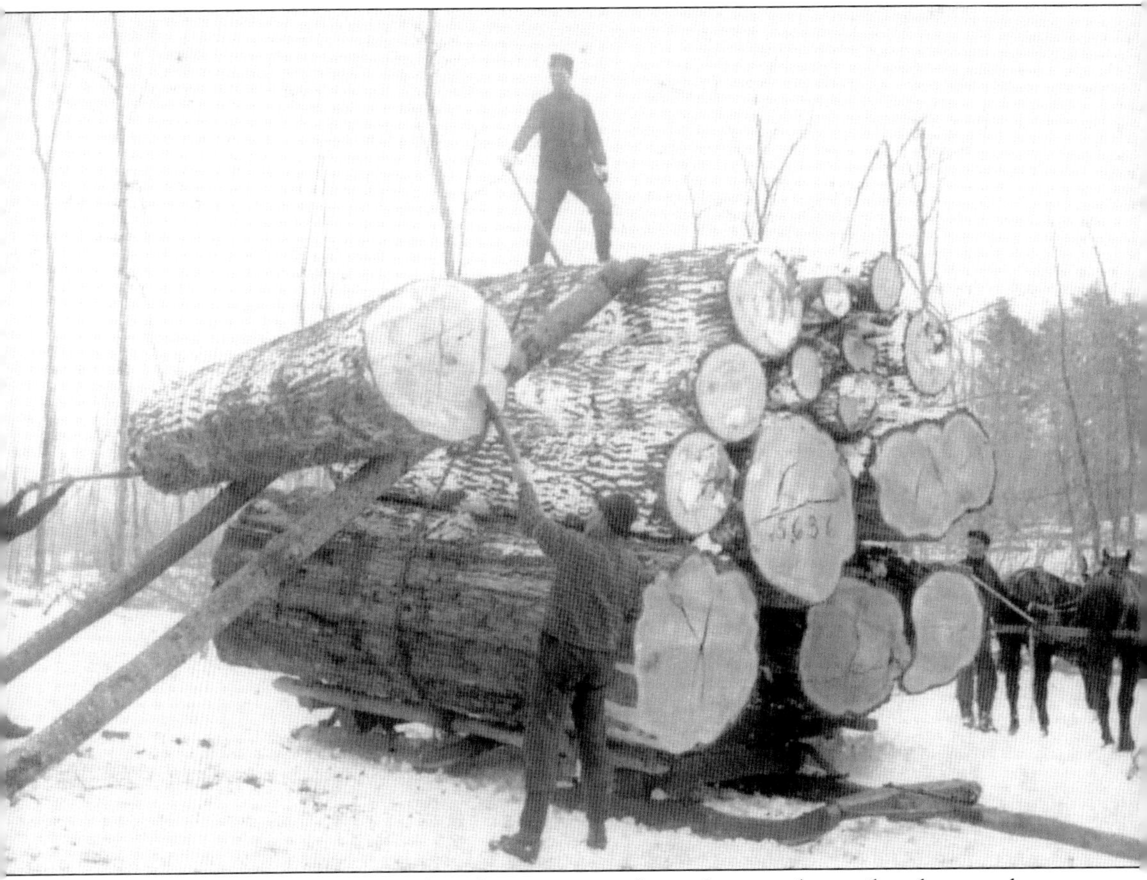

There was work in pineries, and Michigan was ripe for settlement when railroads opened up new territory. The railroads were also gifted large tracts of land in order to provide an incentive for construction. The Flint and Pere Marquette arrived in Ludington in 1874 and in Fountain in 1881. The railroad did much to open up the interior of the county to settlement and commerce. The railroad came north from the spur at Walhalla (Manistee Junction) toward Manistee, and Sugar Grove Road was carved from the swamps and wilderness to become the first road that crossed Sherman Township from east to west. In 1873, the population of the township was 290, and by 1880 it had risen to 409. The community of Fountain was christened by the approval of the post office in 1882 and for 30 years was governed by the township officers, which changed in 1913 when a charter was approved and the village was incorporated. (Author's collection.)

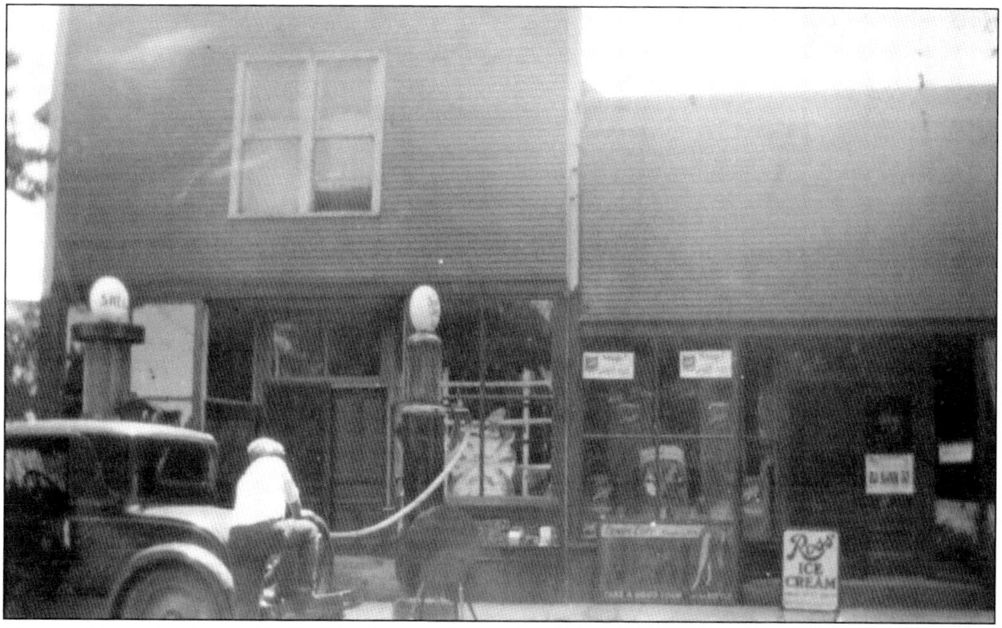

Pictured here is Henry Eoff's Hardware, Grocery, and Ice Cream Parlor across from Letson's Boardinghouse. Henry was the son of Marshall Eoff. Marshall operated the Little Red General Store in Fountain until his death in 1882. Henry built a general store in 1893, added on in 1898, and built the grain elevator in 1900. This image features two great examples of early gasoline pumps from about 1920. (Courtesy of Keith Adams.)

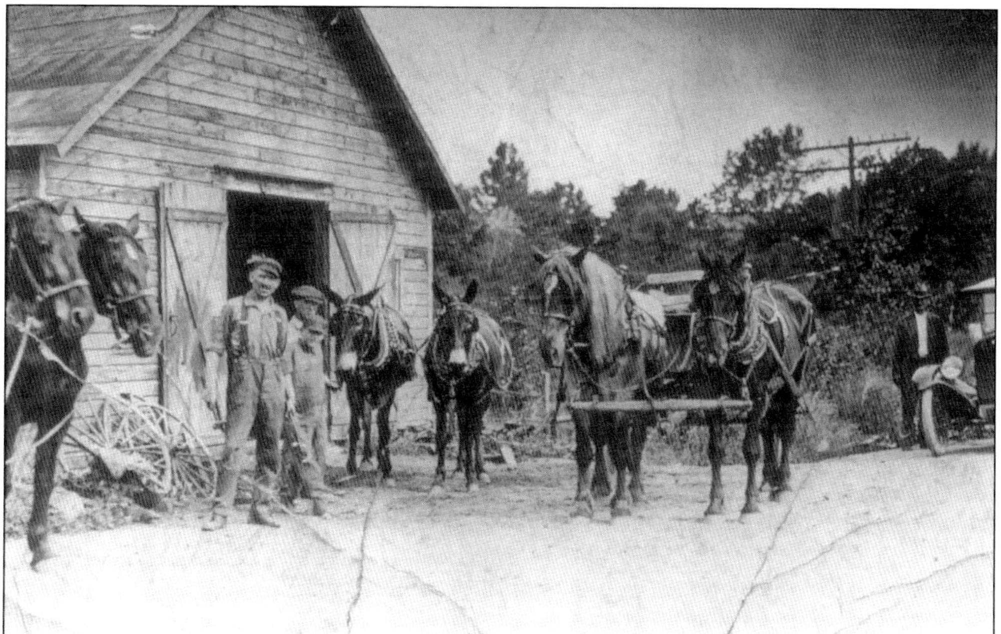

John Swelnis (in the suspenders) is at his blacksmith shop. Swelnis came from Lithuania to the Fountain area, where he opened his blacksmith shop about 1920. There was a large influx of emigrants from Lithuania who left their homeland after 1907 to escape Russian oppression. Many purchased farms and a few opened businesses. (Courtesy of Keith Adams.)

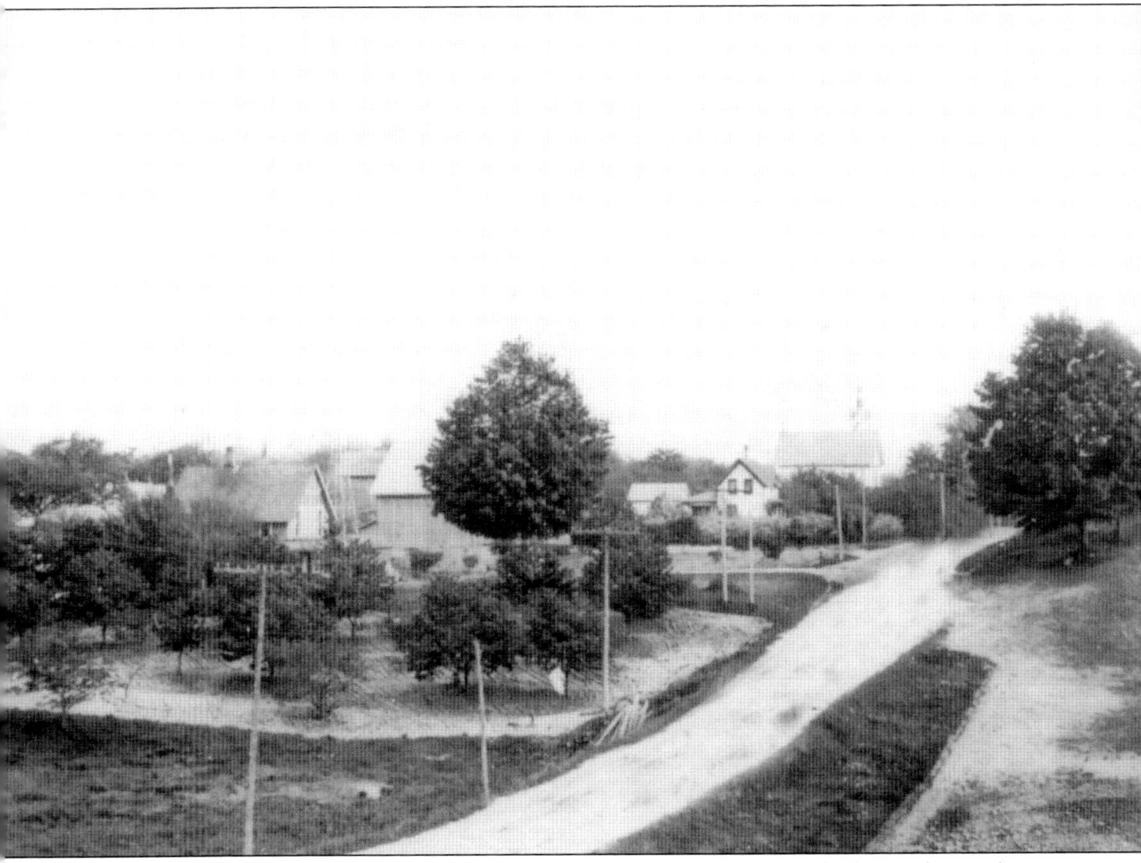

Summit Township is the smallest of the townships in Mason County and takes in the northernmost section of Bass Lake. Summit was originally part of Pere Marquette Township but set apart from it in 1859 to form the new township. Early settlers in the area included William Quevillion, who had trapped and bought furs in the area as early as 1835 and came back to settle permanently in 1850. Quevillion purchased 160 acres of land and built a cabin from which he operated a store. His log cabin was moved to and restored at Historic White Pine Village. Quevillion went on to become the postmaster of Fairview in 1860. Another early settler was Hiram Beebe, who kept an extensive daily diary until his death that provides a glimpse of early life in the region. In 1858, William Labelle settled here and began logging in the area. Labelle's Landing is recognized as the first settlement in the township. Meisenheimerville is another long-past settlement that existed on the corner of Meisenheimer and old US-31. (Courtesy of MCHS.)

The diary of Hiram Beebe of Summit Township relates a logger's day: "Chopped on the job all day in heavy hardwood timber. It has been a nice day to chop . . . I cut down 50 trees. Had very good luck jamming timber. I will finish the strip 16 rods wide tomorrow forenoon. I broke my ax and now I am a bankrupt timber slasher." (Author's collection.)

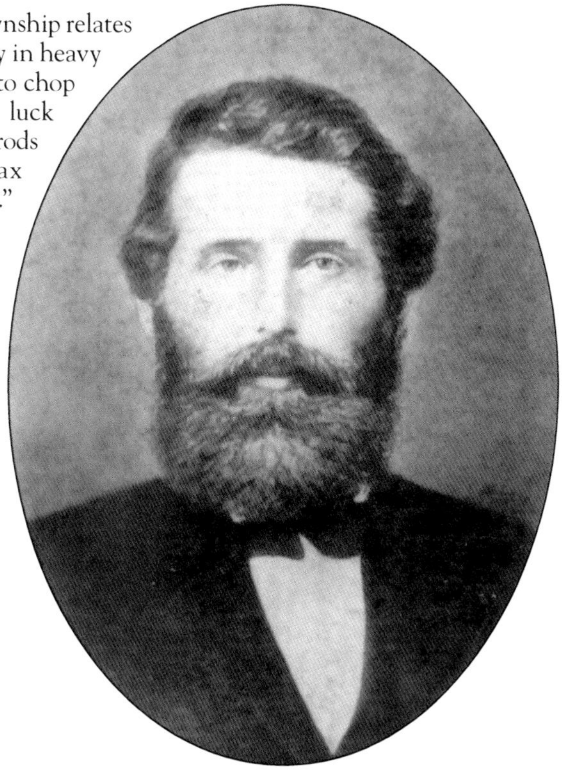

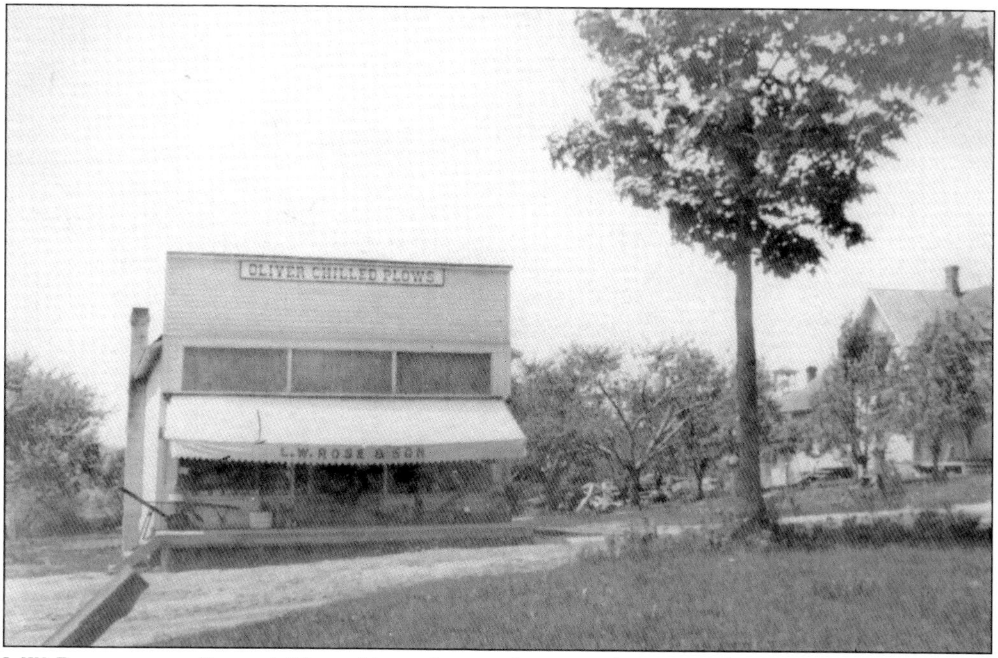

L.W. Rose came to Summit Township and opened a general store on the corner of Hawley Road and sold farm implements. The post office there was named Wesley, and Rose was the postmaster. He also was a well-respected fruit farmer and known for raising quality berries and other fruit. (Courtesy of MCHS.)

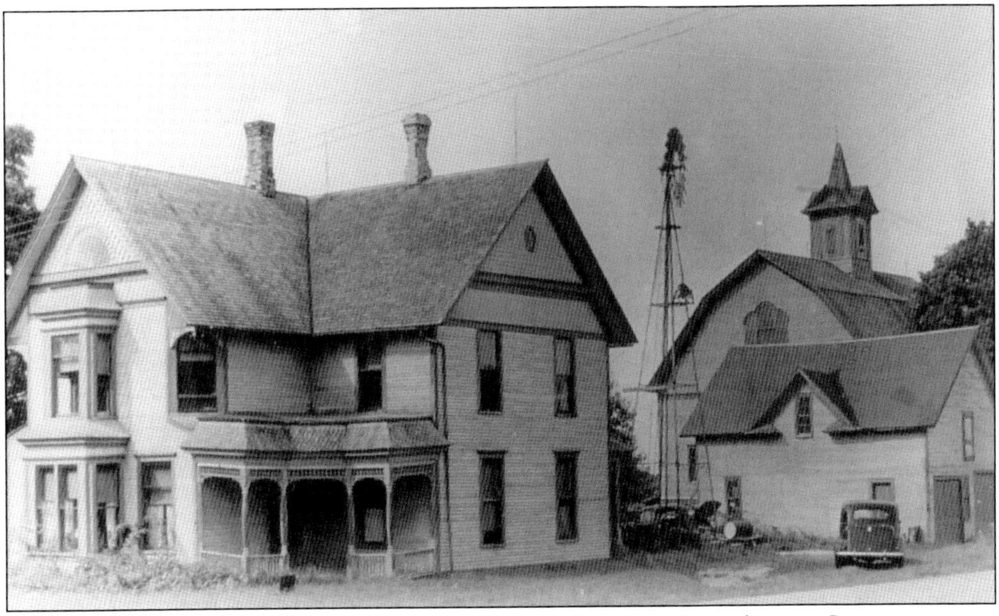

Dr. Abbott was an early Mason County physician who lived on Meisenheimer Corner; in many respects he operated his home as a hospital in the years before the hospital opened in Ludington. He would take in patients in need of extended care into his home so that he might better take care of them. (Author's collection.)

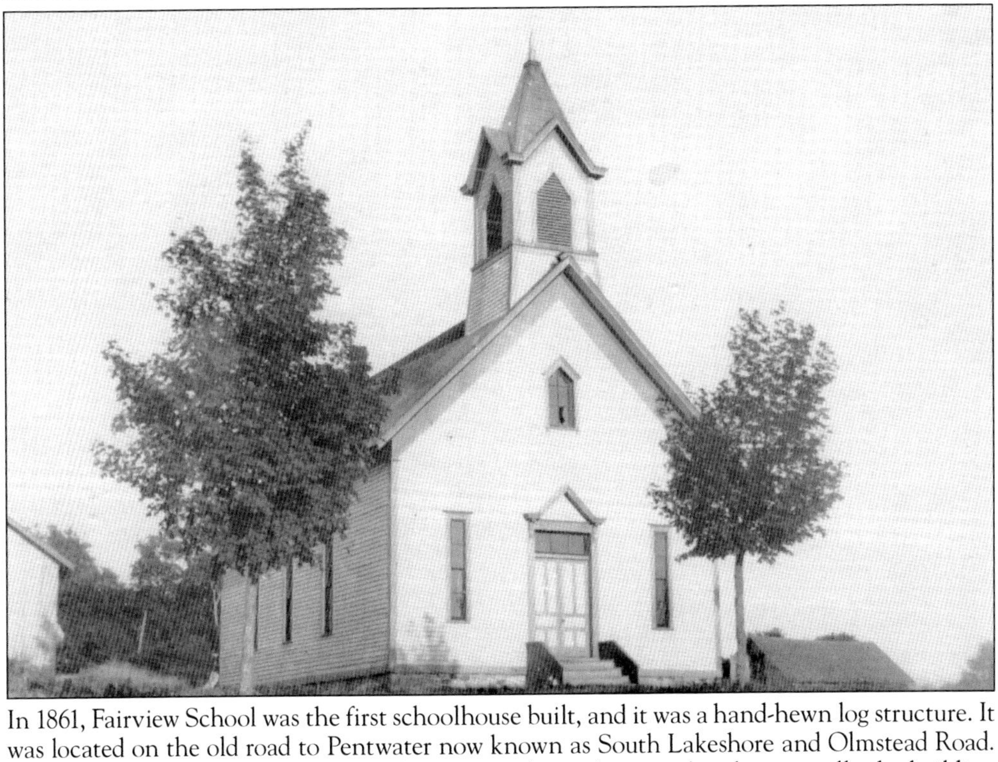

In 1861, Fairview School was the first schoolhouse built, and it was a hand-hewn log structure. It was located on the old road to Pentwater now known as South Lakeshore and Olmstead Road. The building that replaced it was used continuously until it was closed; eventually the building was sold in 1957 and converted to a home. (Courtesy of MCHS.)

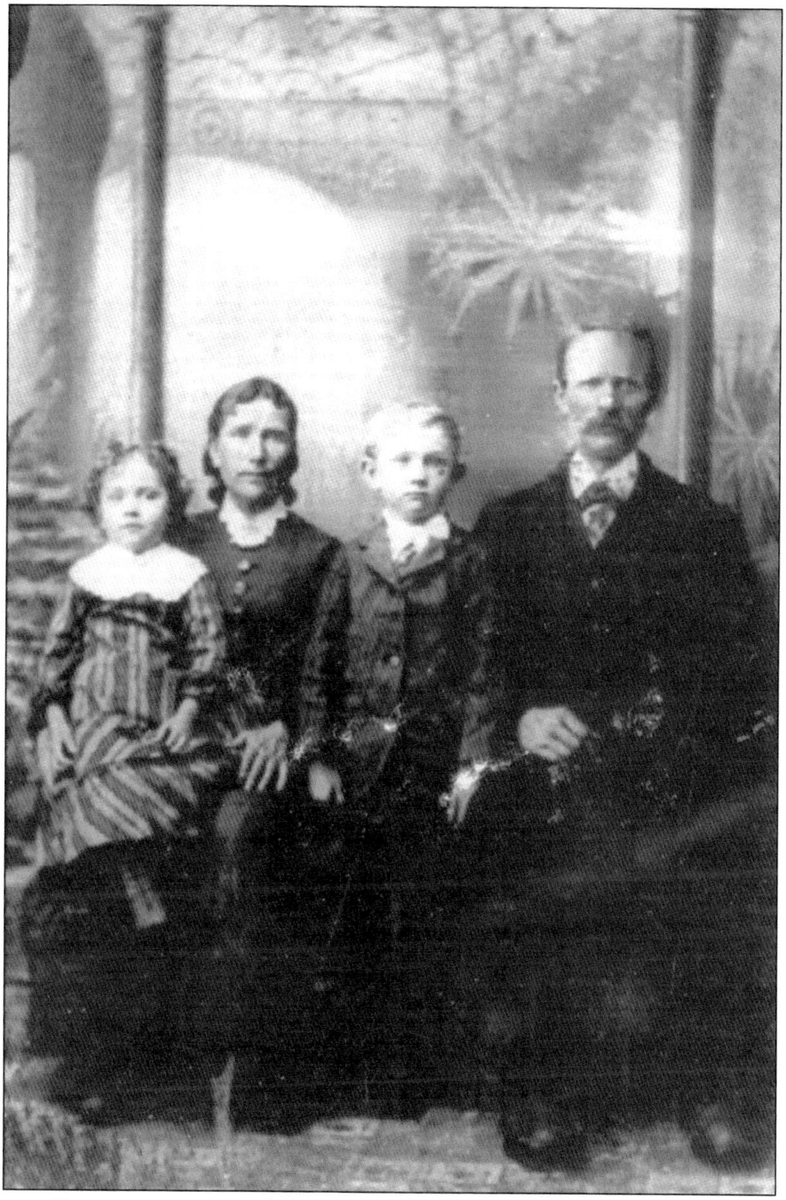

When Rasmus Rasmussen came to America from the Island of Fyn off the coast of Denmark, he determined that his name was not American-sounding enough. He promptly changed it to Robert Peterson. Robert and his wife, Marguerite Hansen Peterson, had four children: Andrew, Mary, Hans, and John. Robert was killed in 1908 when his horse was spooked while hauling cornstalks; he was thrown under the wagon and crushed by the wheels. He had come to Victory Township in 1872, just a few years after the township was organized in 1867. Victory developed as a farming community and was home to many Scandinavians, who settled there for cheap soil-rich farmlands. In the early days of the township's history, goods would be transported up the Lincoln River from Lincoln Village to Birds Settlement (Victory Corners). Birds Settlement was growing rapidly in 1867 and renamed Forest City. The settlement boasted two blacksmith shops, a general store, a boardinghouse saloon, and its own newspaper, the *Victory Gazette*. It was not destined to survive, and Forest City slipped into the memories of Victory's residents. (Author's collection.)

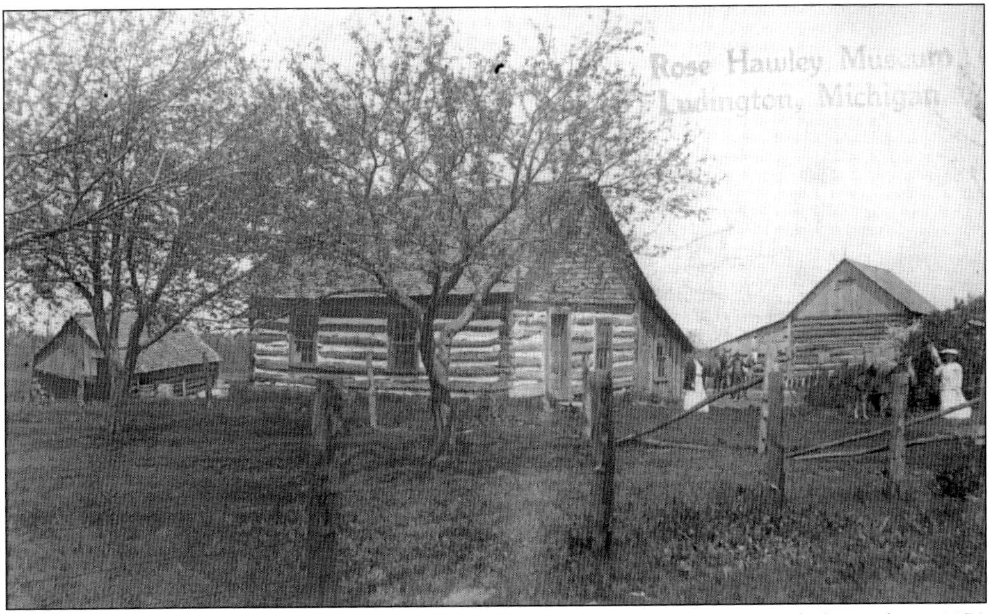

Many immigrants to Mason County's Victory Township came from Denmark from about 1870 to 1905. One group would become established and write home about the good farmlands, and others from the same family and village would follow. This is the home of George and Karen Christenson in the Danish settlement. They had six children: George, Juliane, Carl, Hedevig, Christ, and Meta. (Courtesy of MCHS.)

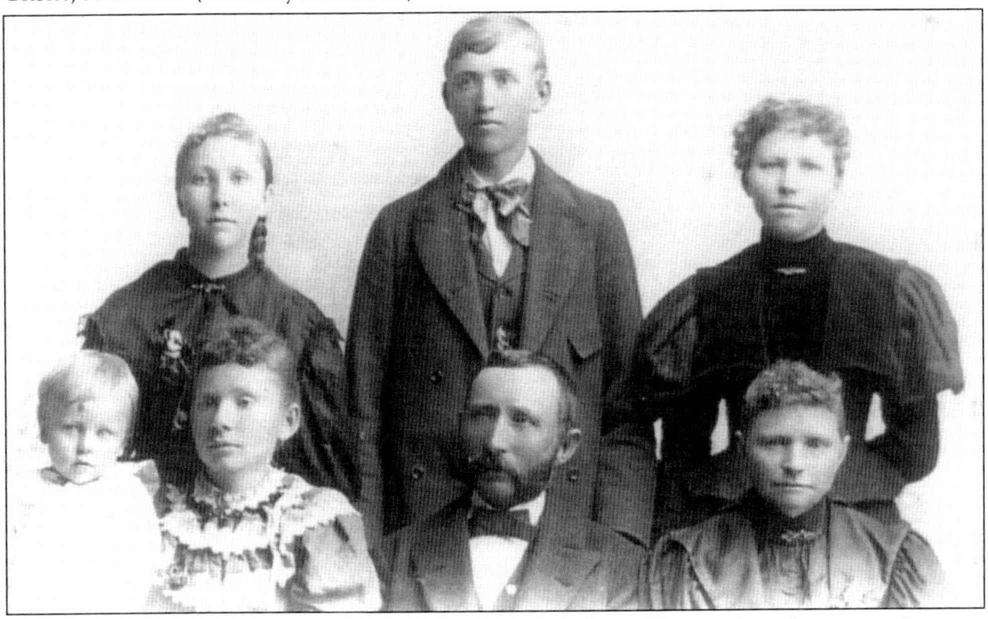

Anders "Andrew" Hansen (1851–1918) was born in Gudbjerg, Denmark and came to America in 1871 and listed his destination as Grand Haven, Michigan. He worked in lumbering for several years after his arrival. Pictured here are, from left to right, (first row) William Anderson (grandson), Marn "Minnie" Kerstine Hansen Anderson, Andrew Hansen, and Karen Andersen Hansen; (second row) Ane Mary Hansen Petersen, John Gronbek Hansen, and Marie Hansen. (Courtesy of Linda Dennis Wright.)

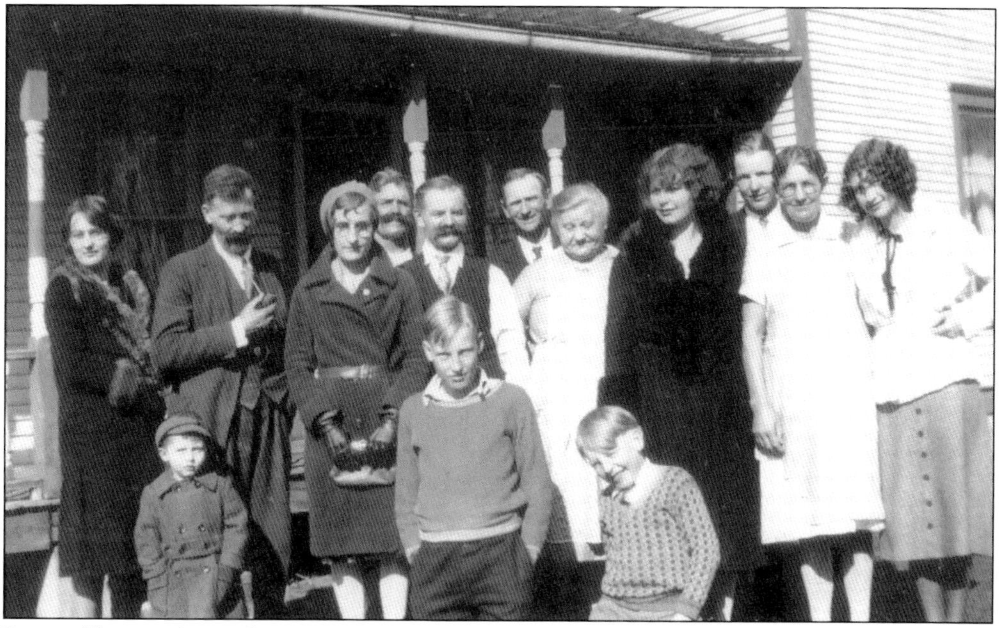

Pictured here in front of a Victory Township home are, (first row) Richard Petersen, Ivan Jensen, and Rigner Jensen; (second row) Maggie Petersen, Lars Jensen, Astrid Jensen, Pete Moggeson, Nels Jensen (Lars's brother), Andrew Petersen, Dorothea Jensen (Nels's wife), Ane Jensen (Nels's and Dorothea's daughter), Viggo Jensen, Johanna Jensen (Lars's wife), and Helen Peterson Williamson. (Author's collection.)

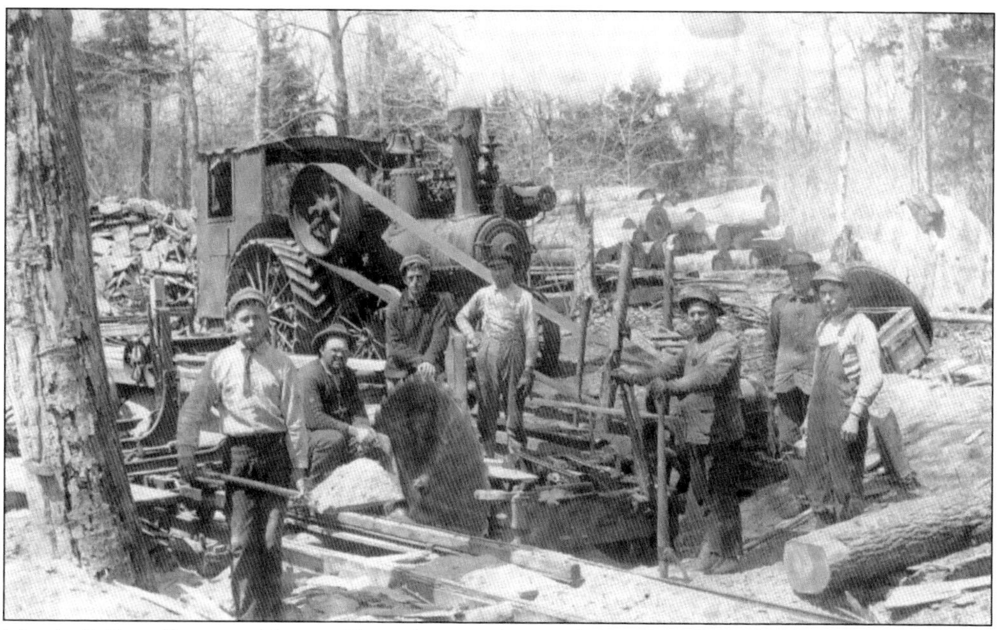

Marshall Costello was a Victory Township resident and ran a small lumber mill. He also had a portable mill that allowed him to travel the county and saw logs on site. This was handy for both he and the landowner, who would not have to transport logs to the mill and finished lumber back to the farm. Costello became road commissioner and served in that capacity until his death in 1930. (Author's collection.)

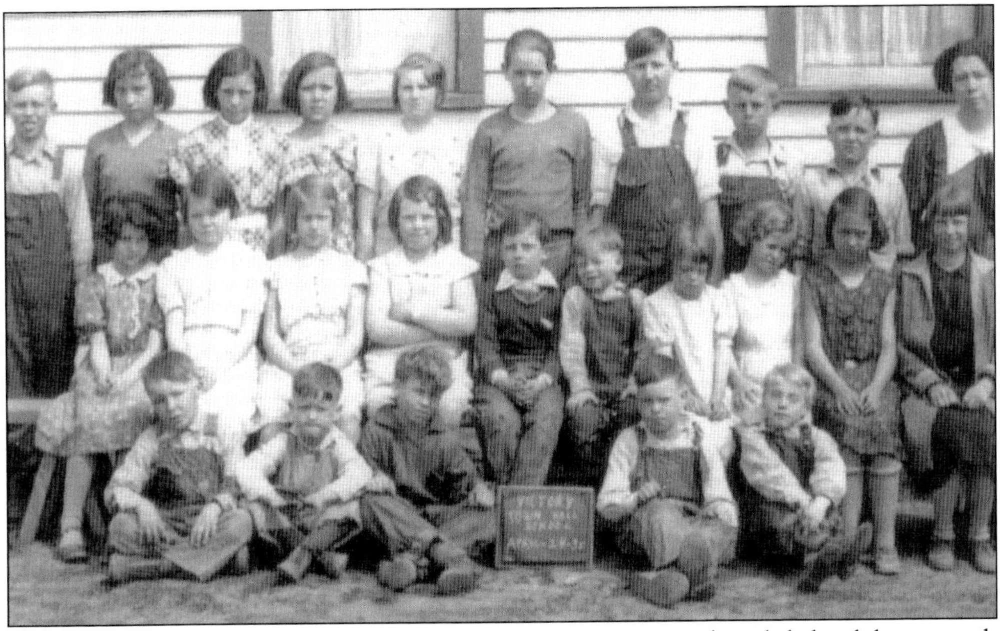

In this 1935 photograph of Victory Town Hall School, the youngster directly behind the sign with his hands folded and the pensive look is eight-year-old Richard "Dick" Petersen looking like he wants no part of what is happening. On the far right, Ada Kirk is the teacher, and some of the others in the class include Bud Anderson, Russell Anderson, and Charles Hargreaves. (Courtesy of Linda Dennis Wright.)

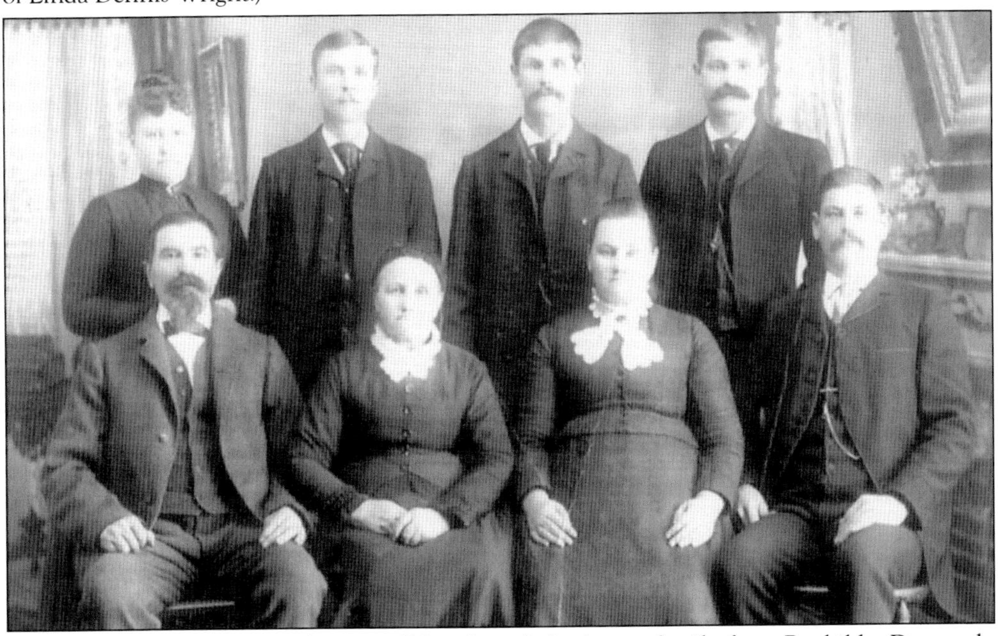

Pictured here is the Lars and Maren (Hansdatter) Andersen family from Roskilde, Denmark. Lars came to America in early 1869 and worked in the woods to earn money to send for his family. Maren and their six children arrived later that year. They originally went to Milwaukee, Wisconsin, before coming to Mason County. They purchased a farm in Victory Township in 1877. (Courtesy of Linda Dennis Wright.)

Three

Villages and Towns

There were many communities and settlements that started in various parts of the county, from Freesoil Mills to Seatonville and Birds Settlement, that looked promising but for one reason or another faded away. Sometimes it was a result of the good fortune of another settlement's geographical location, such as when Amber gave way to Sweetland (Scottville). For others, it was a calamity such as the dam bursting at Hamlin Lake and washing the village away. Sometimes it was simple economics, such as when fire took the Buttersville Sawmill at the end of the lumbering era. Workers had to relocate for employment because rebuilding was not feasible. Regardless of the reason, a community's success or failure often relied on location, being centrally situated and easily accessible and having a wide range of economic potential.

Early in the region's history, travel was primarily along the lake, and a good harbor was critical. Originally, trading and transporting goods took place in and around the village of Pere Marquette, but Charles Mears was a hands-on landlord who invested and developed Lincoln to be the new county seat. A better harbor, however, was the key to Ludington winning over the village of Lincoln. Lincoln Village grew in part due to having the gristmill and county courthouse; economically it was the center of commerce in 1860, but by 1873 that distinction fell to Ludington, and thus Lincoln faded. Many other communities grew and gained prominence because they were a stop on the Pere Marquette Railroad; farmers brought their goods to the station to ship out, and passengers came and went daily. Commerce follows the path that people take in their daily lives, and as the railroad's influence faded, small towns and villages along the way that relied on the railroad saw their importance diminished.

Ludington is the largest city in Mason County, followed by Scottville. Other villages include Custer, Branch, Tallman, and Walhalla to the east and Fountain and Freesoil to the north. Epworth Heights is more of a private community, but it has an important place in local history.

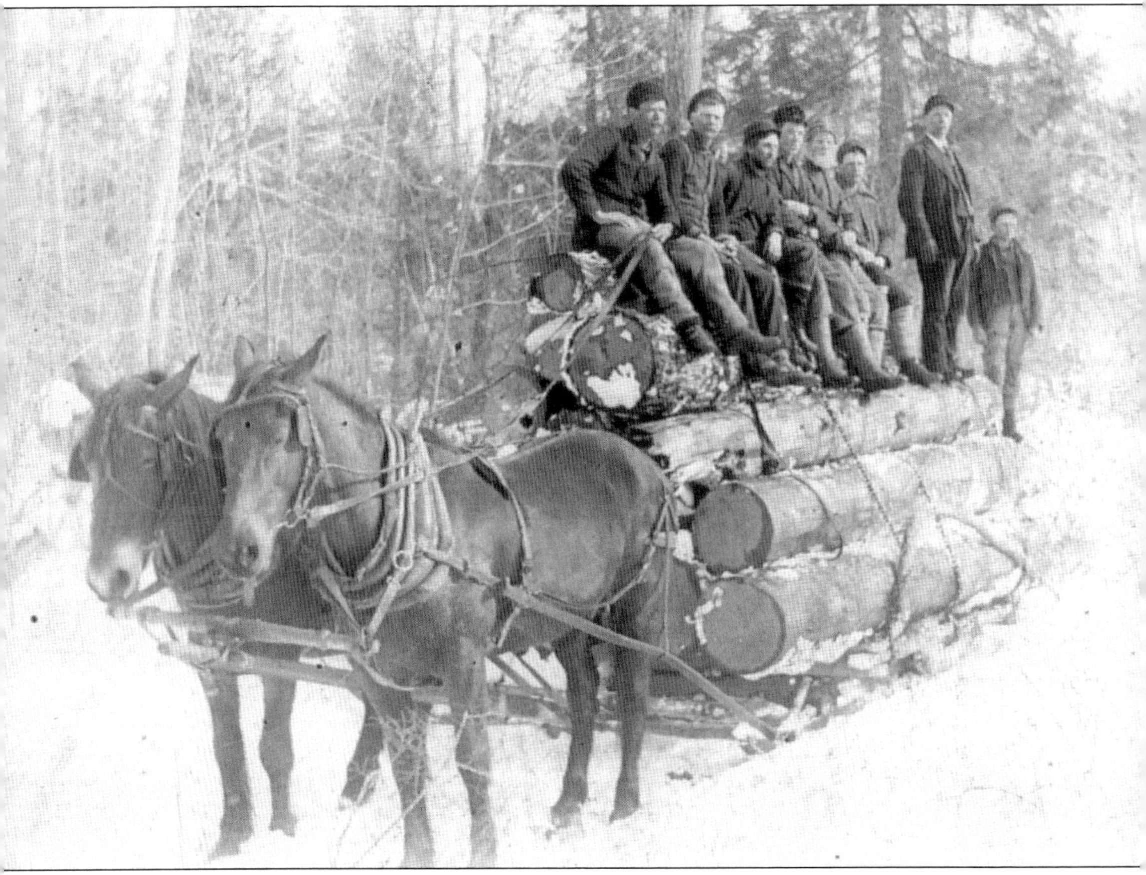

Branch is an unincorporated community on the Mason County and Lake County line that lies partially within the township of Branch and partially in Sweetwater Township of Lake County. Like its neighbors, Branch's history is primarily that of logging in the region and being a stop on the Flint and Pere Marquette Railroad. In fact, the first hotel built there to service the lumbering community was constructed by Benjamin F. Barnett of the Carr Settlement. When Barnett heard where the railroad was going to come through, he jumped at the opportunity. In 1876, Barnett became the first postmaster of Branch, named for the north branch of the Pere Marquette River. Carr is another of the small communities that shares boundaries with Lake County. The area around the settlement of Branch remains sparsely settled, as much of the land within its borders belongs to the Huron Manistee National Forest. It is primarily a recreational and resort area that offers hunting, fishing, and other outdoor sporting opportunities for vacationers. (Author's collection.)

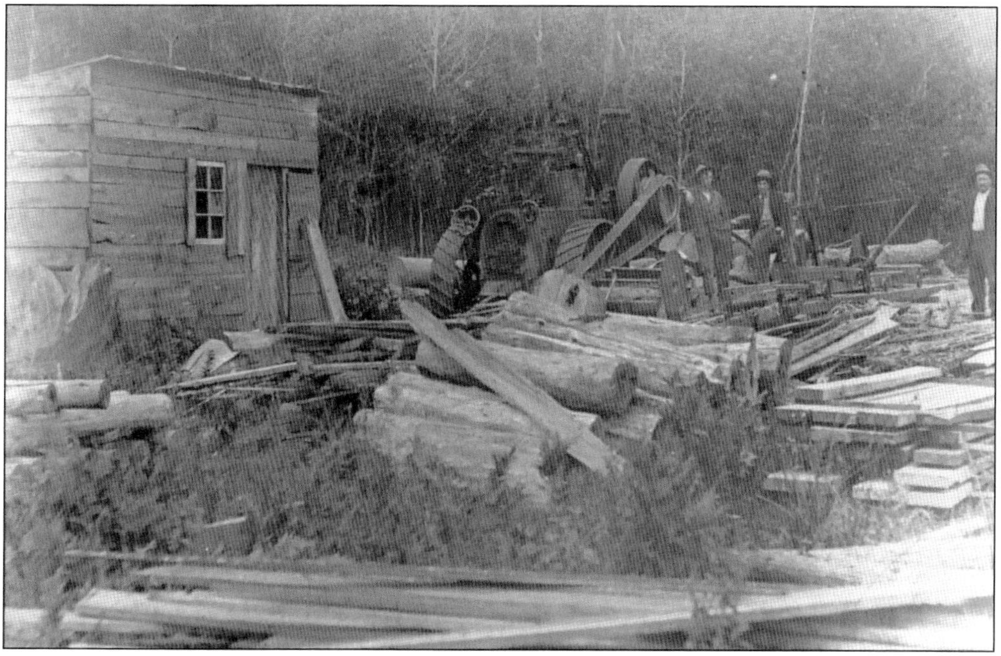

Branch is located on the Lake County line and is split between the two counties, not only geographically but historically was well. One cannot explore the history of one without including the other. Matt Stevenson (upper right) lived in Branch but owned a mill just north of the township. (Courtesy of Lake County Historical Society.)

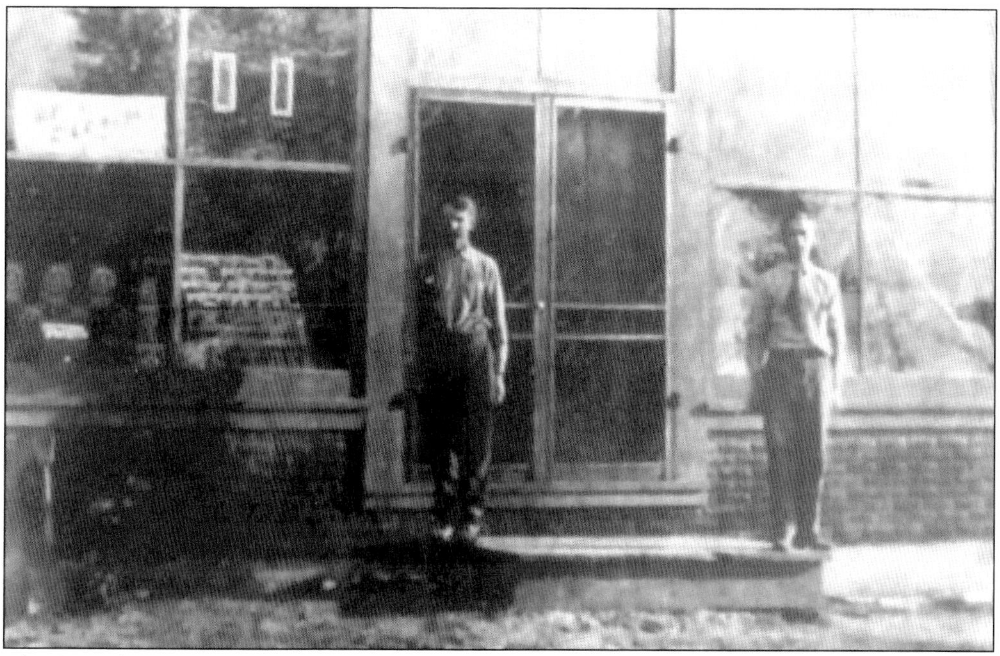

The Branch Store was a gathering place for community members to meet and hunker down to chew the fat about local happenings. The men pictured are identified only as Tyndalls. The Tyndall family was one of the early settlers in the eastern section of Mason County. (Courtesy of Lake County Historical Society.)

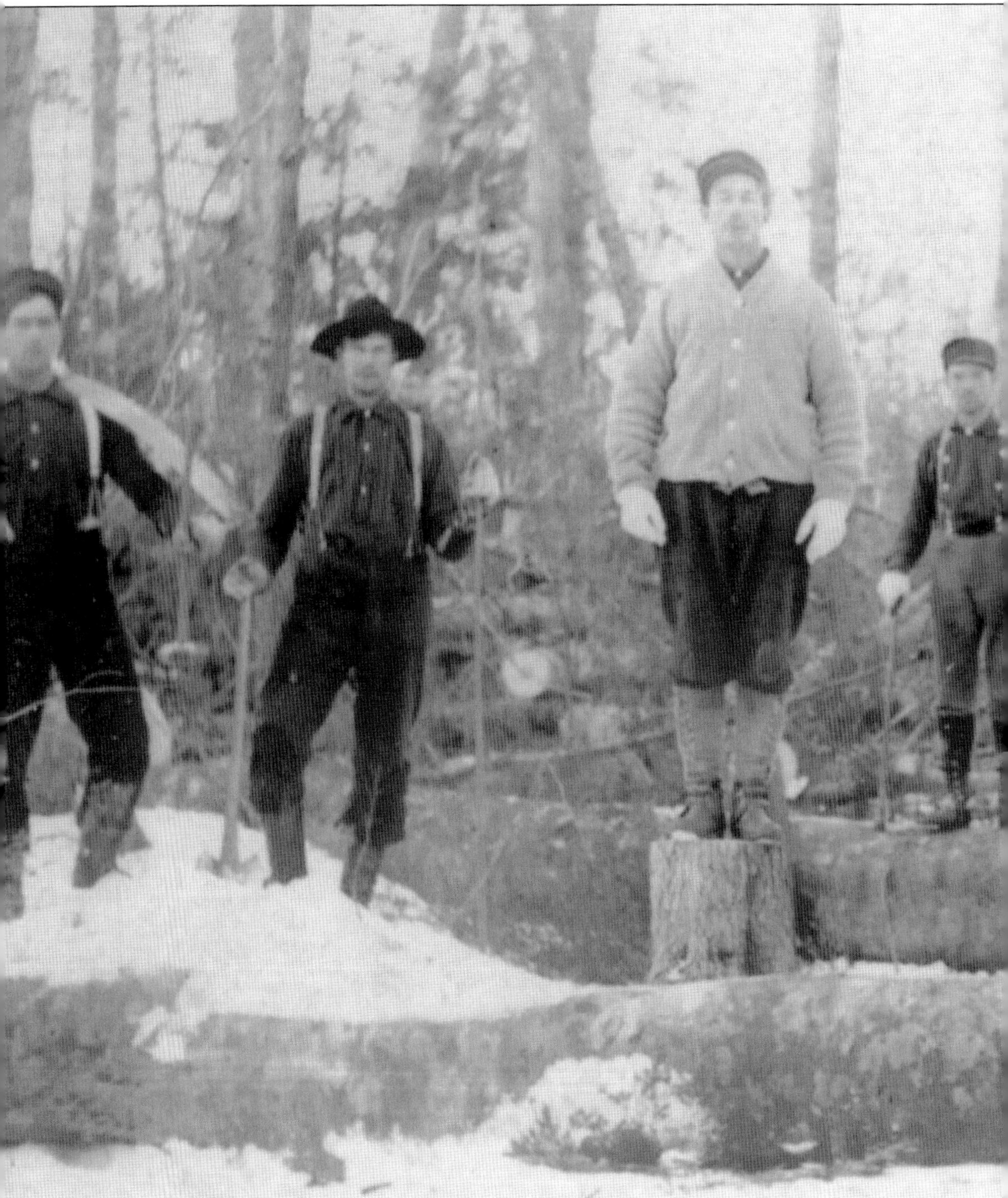

Carr Settlement, named after Charles Carr, is located in the far-east section of Logan Township and not only borders Lake County but also is partially situated in Lake County. Charles Carr and Benjamin Barnett were brothers-in-law who had both served in the Union army. They came to Michigan in 1867 to establish their claim, set up housekeeping, and begin logging. The Flint and Pere Marquette Railroad came through the area in 1872, which was also the year that the first school was established. Even so, the region was sparsely settled when the Carrs and Barnetts

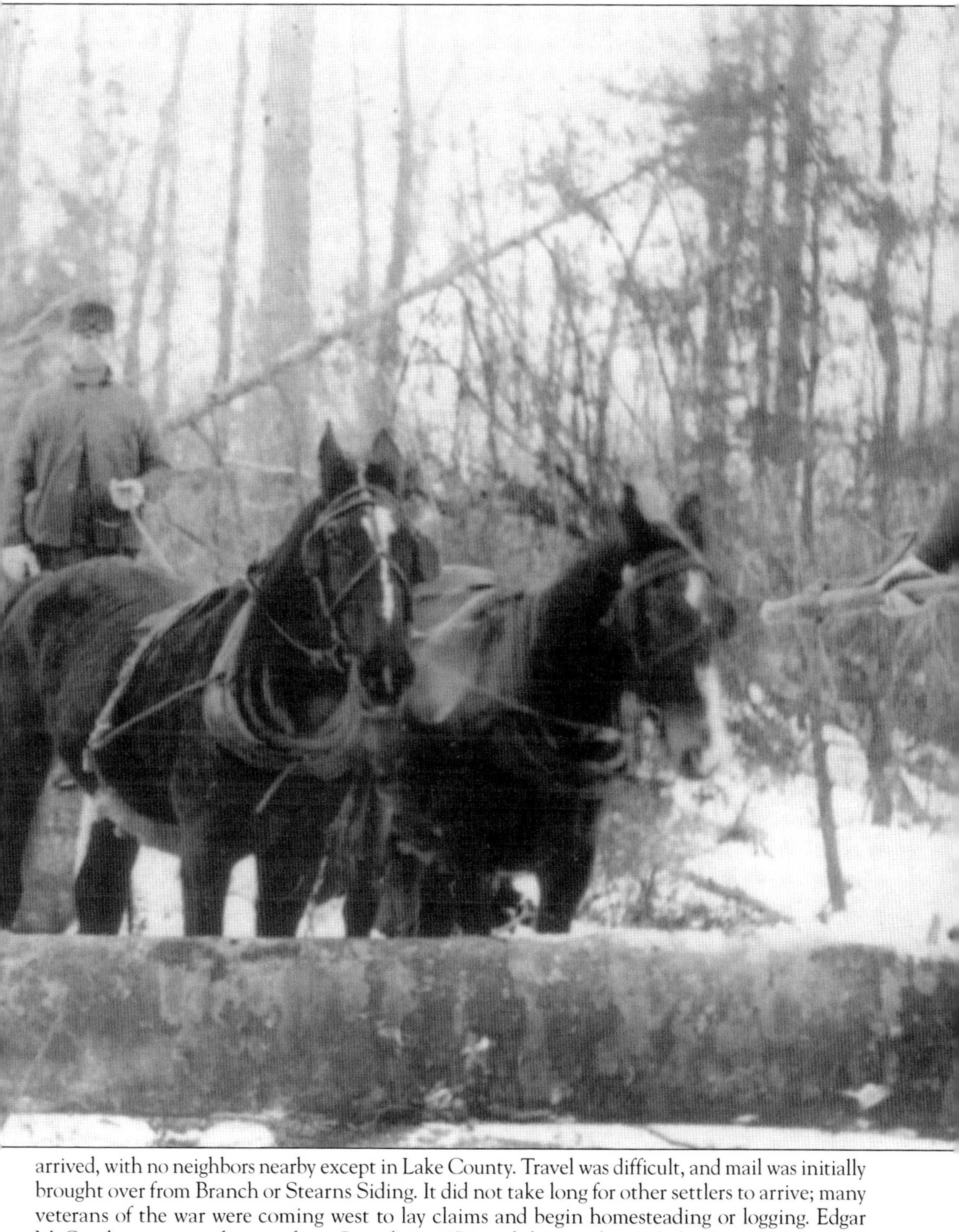

arrived, with no neighbors nearby except in Lake County. Travel was difficult, and mail was initially brought over from Branch or Stearns Siding. It did not take long for other settlers to arrive; many veterans of the war were coming west to lay claims and begin homesteading or logging. Edgar McCumber came to the area from Canada in 1874, and the area he settled in became known as McCumber Settlement. (Author's collection.)

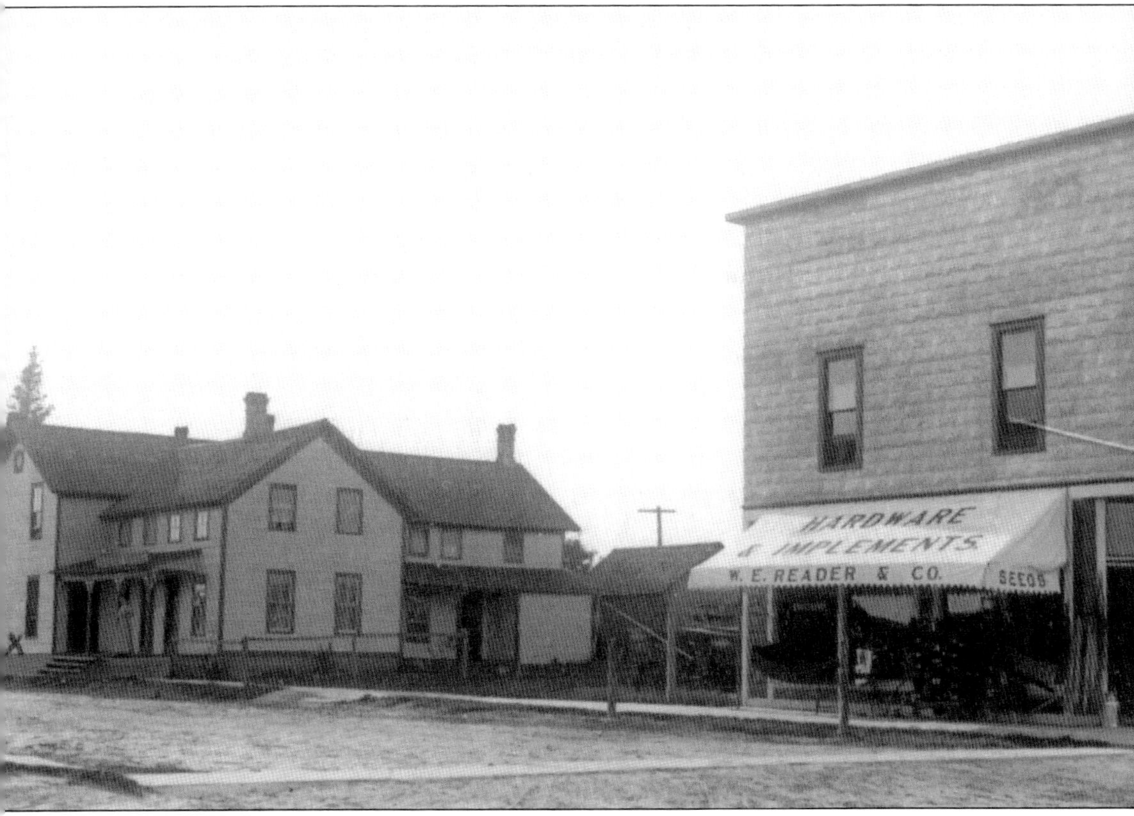

At the turn of the 20th century, Custer was quite a thriving little village, with a main street roughly one block long that included a general store, sawmill, post office, bank, grocery store, hotel, and hardware store. Other area businesses included a cheese-box factory, pickle station, Briggs and Booth Lumber Company, a saloon, blacksmith shop, livery, and a bakery. One could also frequent a pool and dance hall for entertainment. A little more than 50 years ago, the business community migrated yet again, this time to US 10, where the post office, Johnny's, Bonser's grocery store, and others have set up shop and continue to conduct business and keep the village of Custer running into the 21st century. The old main street was abandoned, but Sander's Meat Company is still located in that section of town. (Courtesy of MCHS.)

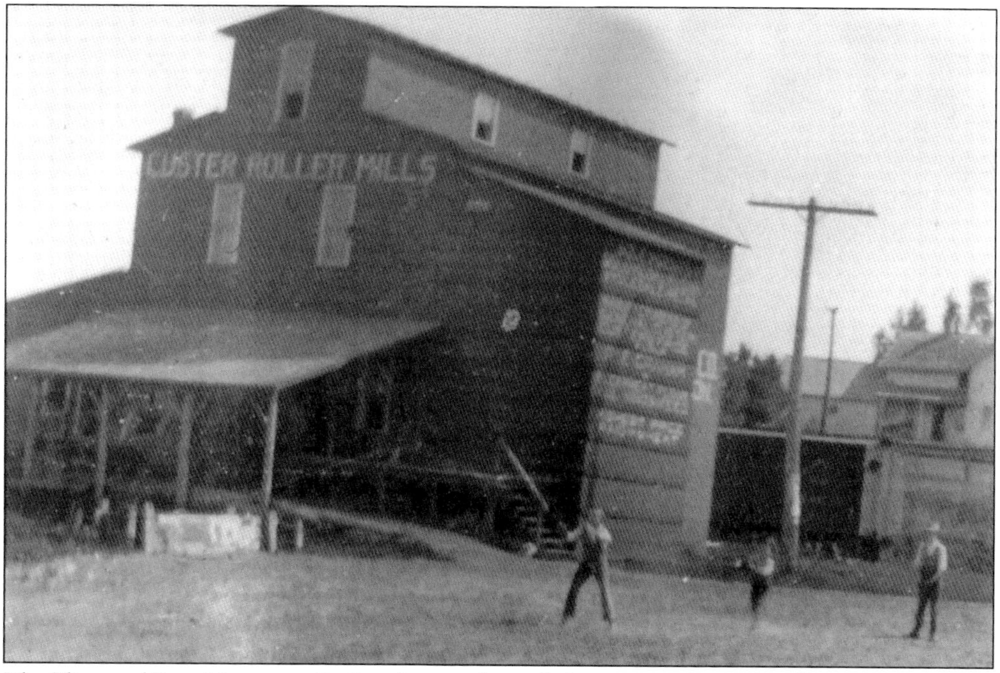

The Flint and Pere Marquette Railroad came through Custer in 1874, and William Davison built a station there. Agriculture was one of Custer Township's main activities after the lumbering era ended, and pine stumps were cleared from the land to establish new farms. (Courtesy of Village of Custer.)

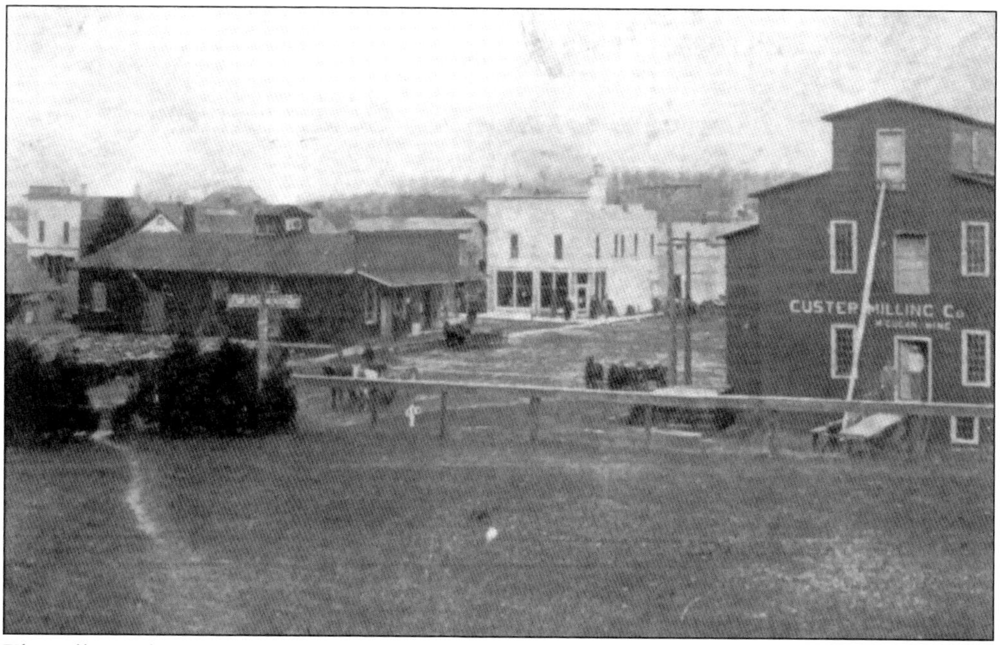

The village of Custer was a center of activity for the community. The main street was located a short distance south of US 10 and was only one block long. The old main street is still for the most part intact as the abandoned buildings were purchased and used for storage. (Courtesy of Village of Custer.)

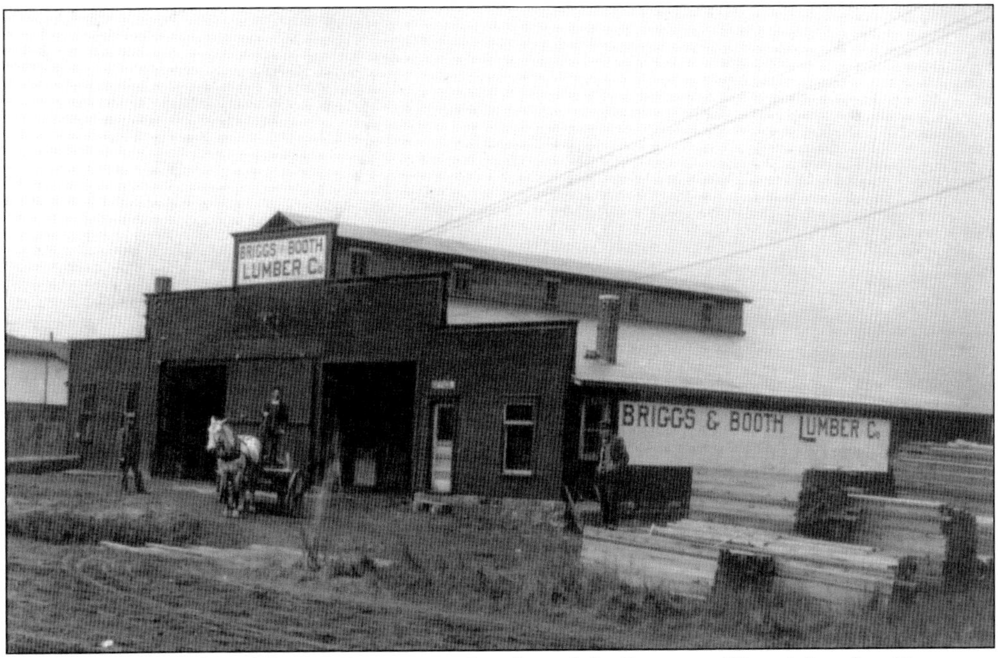

Partners John Booth and Eugene Briggs were founders of the Briggs and Booth Lumber Company. After, Booth went on to partner with Gus Schoenherr in Fountain. (Author's collection.)

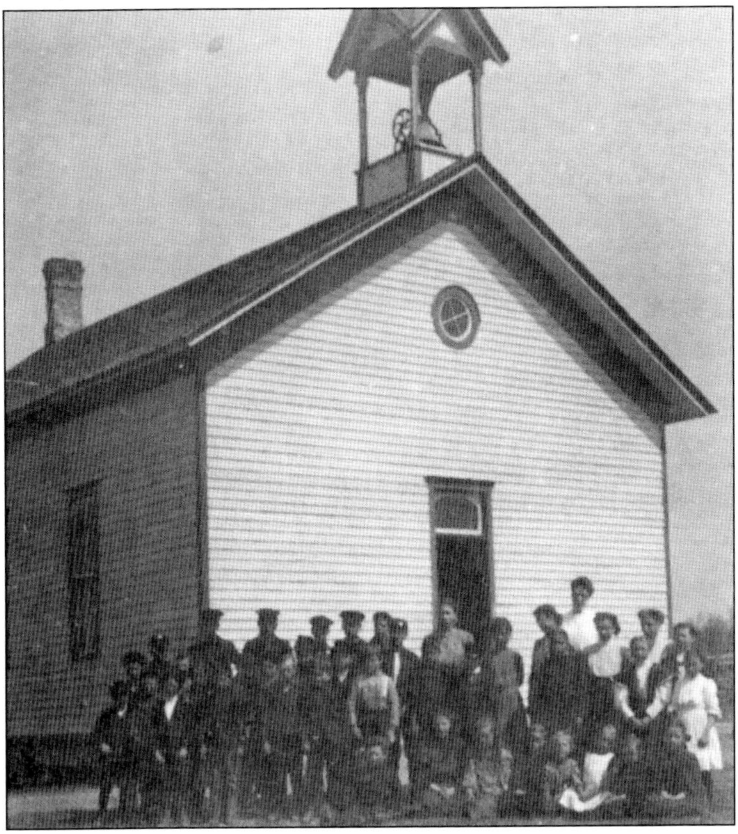

Wilson School was located on Wilson Road between Darr and Tuttle Roads. John Wilson came from Allegan, Michigan, in 1882 and purchased 120 acres on Wilson and Darr Roads. Other Custer Township schools included Weldon Creek, McClellan, Riverside, Resseguie, and Meninger. By 1959, all of the rural one-room schools had been consolidated, and an era of rural education came to an end. (Courtesy of MCHS.)

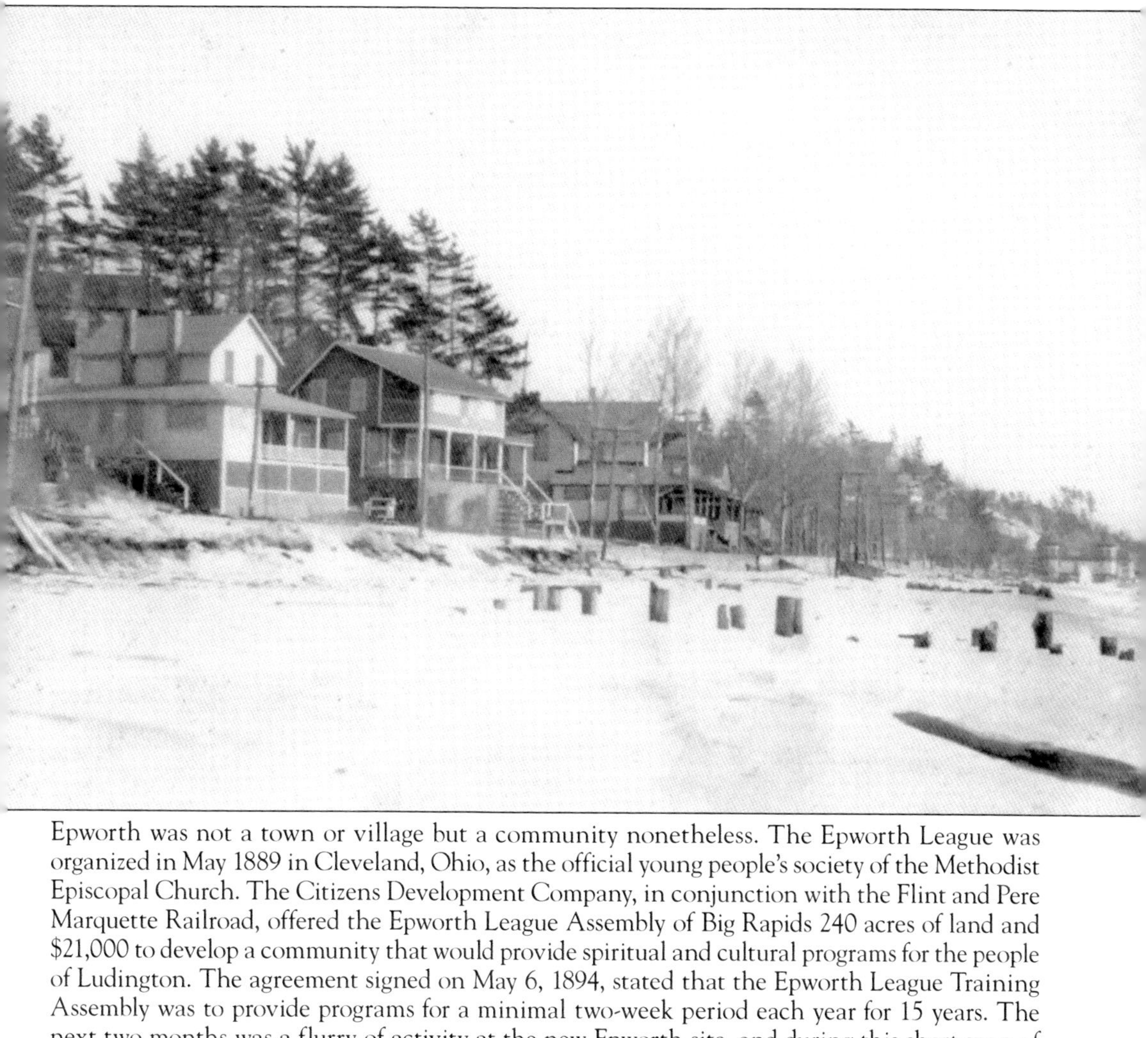

Epworth was not a town or village but a community nonetheless. The Epworth League was organized in May 1889 in Cleveland, Ohio, as the official young people's society of the Methodist Episcopal Church. The Citizens Development Company, in conjunction with the Flint and Pere Marquette Railroad, offered the Epworth League Assembly of Big Rapids 240 acres of land and $21,000 to develop a community that would provide spiritual and cultural programs for the people of Ludington. The agreement signed on May 6, 1894, stated that the Epworth League Training Assembly was to provide programs for a minimal two-week period each year for 15 years. The next two months was a flurry of activity at the new Epworth site, and during this short span of time the hotel, auditorium, and classrooms were built. (Author's collection.)

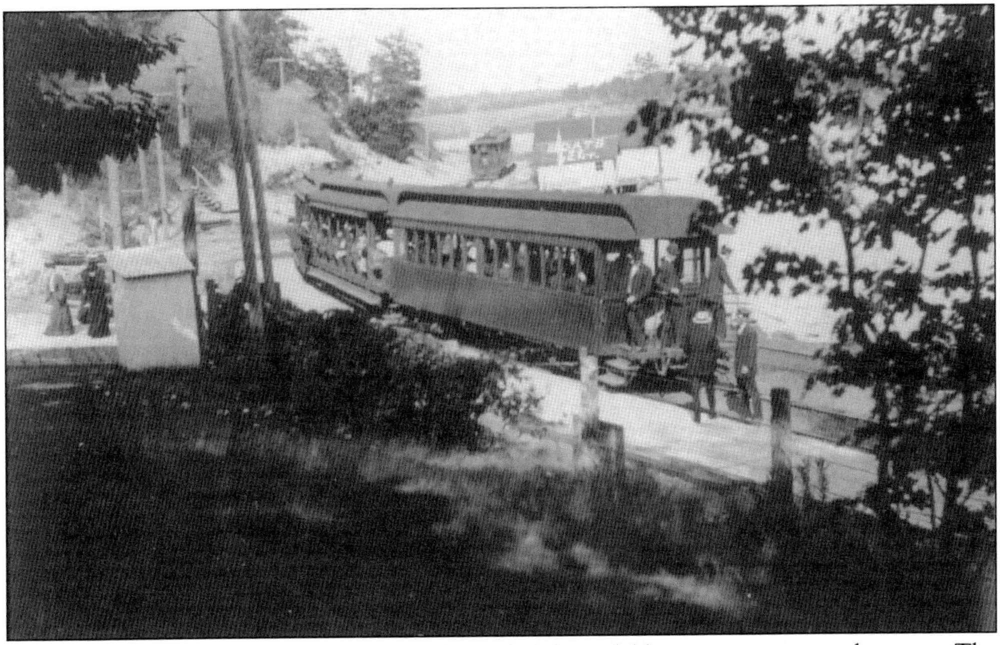

The Epworth League Railroad was built and provided dependable transportation to the resort. The engine of the train was built inside of a passenger coach, and it was quite unusual in appearance—a short, stubby enclosed coach pulling two or three open-air coaches through the woods to the Epworth Station. It did not look like a real train and appeared as a "Dummy Train" and is still referred to that way almost 100 years after it was discontinued. (Author's collection.)

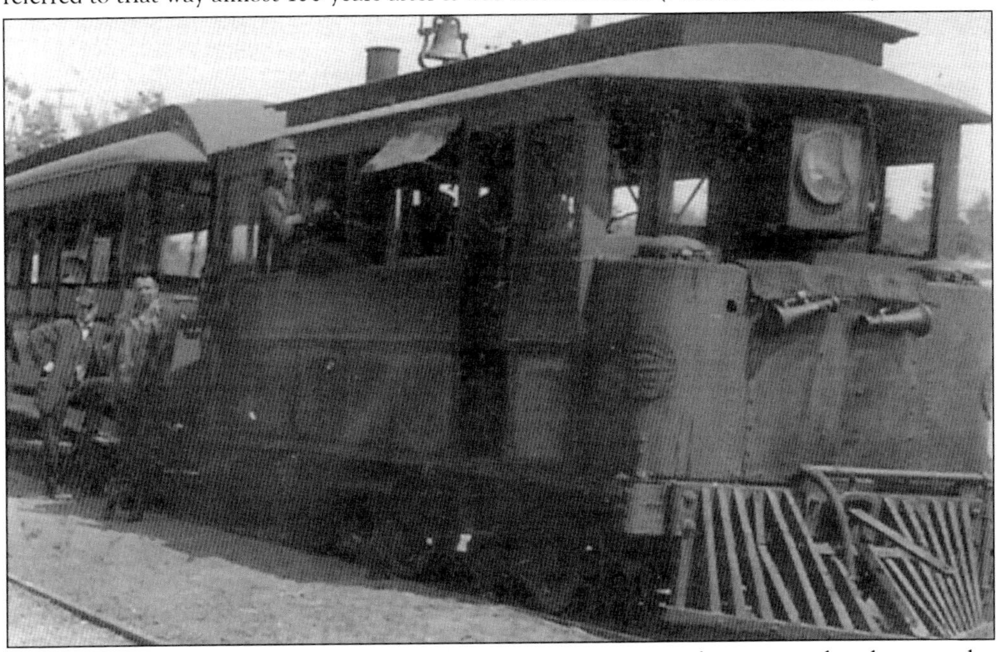

In 1902, Justin Stearns purchased the Epworth League Railway and reorganized and renamed it the Ludington and Northern Railway. Logging trains used the tracks to haul timber for Cartier Lumber Company, and the tracks were also extended to the middle bayou to provide additional passenger service to resorts on Hamlin Lake. (Author's collection.)

The lots at Epworth are not owned by the cottage owners but rather the association. When Epworth began, the initially intention was to subdivide the area that comprises Cartier Park but a trade was worked out with Cartier and the 40-acre parcel was exchanged for the one to the north of Mount Epworth that comprised the old village of Lincoln. (Author's collection.)

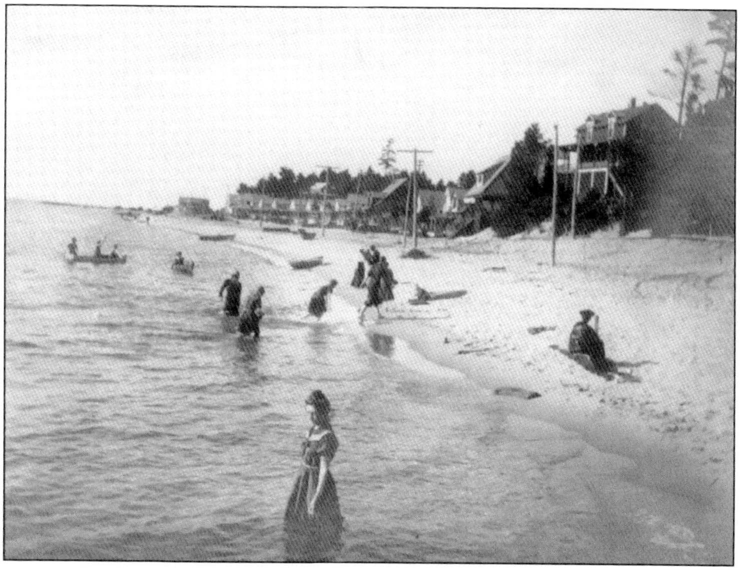

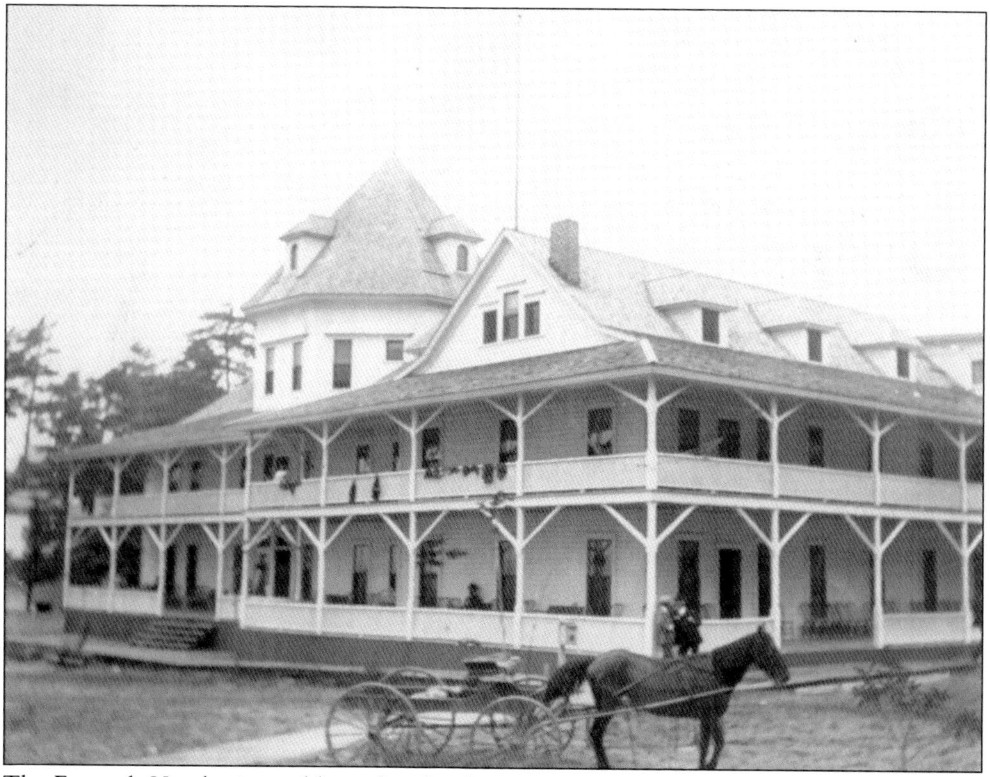

The Epworth Hotel, pictured here shortly after construction, was a beautiful building on the shores of Lake Michigan. Justus Stearns took over the operation of the faltering hotel for a 10-year period and turned its fate around and when he turned it back over to the Epworth League. (Author's collection.)

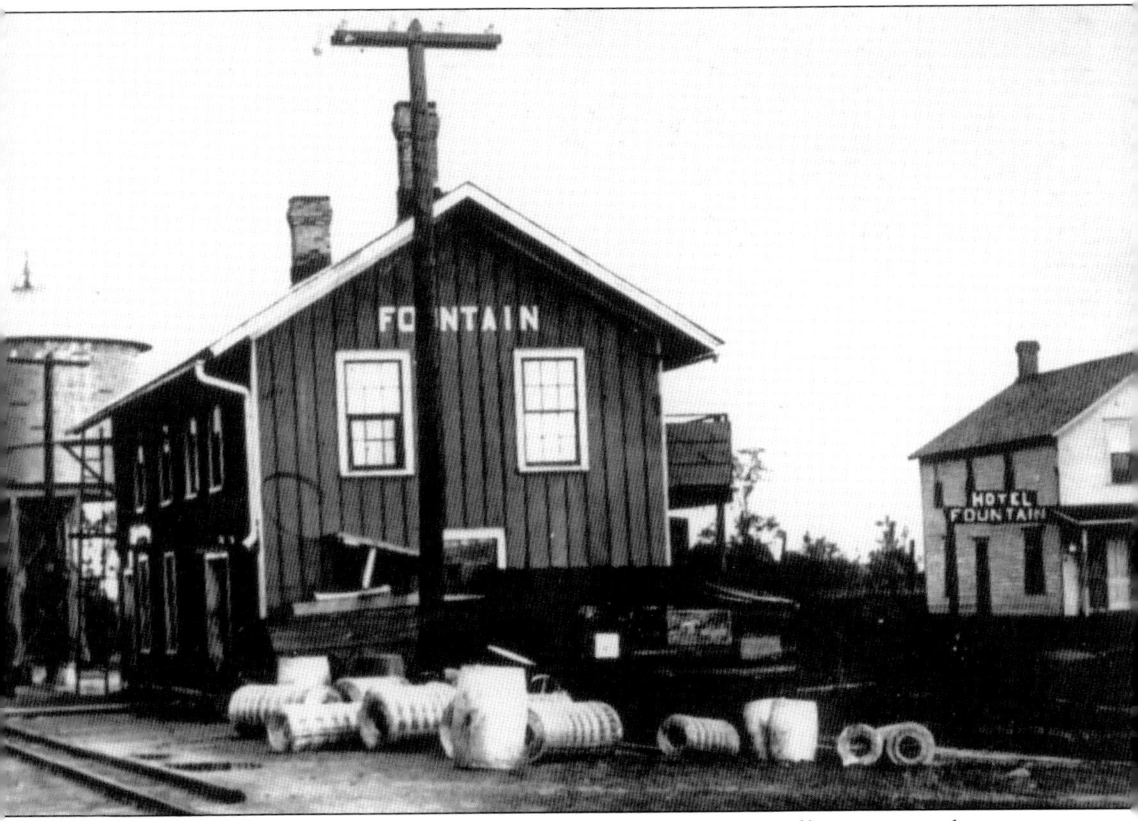

The post office was approved in 1882, and in order to have a post office, one must have a name for it. Fountain, Michigan, was chosen, but where did this originate from? Well, some might have guessed that it was derived from the fact that there was a bubbling spring located near the Pere Marquette Railroad water tank. Fountain is located in present-day Sherman Township, originally a part of the original Freesoil Township. In October 1867, the application was presented to the Mason County Board of Commissioners, and after it was approved the new township held its first election, in April 1868, at the home of Fred Wiedmer. A few years later, in 1889, the township was split again, with the eastern portion being named Sheridan. In those years after the Civil War, names of Union generals and others associated with the victory over the "Southern aggressors" found their names attached to roads, schools, towns, and townships, as many veterans settled in Northern Michigan. (Courtesy of Keith Adams.)

Keith Adams and a couple of friends are horsing around on the hitching post in front of his parents' general store in Fountain. Other local business owners included Henry Eoff, who built the grain elevator about 1900, and D.D. Manchester, who was a dealer of coal and operated his business until 1917. (Courtesy of Keith Adams.)

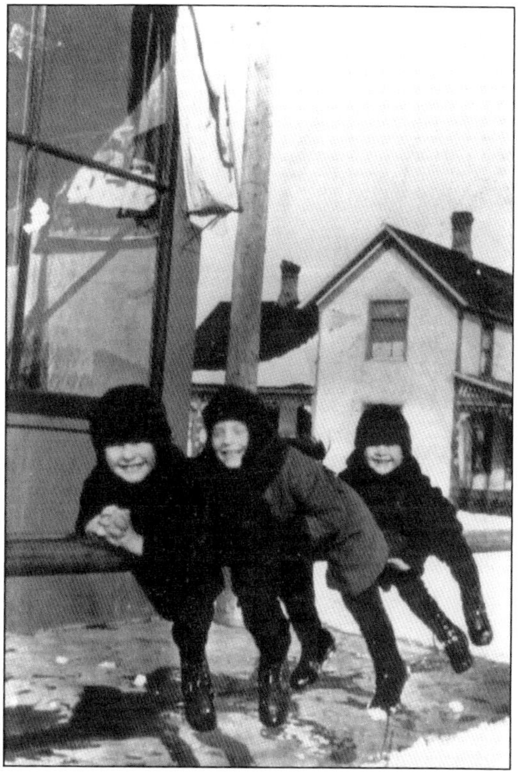

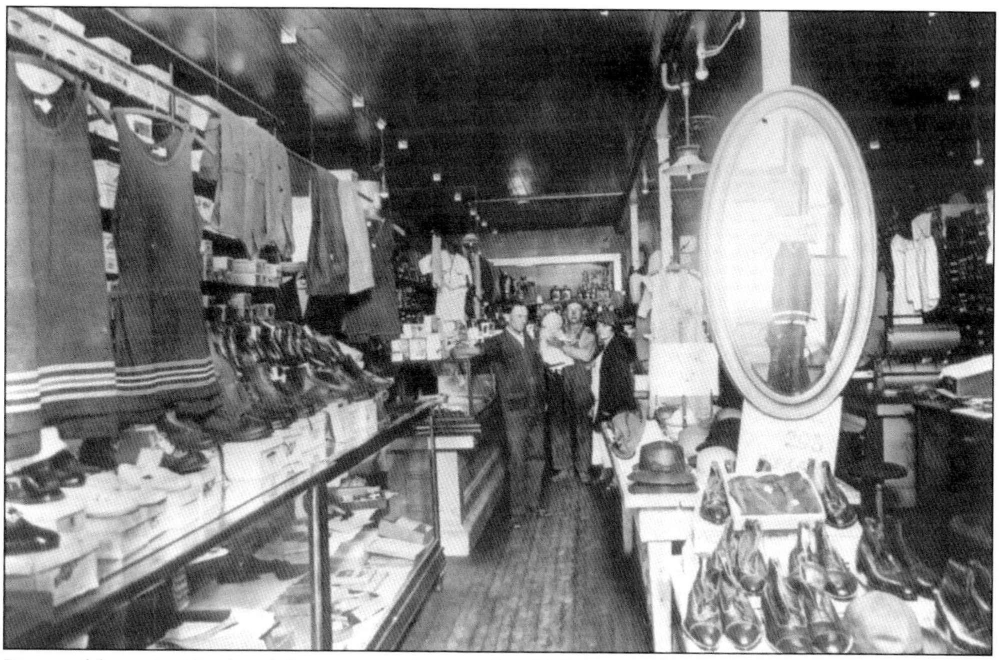

Pictured here inside the Adams general store, Emil Blohm is the man leaning on the counter. Everything a person needed was probably within walking distance in the village, whether it was a haircut from Roy Sinclair or to make a deposit at the new bank, where Luther Foster of Ludington was a cashier. (Courtesy of Keith Adams.)

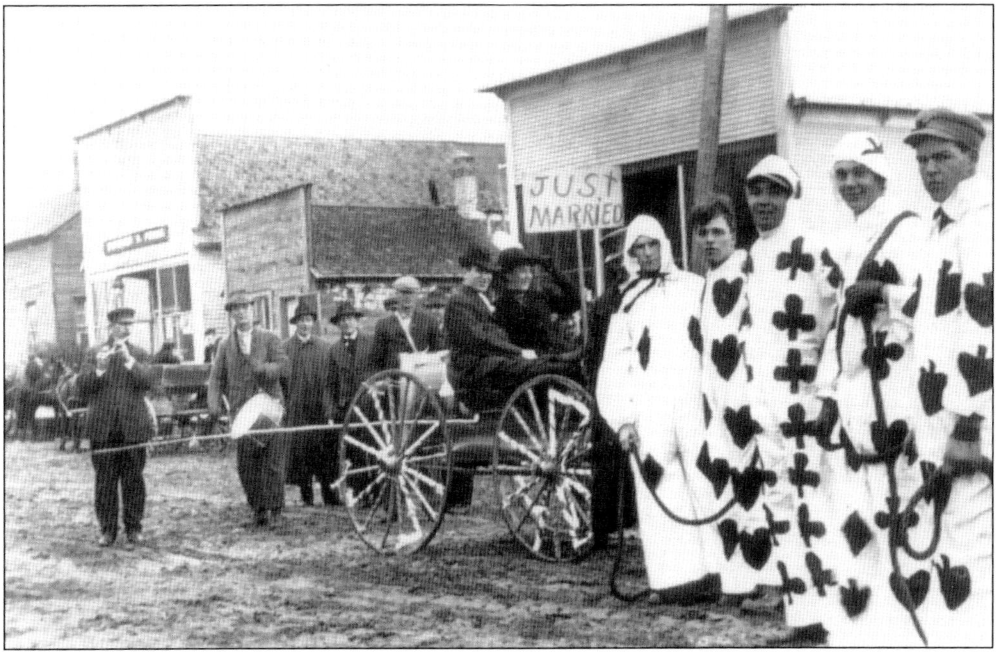

At the wedding of Maude Laguire and Van Brant in Fountain, it looks like their friends are having a bit of fun. It was all taken in the spirit in which it was meant; a wedding celebration was an opportunity for everyone to get together and enjoy good food, good company, and home-grown entertainment. (Courtesy of Keith Adams.)

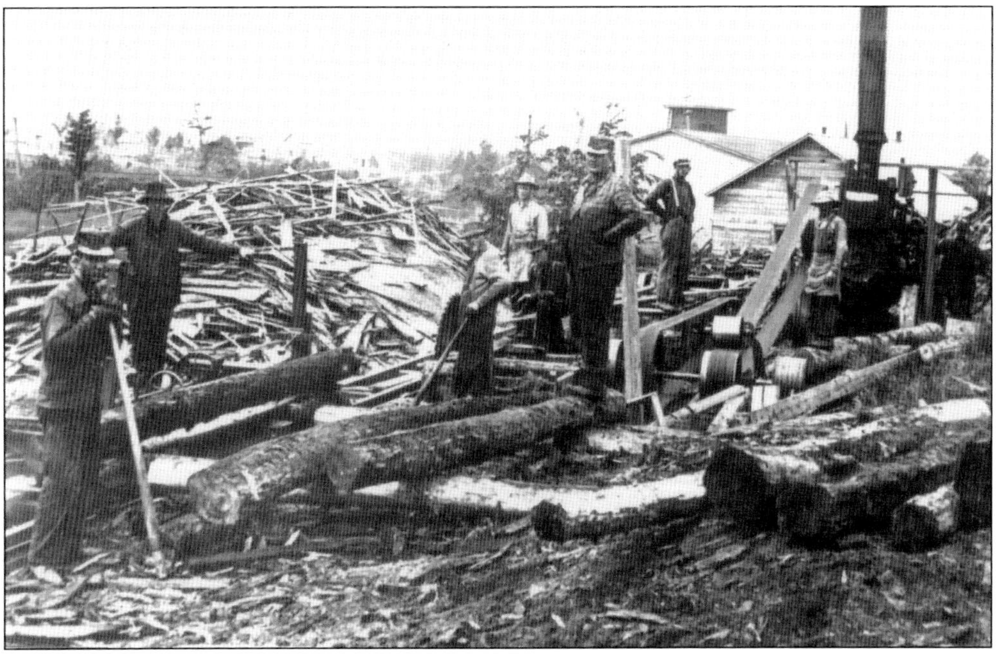

The Fountain Lumber Company was built on the site of the original Foster Sawmill. It was hard work, and it could be dangerous as well. At the time this photograph was taken, the area did not have a hospital, and care of the injured was often provided by family or, in the case of itinerant workers, through the kindness of strangers. (Courtesy of Keith Adams.)

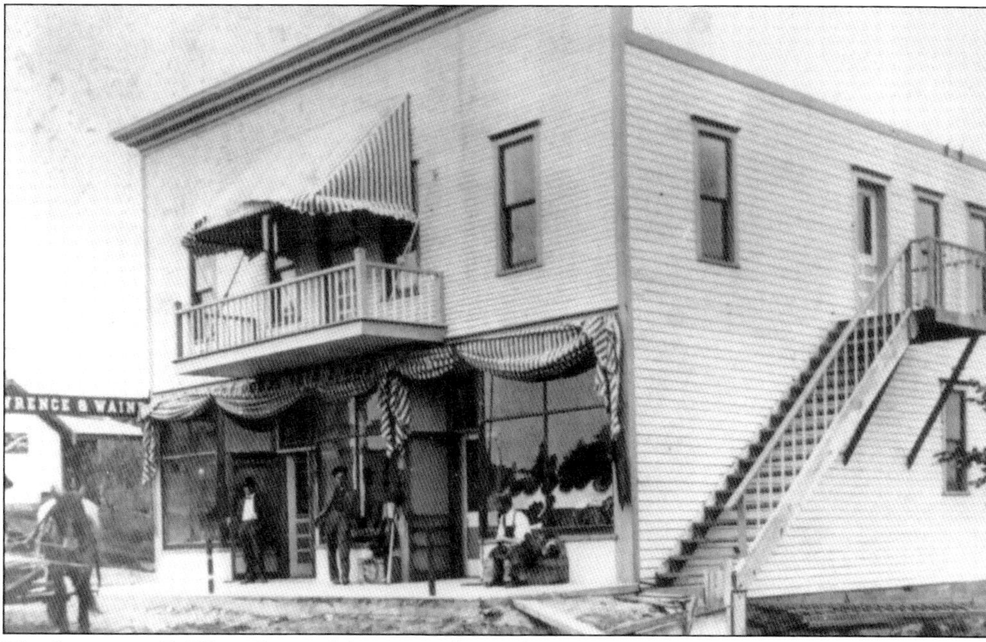

The Lawrence E. Wain General Store was located on South Cleveland Street in Fountain; the village was a bustling center of commerce and a farming center for the area. Travel was more difficult before 1920 because of the poor road system. In the 1870s, a trip from Fountain to the gristmill at Lincoln would easily take up to two days. (Courtesy of Keith Adams.)

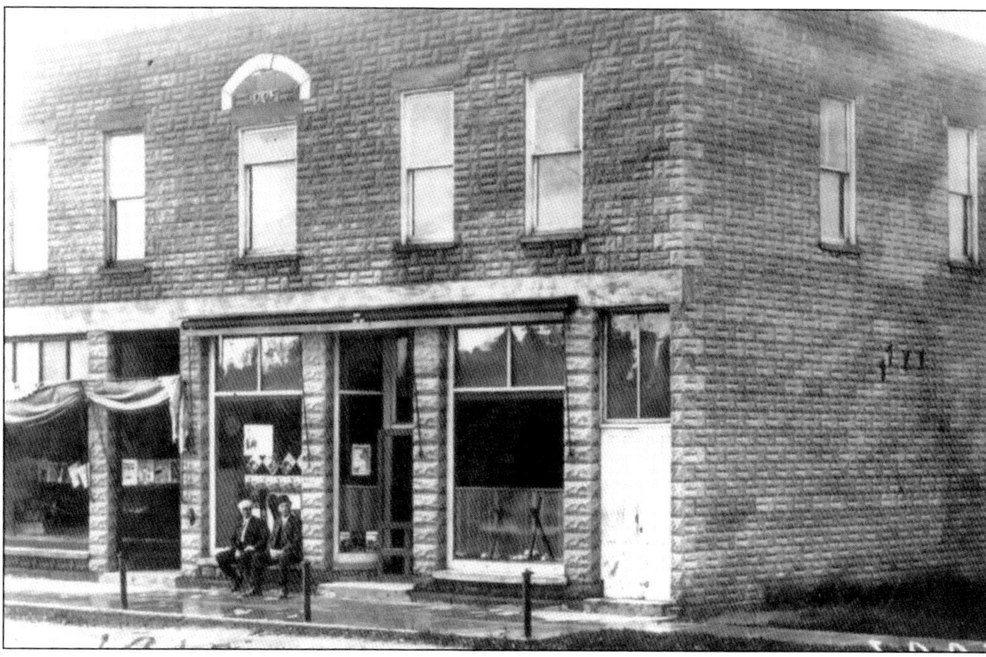

The Hans Luken Grocery Store was located in this building, and in keeping with the times, the family lived in the apartment above the store. On the right side of the building, Edward Rasmussen operated his drugstore, and the upstairs was used by the Odd Fellows, who had the building constructed in 1908 for their lodge. (Courtesy of Keith Adams.)

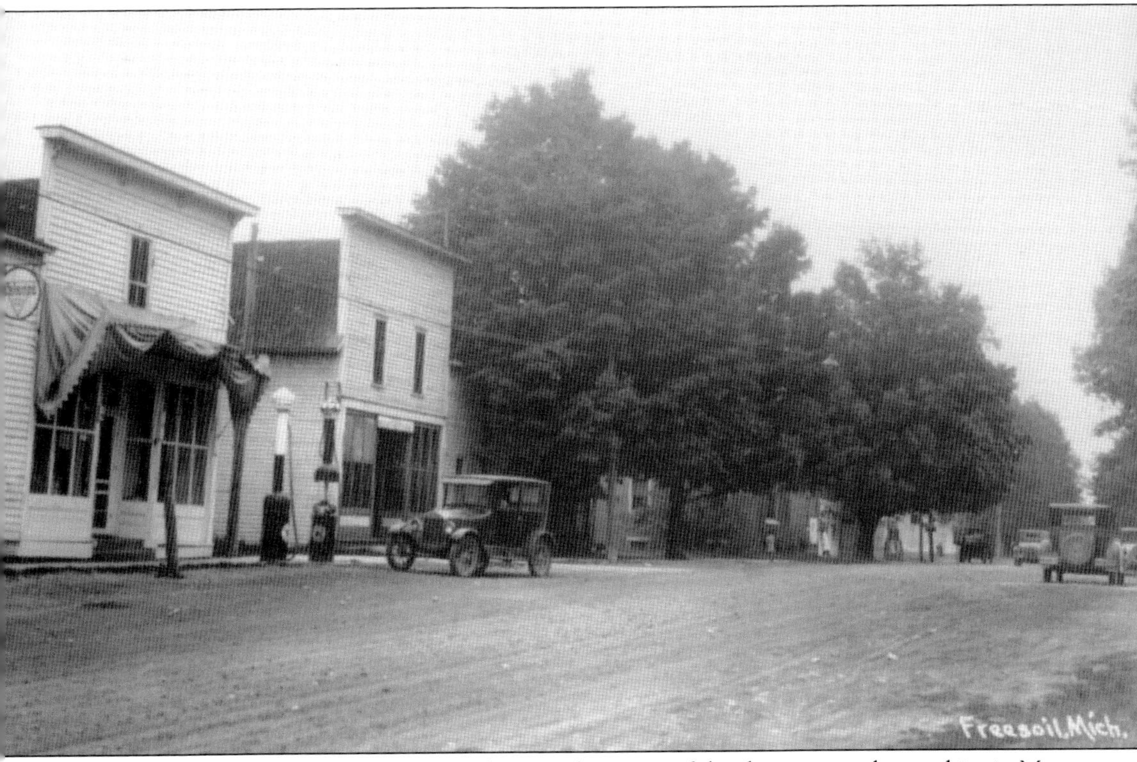

Pictured here is Main Street in Freesoil. Freesoil was one of the three original townships in Mason County, having been formed in 1855. Freesoil was divided into three townships: Freesoil, Grant, and Meade. The village of Freesoil began in the early 1860s, and logging was the principal economy, followed by agriculture. The population had grown to as much as 400 at one time. The village began after Phillip Ritter settled in the area east of what would become known as Ritter Swamp. Because of its location in the county, Freesoil had closer ties to the Manistee area because in those early days travel was difficult. As a result, many of the early families that settled there came south from Manistee as opposed from Ludington. At one time, Freesoil was a busy community; there were several businesses and stores. As travel became easier and roads better, the larger stores to the west took in more business, and the result was the same in Freesoil as in many small towns: commerce declined and stores closed. (Courtesy of Benita Eddy Hurd.)

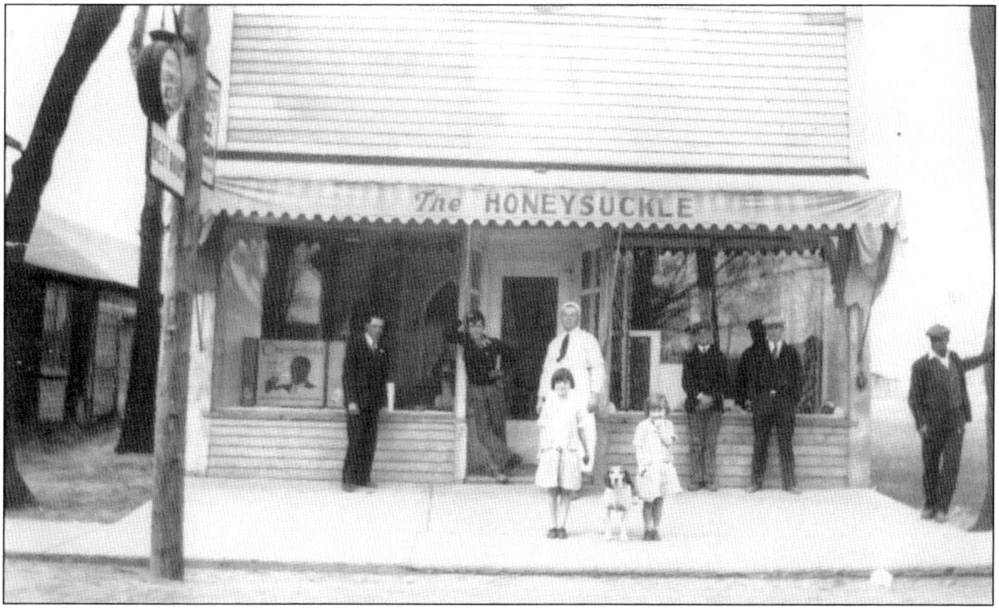

The Honeysuckle was a well-known establishment in Freesoil on the north side of the street across from the Church of Latter-day Saints. It was owned at various times by Bernice and Frank Eddy, Jon and Peg Felty, the Lubert family, and finally the Dombrowski family before being converted to a private residence. (Courtesy of Benita Eddy Hurd.)

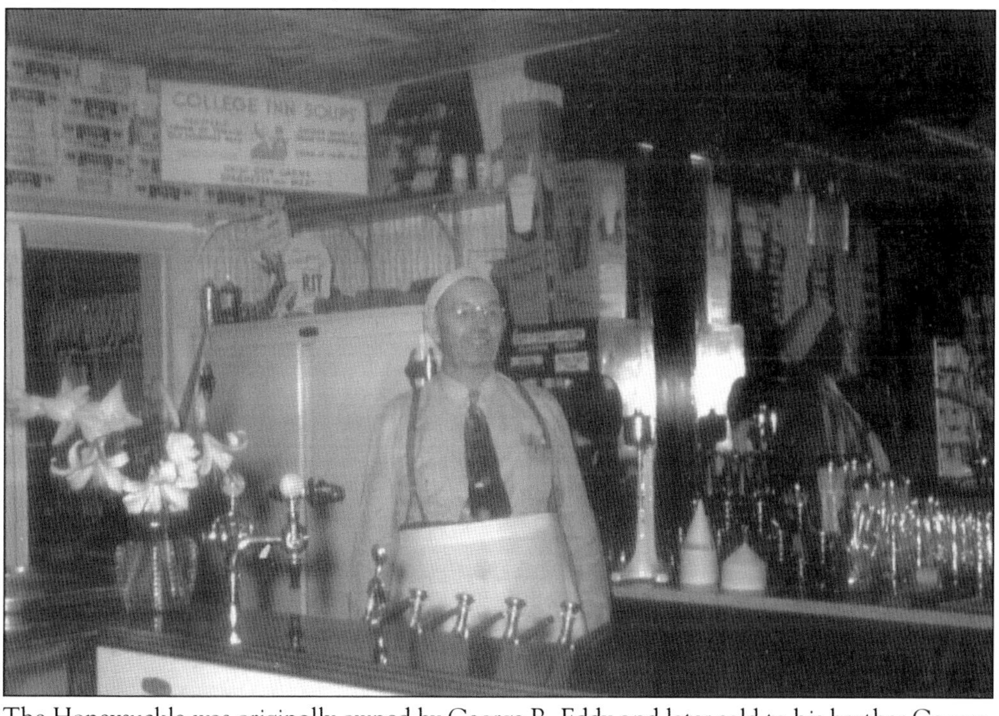

The Honeysuckle was originally owned by George R. Eddy and later sold to his brother George. It was more than just a store; the Honeysuckle was a community treasure and central gathering place for residents who frequented the establishment for refreshments served up at the ice cream counter by longtime owner Frank Eddy, pictured here. (Courtesy of Benita Eddy Hurd.)

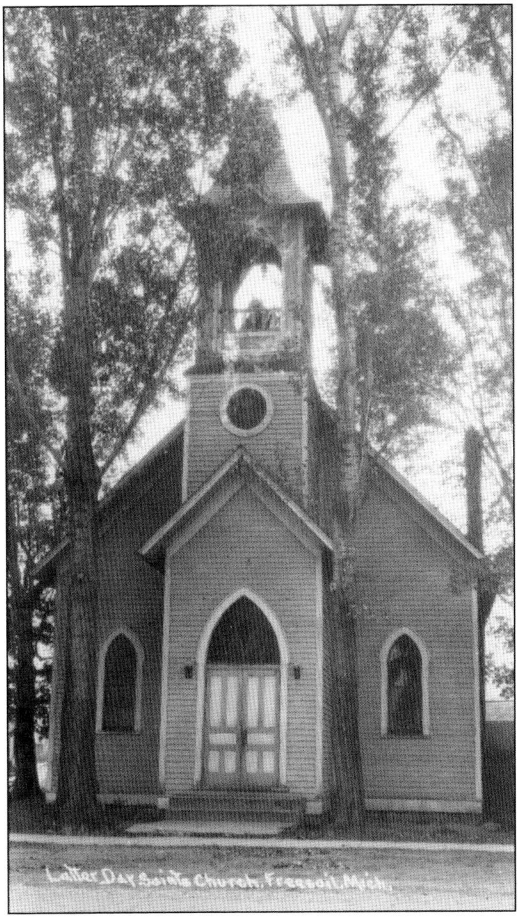

The Freesoil Community Band provided entertainment at rural gatherings in the late 1920s. Band members included Taylor Winnup, Floyd Wolf on drums, Kenneth Gilmore playing the banjo, Neva Winnup, Taylor Gilmore with the fiddle, and Elmer Wolf. (Courtesy of Benita Eddy Hurd.)

The Freesoil Methodist Church was dedicated in 1884. In an August 27, 1941, *Ludington Daily News* article, "The second church to be organized here was the Latter Day Saints in 1887. Previous to this date, meetings were held in the various homes and the present church building was erected in 1901 and dedicated in 1902. The St. Johns Cantius Church was erected about 35 years ago (about 1906) and many additions and improvements have been made." (Courtesy MCHS.)

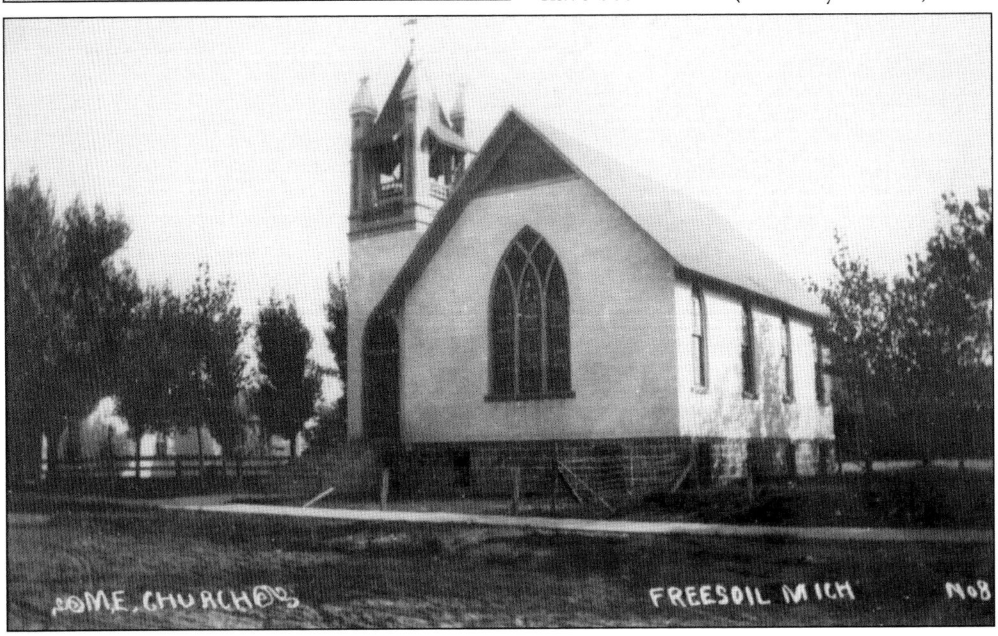

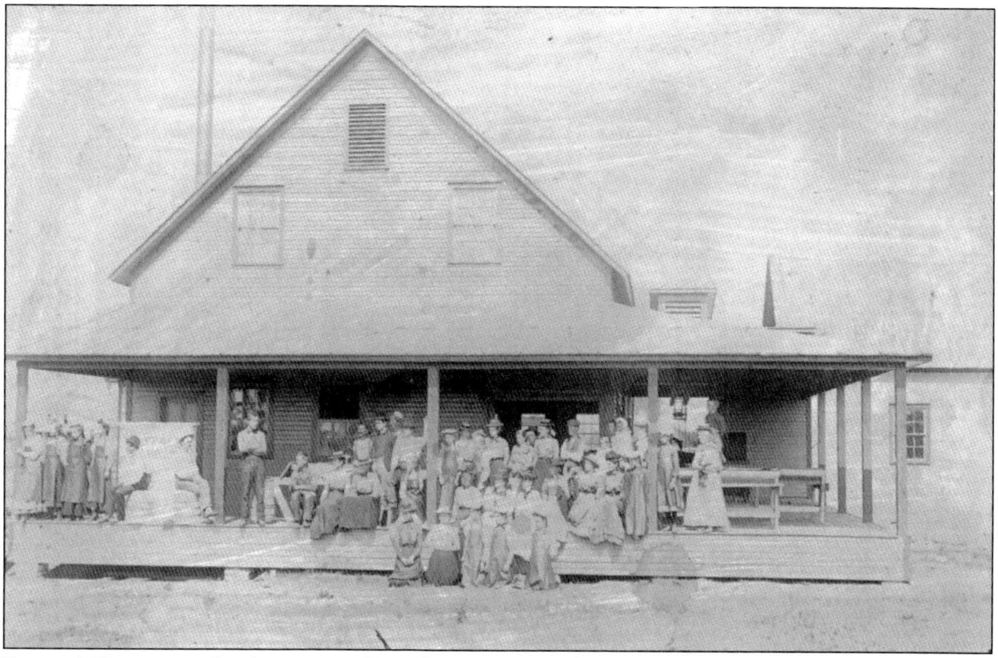

Freesoil Canning, also known as Star Canning, was located south of Main Street along the west side of the railroad tracks. There was a drugstore, blacksmith shop, hotel, railroad depot, and barbershop. Businesses included Rothchild Case and Company, Bennett and Stephens, and Manigold Stephens and Company, among many others. (Courtesy MCHS.)

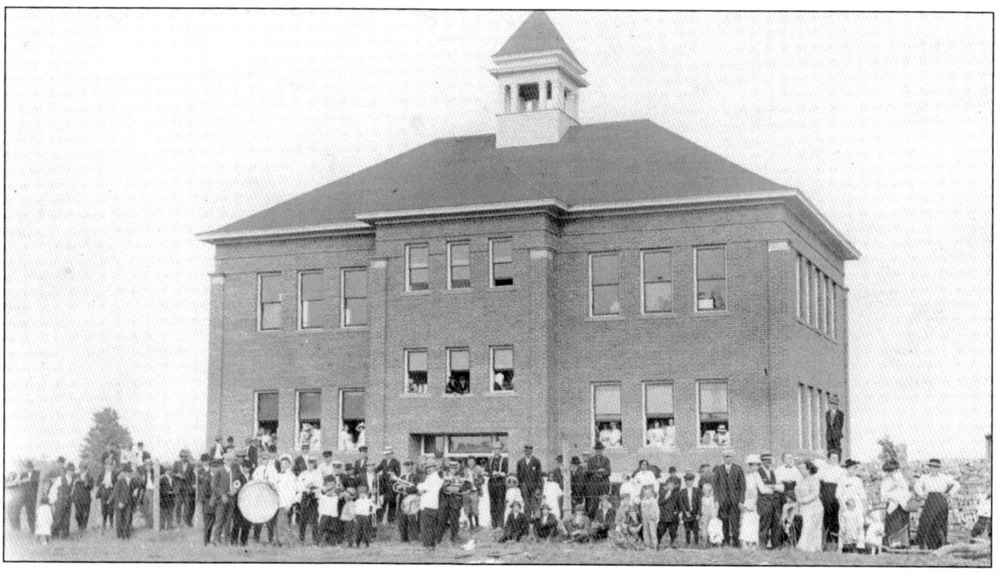

Freesoil High School was established in 1913. The August 27 edition of the *Ludington Daily News* stated, "The first licensed physician arrived in the village and taught school to earn his living. It is said that often while teaching he left the school to run itself while he made a professional call on some sick patient." (Courtesy MCHS.)

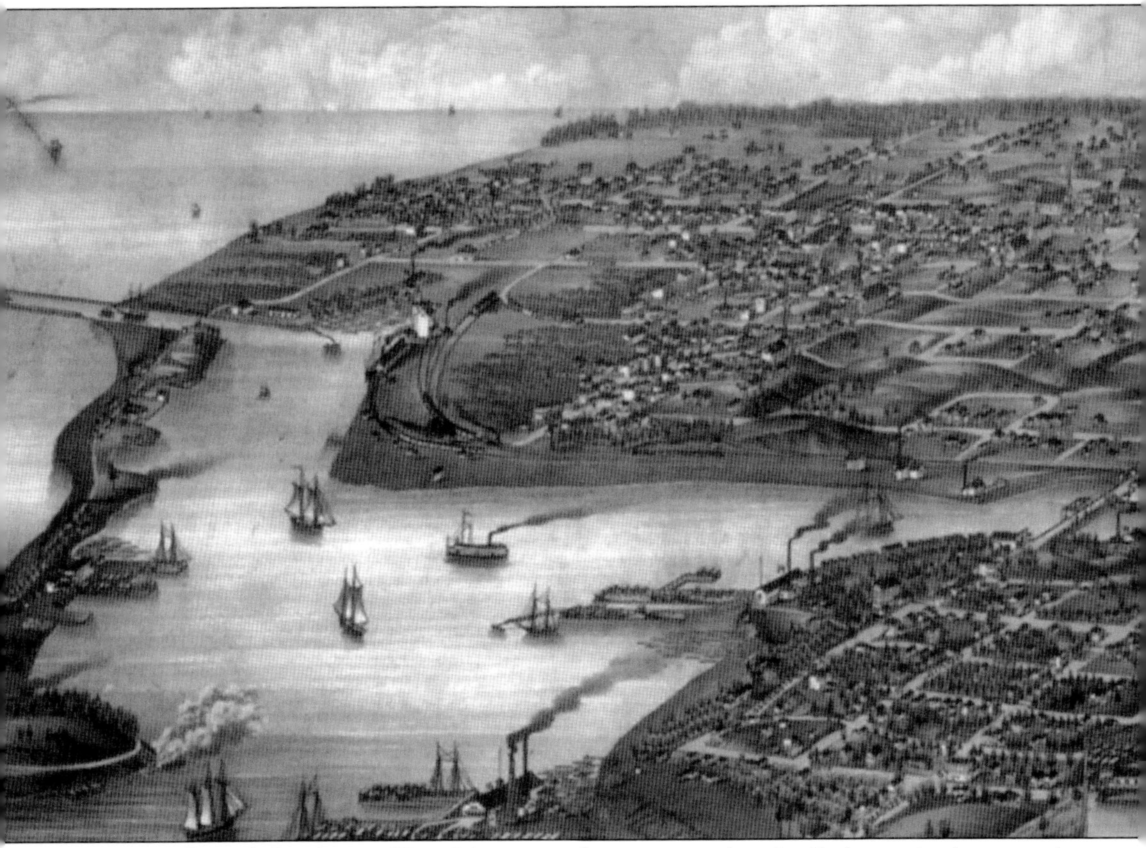

Originally settled and named Pere Marquette after its namesake who died upon its shores at what would become Buttersville Peninsula, the village was platted in 1867 by James Ludington and incorporated in 1873 as Ludington. A new city hall was constructed in 1873 that would also house the Phoenix Fire House. Like many communities along the Lake Michigan shoreline, trapping and trading was followed by shingle makers and lumbering. Pine was king, and the harvesting of the great forest created kings of paupers who had come in droves for the bounty of a new land. The newly constructed Filer House was situated north of the mill and Sawdust Avenue, where most of the building and activity was taking place. The Filer House was probably considered in the boondocks by 1865 standards. When one looks at a sketch of 1865 Ludington and the period photographs of Lincoln Village, the concept of James Ludington platting a village in 1867 seems like an unattainable dream. Yet 1867 is the year that he also brought George Clayton across to the village to set up a newspaper, the *Mason County Record*. (Courtesy MCHS.)

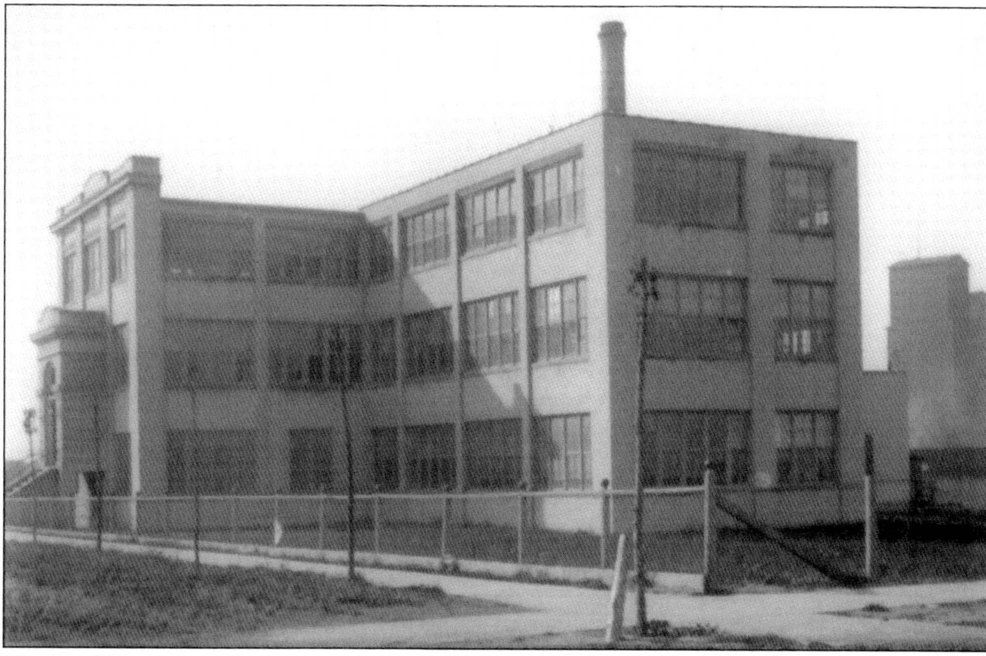

The Star Watch Case Company was originally founded as the Illinois Watchcase Company in Elgin, Illinois, about 1897. The business long stood on South Rath Avenue after its move here in 1906 and employed many thousands of Ludington men and women during its years of operation. The watchcases made in Ludington were supplied to the best Swiss watchmakers in the world. Precision Watch Case Company purchased the business in 1979 to close it in 1982. (Author's collection.)

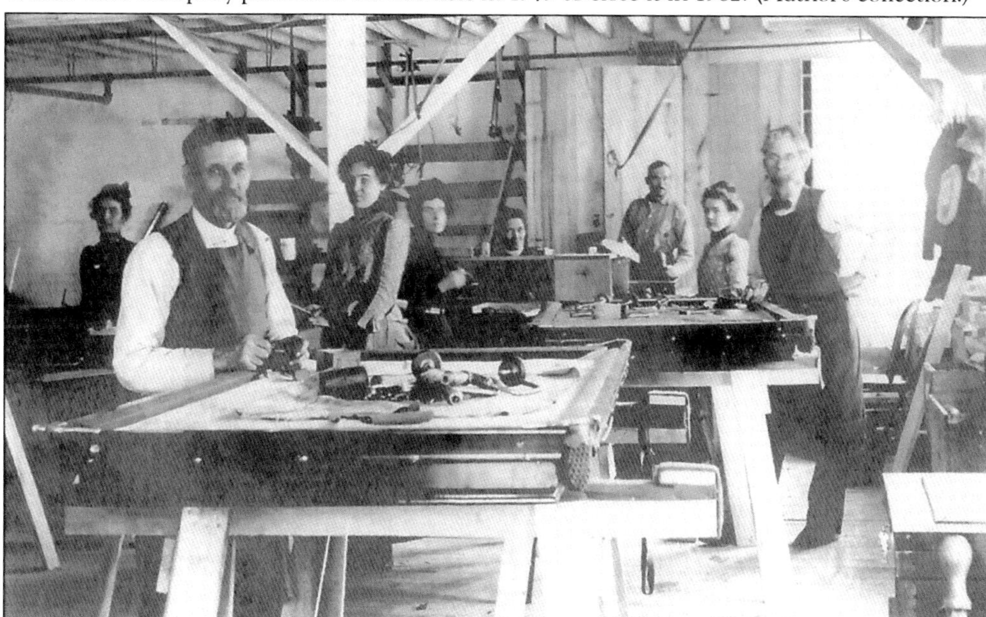

The Carrom Company has been a fixture in Ludington for over 100 years. Its beginnings came in 1890 after Henry Haskell invented a wholesome game, Carrom, that he had hoped would have an appeal to children and deter them from hanging around pool rooms. The game was first produced by Ludington Novelty Works in which Haskell was a part owner. (Courtesy of Ron Lessard.)

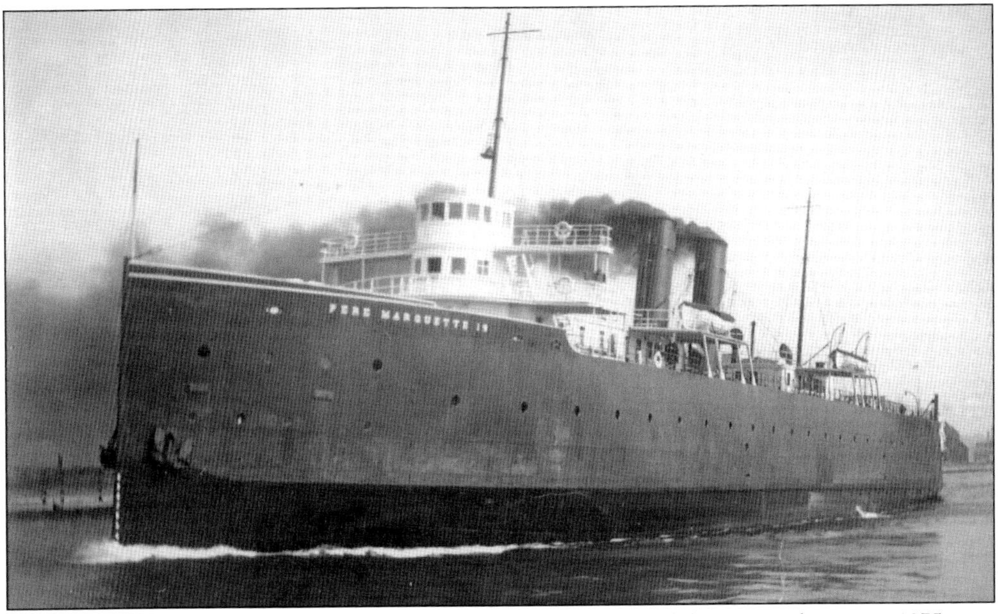

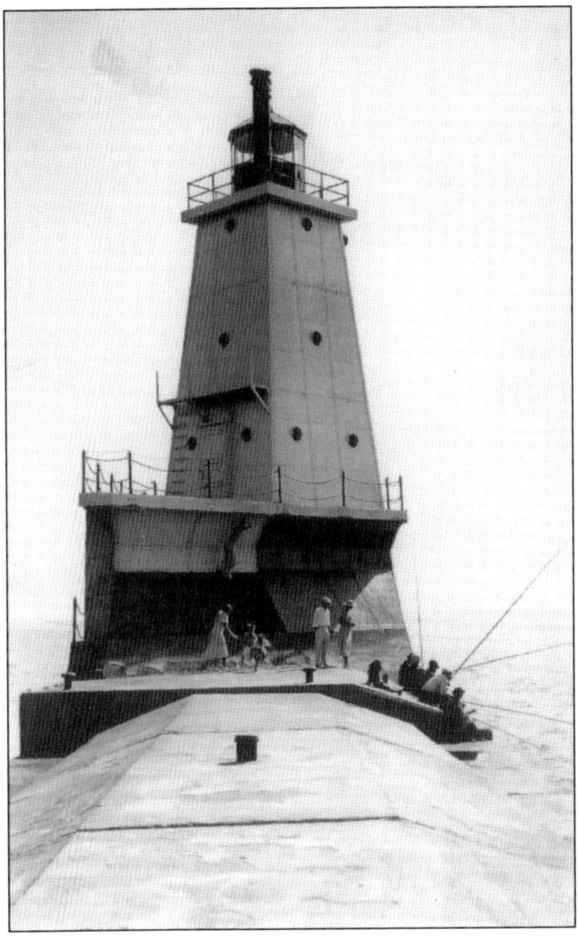

Cross-lake service began in 1875 with the chartering of the side-wheeler *Sherman* by the Flint and Pere Marquette Railroad. It was not long before the railroad began to have its own ships constructed for the growing break-bulk shipping business between Ludington and other Wisconsin ports. The year 1896 saw the launch of its first steel-hulled car ferry, the *Pere Marquette*, and heralded in a new era of shipping and commerce for the Ludington area. (Author's collection.)

The current North Pier Lighthouse was built in 1924. The first light was established in 1871 and destroyed in December 1876. It was rebuilt in 1877 and replaced in 1924. The walk out to the lighthouse is a popular attraction for residents and tourists alike. In years past, the break wall would be loaded with fishermen hooking their limit of perch, and Ludington hosted a perch festival. (Author's collection.)

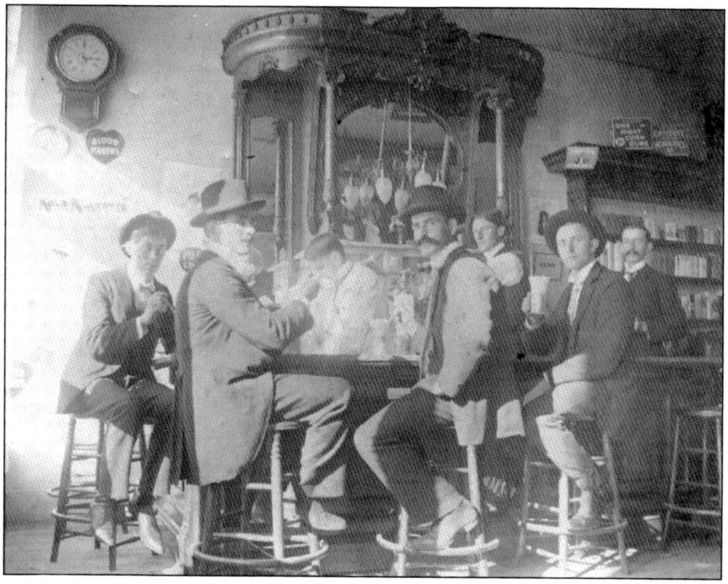

Joseph Sahlmark was a druggist who opened his store in 1897, located at the corner of James and Filer Streets in Ludington. A graduate of Northwestern University, he came to the Ludington area shortly after his graduation. Joseph's wife served as treasurer for the Paulina Stearns Hospital Board for over 50 years. (Courtesy of MCHS.)

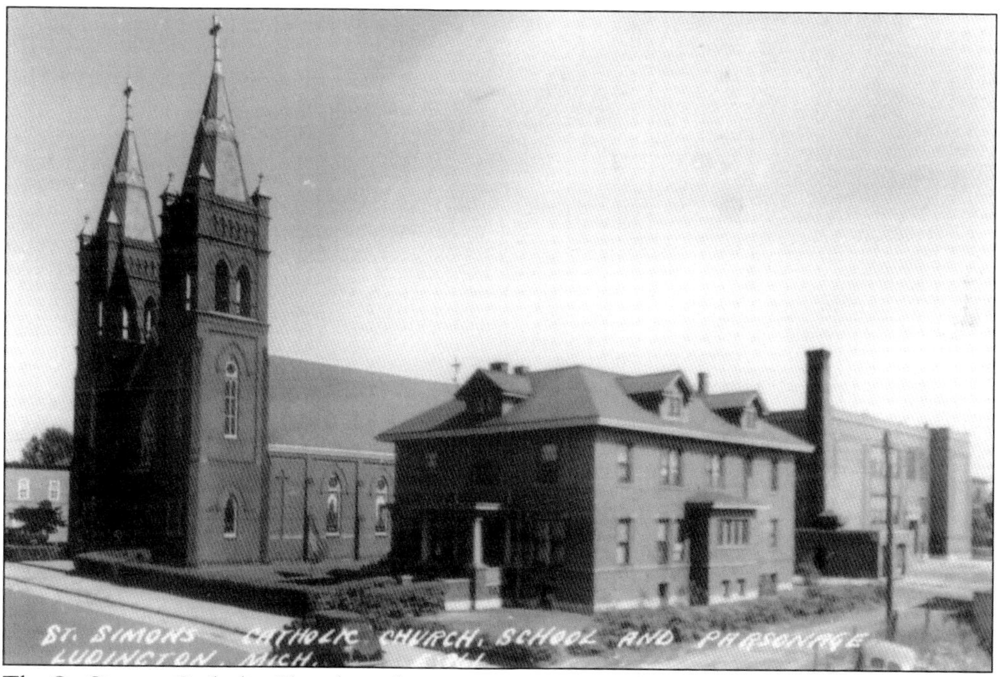

The St. Simons Catholic Church, with its two towers, was a landmark in Ludington and could be seen easily from the harbor. That building was completed in 1902 and had been constructed directly across the street from the first church and parsonage that had been built in 1872. There was an attempt to save the towers, but all three of the structures shown in this view are now gone. The current police and city hall occupy the site of the old church. (Author's collection.)

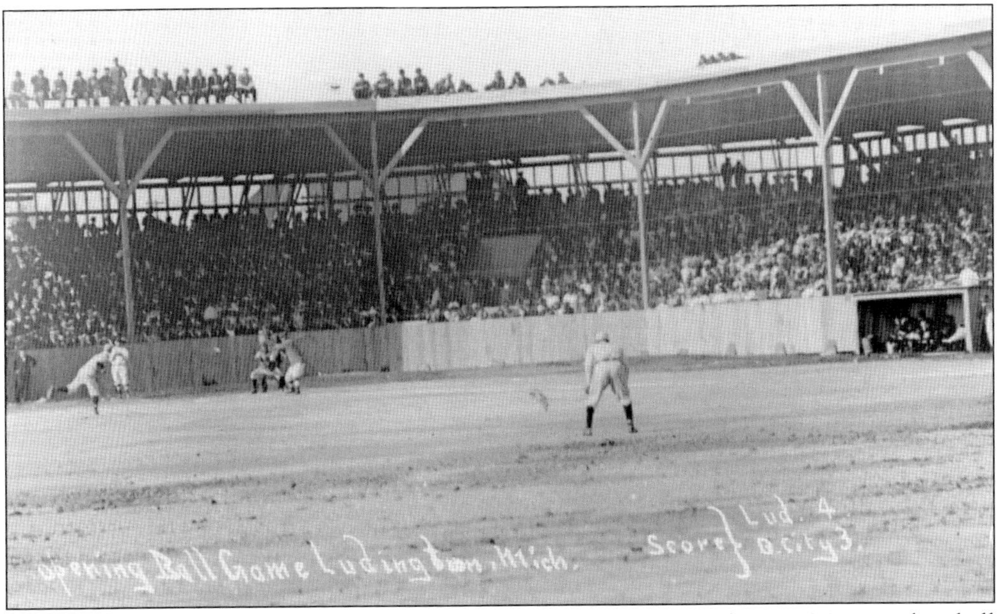

Culver Park was an important recreational site 100 years ago; the Ludington Mariners baseball team is shown here playing a game to an enthusiastic crowd around 1915. Located to the west of Star Watch Case, teams would be getting a little wet should they play a game at the same location today, as it is now the city marina. (Author's collection.)

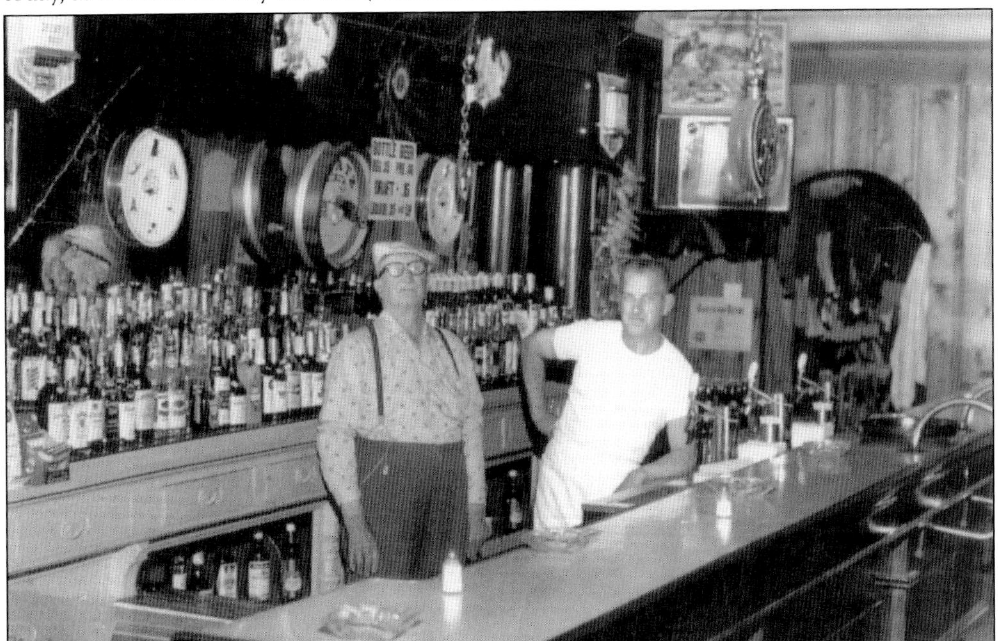

Miller's Place, Miller's Tavern, or Miller's Bar, call it by any name, but it was a popular watering hole in Ludington for many decades. Here is a good interior view of Miller's at 209 South James Street. Russell H. Miller Sr. oversaw the operation of the business, assisted by his wife, Betty. Later it was known as the Crows Nest and has recently changed hands again to continue operations as the Ludington Pub. (Author's collection.)

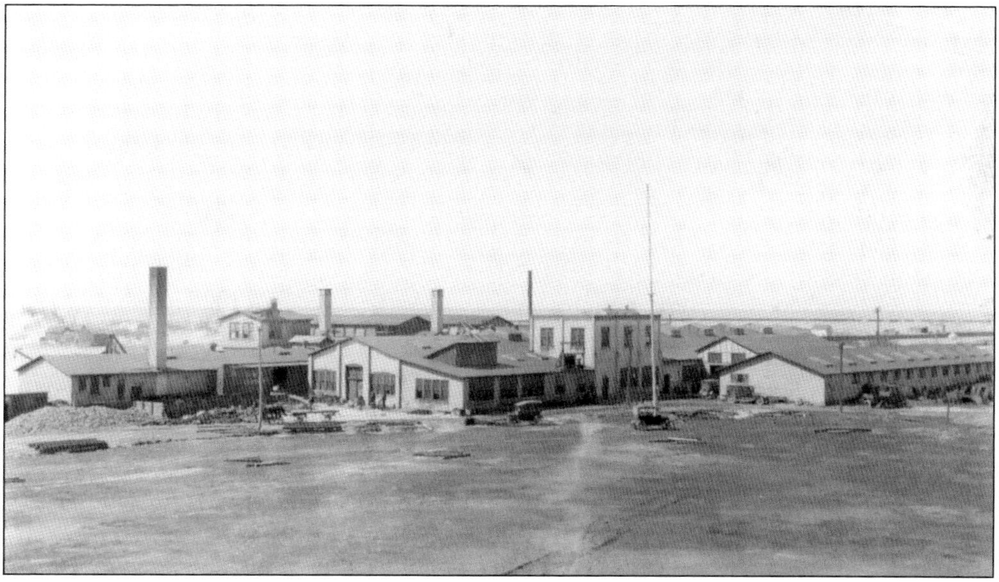

In 1909, Justus Stearns, along with several other Ludington businessmen, including W.L. Mercereau, F.B. Olney, and M.B. Danaher, established the Giles Tractor and Engine Company in order to manufacture marine and heavy-duty stationary engines. Boat engines and boats were manufactured at the plant as well from 1909 to 1914. (Author's collection.)

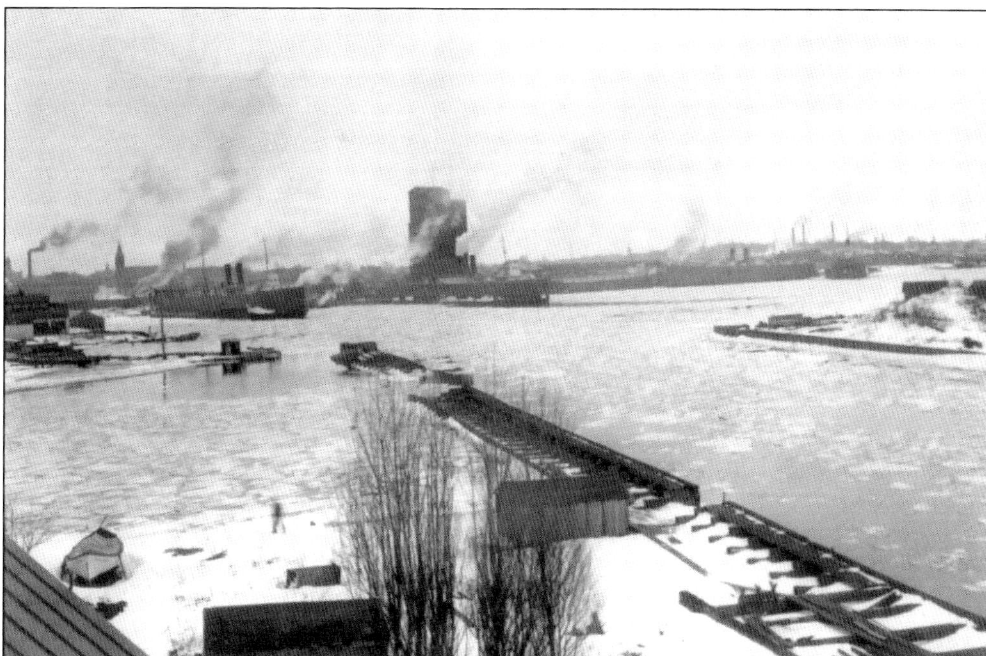

This photograph is rich in eye-catching elements of long-past landmarks. Taken from the lifesaving station looking east, one can see part of the Giles Tractor Factory; to the left, just out of sight, is Culver Park; and several car ferries are in port, as well as one of the wooden-hulled Pere Marquette black boats at the freight shed. To the right is part of Finn Town, home of Ludington's fishing fleet. The Star Watch Case, St. Simon's Church, and the freight elevator are all landmarks that have vanished. (Author's collection.)

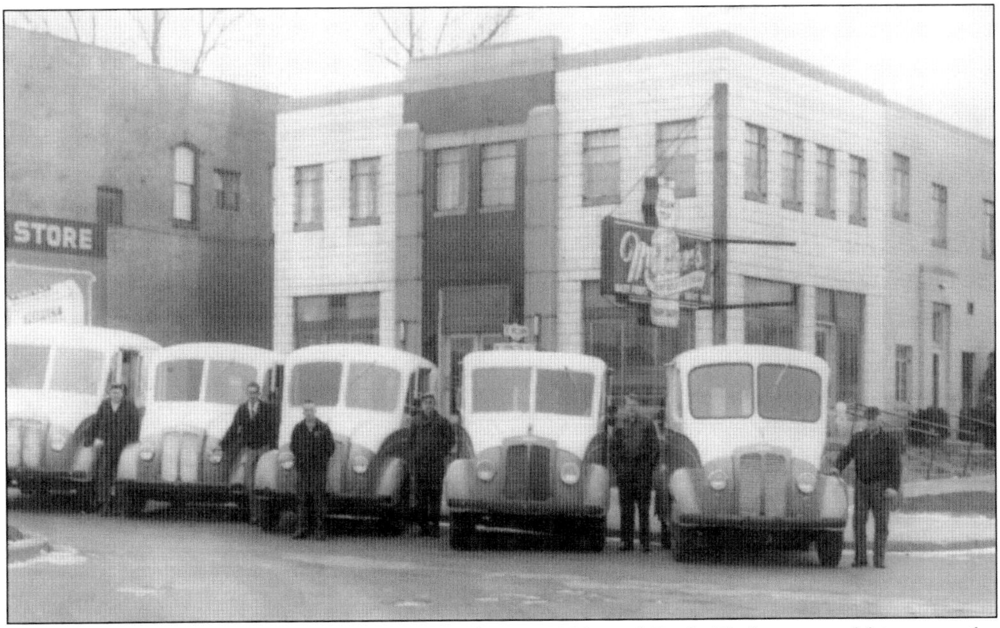

The Park Dairy was started by Guy W. Hawley in 1929, and Earle Taylor started his route for Miller's Park Dairy in August 1947 in a horse-drawn wagon. He delivered milk for 31 years, having worked for the Park Dairy, then Farr View and McDonald's Dairy before finally retiring from the route in 1978, just a short time before home deliveries were discontinued completely. (Author's collection.)

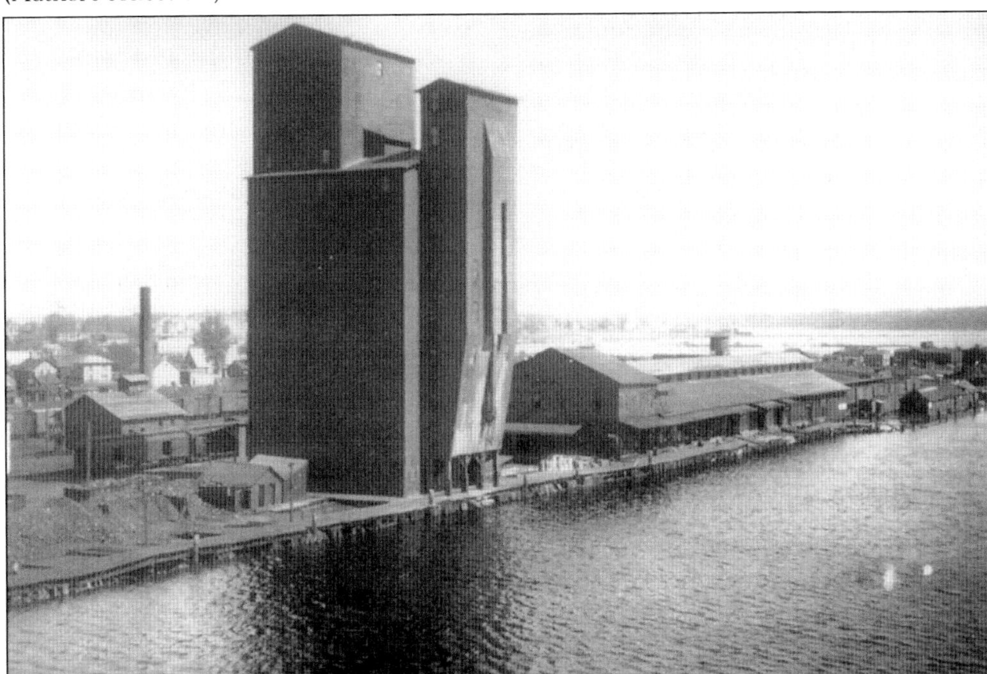

In this c. 1930 view taken by Erhardt Peters the detail of the grain elevator and loading docks can clearly bee seen. This is where ships like the SS *Nevada* would take on automobiles and break bulk cargo. (Author's collection.)

The First Ward School was built in 1872 and replaced in 1886 with Lakeview School on the corner of Haight and Gaylord Streets. The south entrance is pictured here sometime after the 1909 renovation. This building was located in Ludington on the same site as the present Lakeview School, which was built in 1966. (Author's collection.)

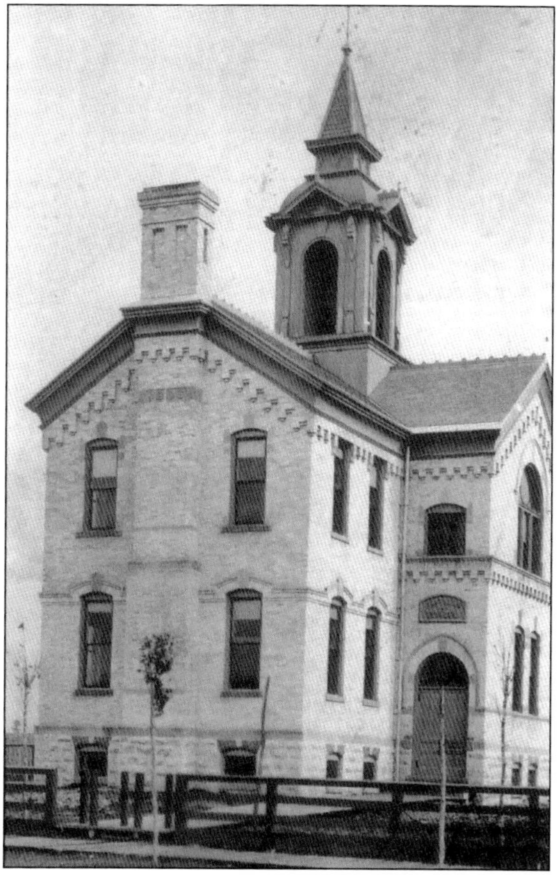

Heysett's Drug Store on South James Street was a local landmark where one could find most anything: patent medicines, nostrums, snake-oil (and salesmen), blood purifiers, and more. Many of these elixirs may seem odd, but in the dawn of science and technology, people often pushed the boundaries of what was acceptable. Even in Ludington, snake oil had its fans and promoters. (Courtesy of MCHS.)

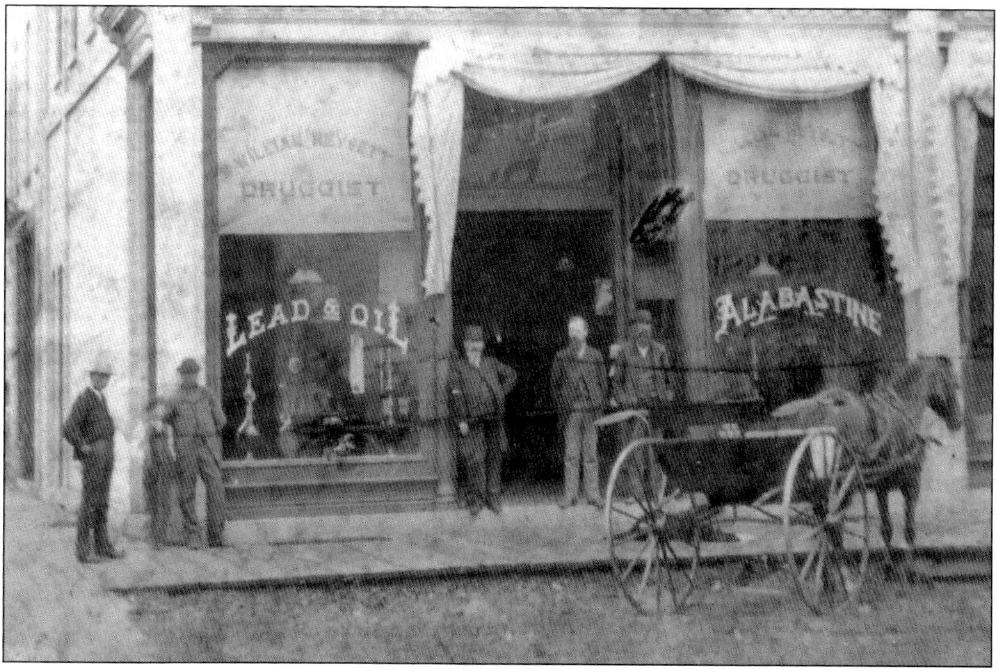

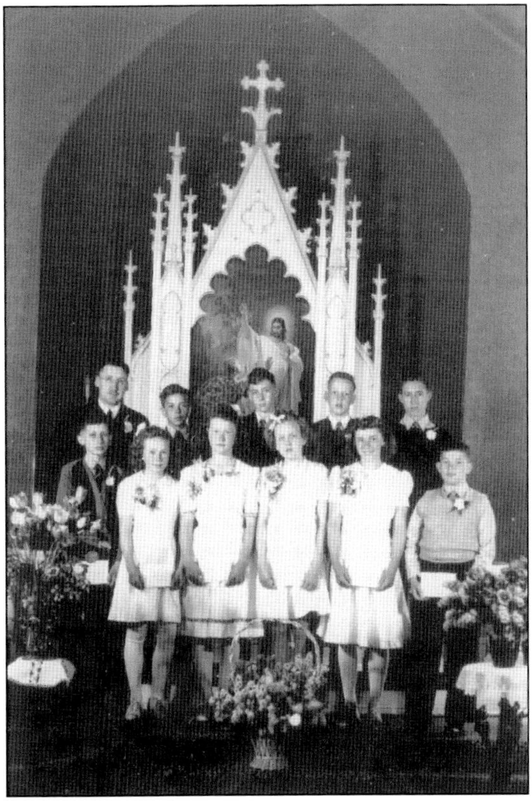

Reverend Christianson came to Ludington in 1938 from Denmark and is shown here in a confirmation class photograph inside of the Bethany Lutheran Church in the Fourth Ward. Reverend Christianson continued to work long past retirement and was a much loved and respected community figure. The boy directly in front of Christianson (far left) is Richard Petersen. (Author's collection.)

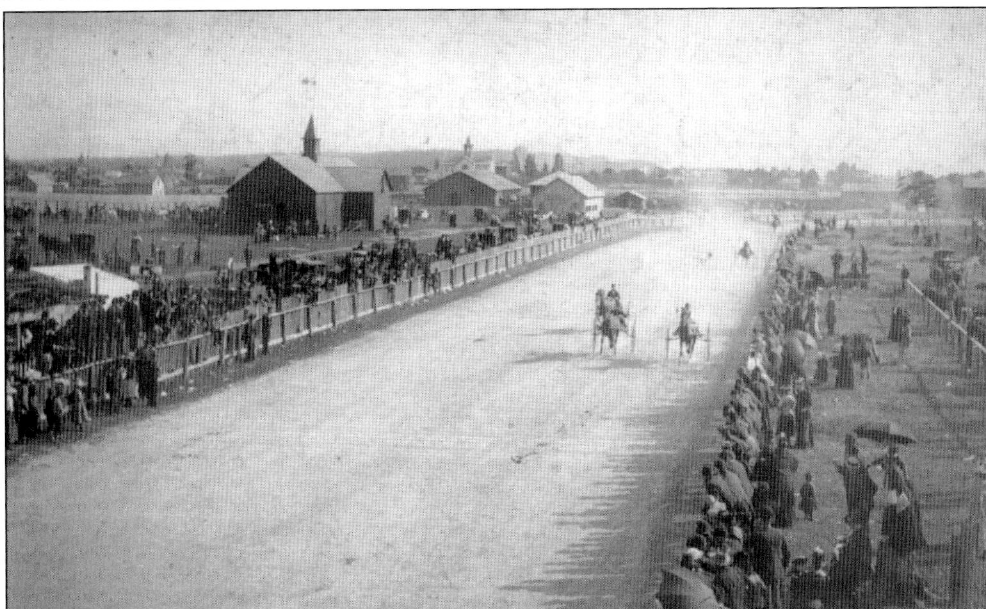

This is an incredible early view of the fairgrounds that existed where the present-day Oriole Field is on West Tinkham Street. It was a center of social activity and sulky racing. The tall structure in the distance is Lakeview, the First Ward School. The fairgrounds were eventually moved to US 10/31, just east of the present airport. (Author's collection.)

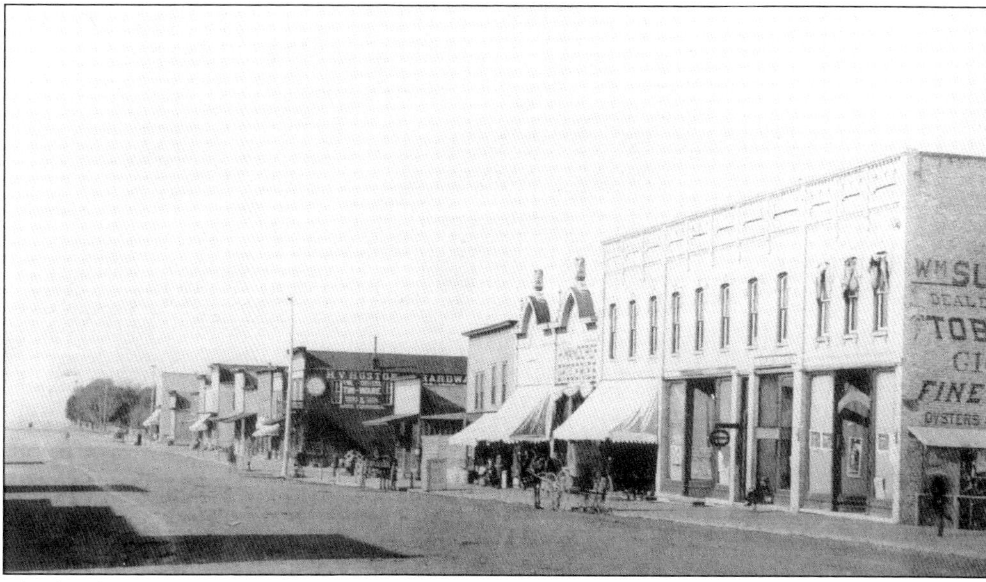

The hardware store seen here was owned by George Tripp. Tripp served as the first treasurer of Riverton Township and also prior to 1882 had served three terms as an alderman in the city of Ludington. His experience in Ludington influenced his brother Charles Tripp to relocate here in 1868. Charles was an early Ludington businessman who owned a tobacco, cigar, and fancy-goods store downtown. (Author's collection.)

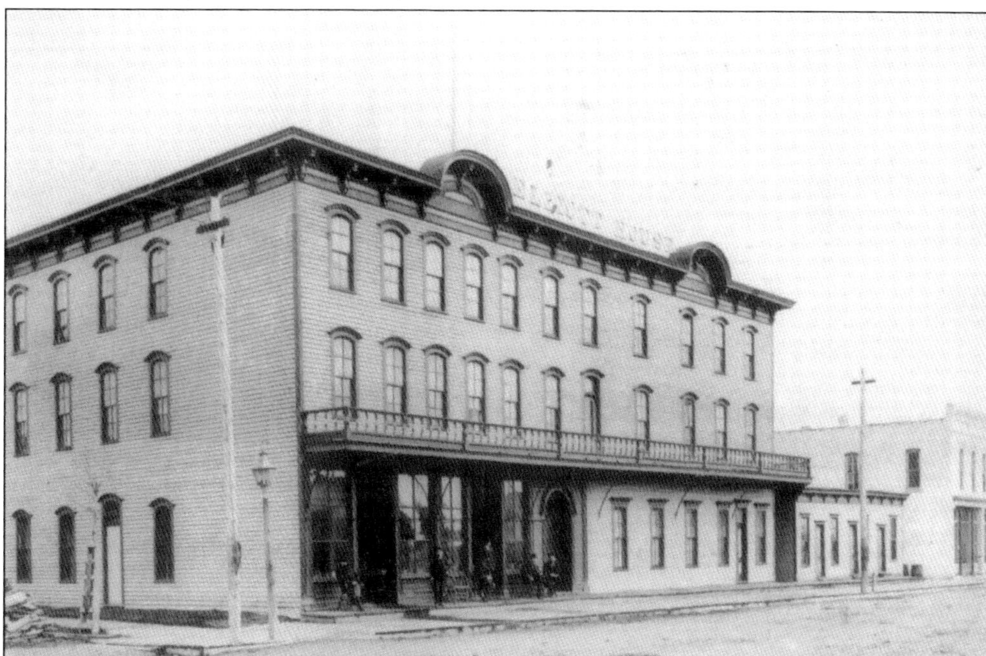

The Elliott House was one of the premier 19th-century hotels in Ludington. Charles Wing had this to say of the Elliott House: "Our first home in the city was the Hanson House, afterwards called the Elliott, then new, with "Pap" Elliott in charge—a very good hotel." To the north, one can see the old Bach's Bakery and the Johnson Building, which houses the Brew Pub and the Antique Store. (Author's collection.)

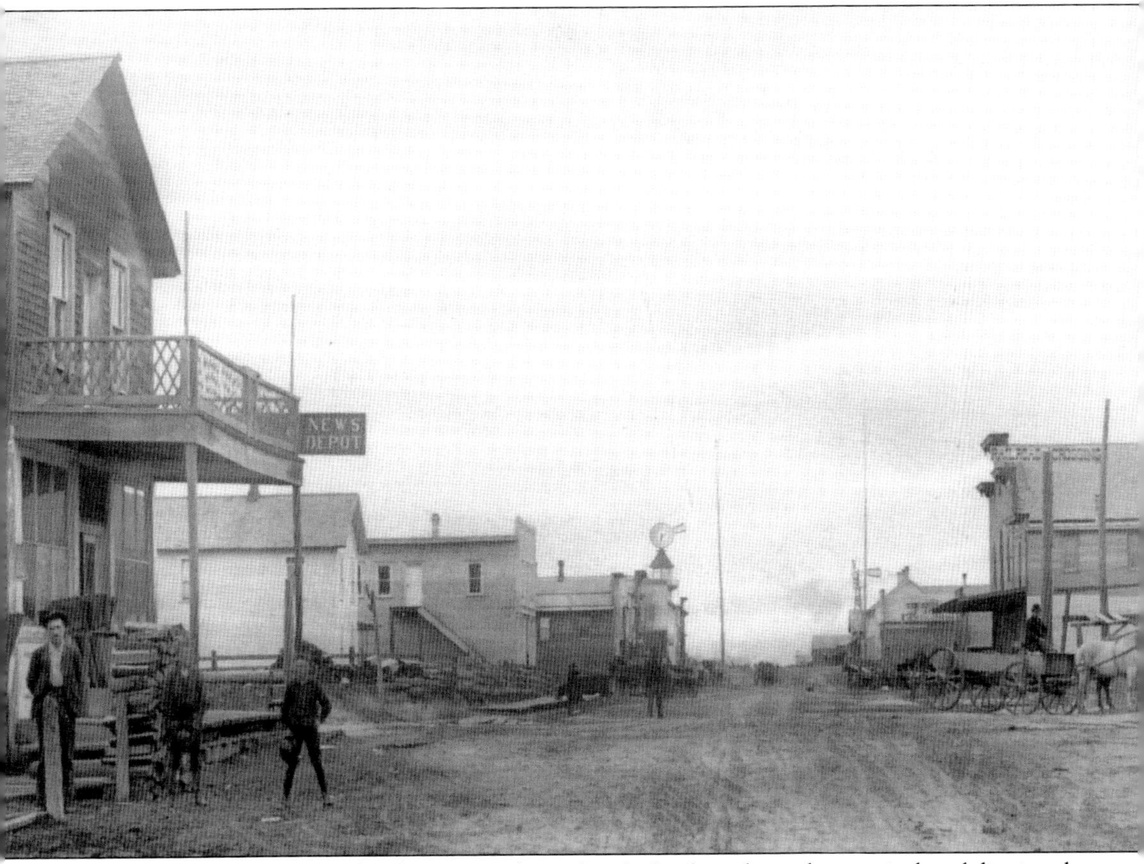

Situated nine miles east of Ludington, in the midst of a fertile and populous agricultural district, the beautiful little village of Scottville is the second biggest town in Mason County and has Adventist, Evangelical, and Methodist churches, a graded school, various manufacturing institutions, and a weekly newspaper, the *Enterprise*. The village now contains a population of about 500 and is noted for its excellent stores and the thriftiness of its businessmen, nearly all of whom are men yet young in years. It is situated on the Flint and Pere Marquette Railroad line (from an 1896 promotional). In 1880, Jacob Welch and his family moved to Amber Township in Mason County. It is believed but not documented that Jacob, his wife Cornelia (Wilson), and son William Uriah opened a farm-implement store that they operated in Amber until moving to nearby Scottville and reopening their business on Main Street. (Author's collection.)

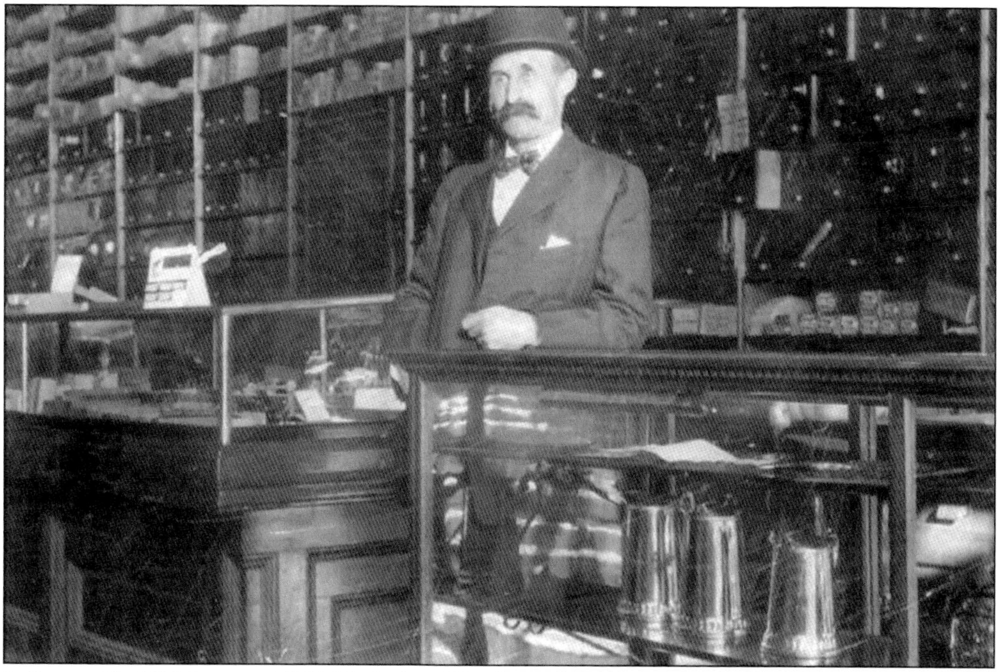

In Scottville, Welch opened J Welch & Son, "Dealers in Hardware." According to Beatrice O'Hearn, "Another hardware store was built in 1884 by Mr. Welch and Son. This building burned and in its place a bakery was built, with an opera house on the second floor. The bakery was owned by Joe Poirier." (Author's collection.)

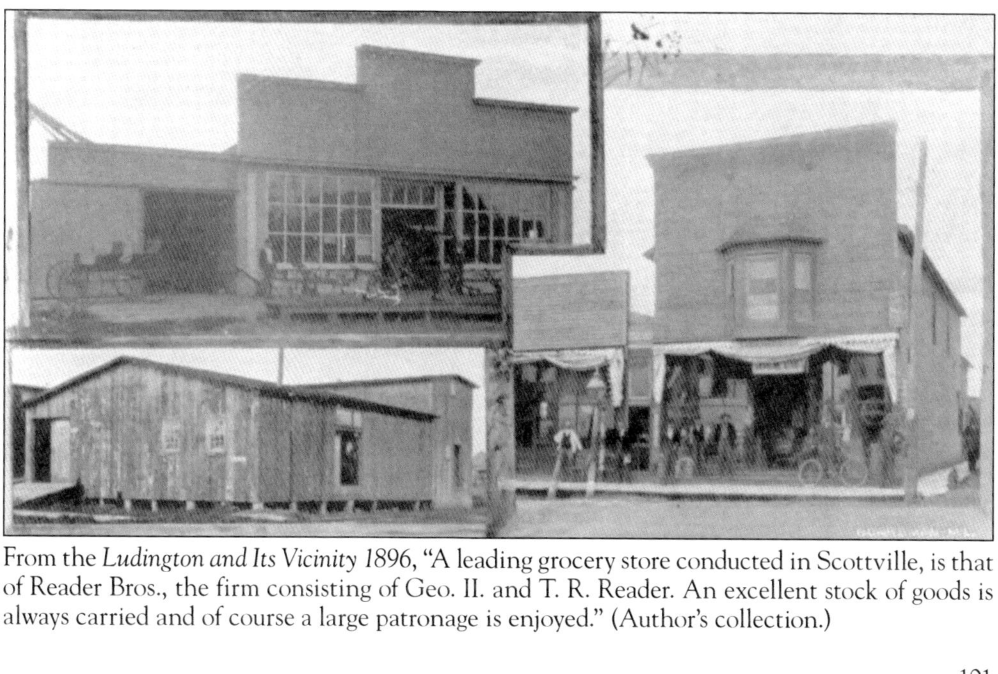

From the *Ludington and Its Vicinity 1896*, "A leading grocery store conducted in Scottville, is that of Reader Bros., the firm consisting of Geo. H. and T. R. Reader. An excellent stock of goods is always carried and of course a large patronage is enjoyed." (Author's collection.)

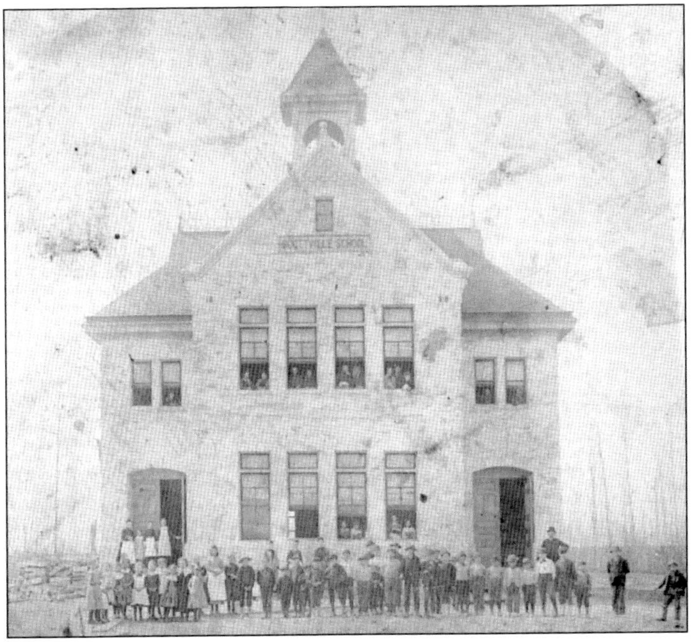

A new school building was erected in Scottville in 1878, with W.F. Fairbanks being the first teacher. By 1887, the building was too small to serve the needs of the growing city, and a new brick schoolhouse was erected, which proved to be too small to accommodate the large number of pupils. (Author's collection.)

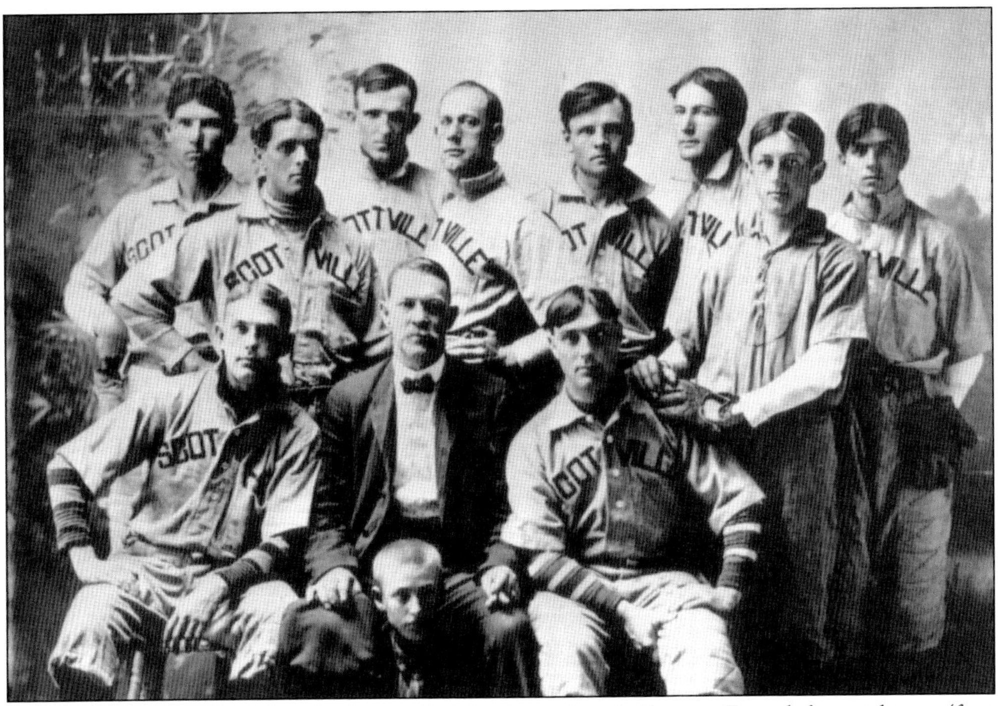

Pictured here around 1905 is the Scottville Merchants baseball team. From left to right are (first row) McPhail, Sidmore (manager), and Garlock (captain); (second row) Willette, Rowe, Greenway, Andree, Blaskins, Smith, Wagner, and G. Rowe. Most communities and many businesses sponsored baseball teams that played to the delight of local spectators. (Author's collection.)

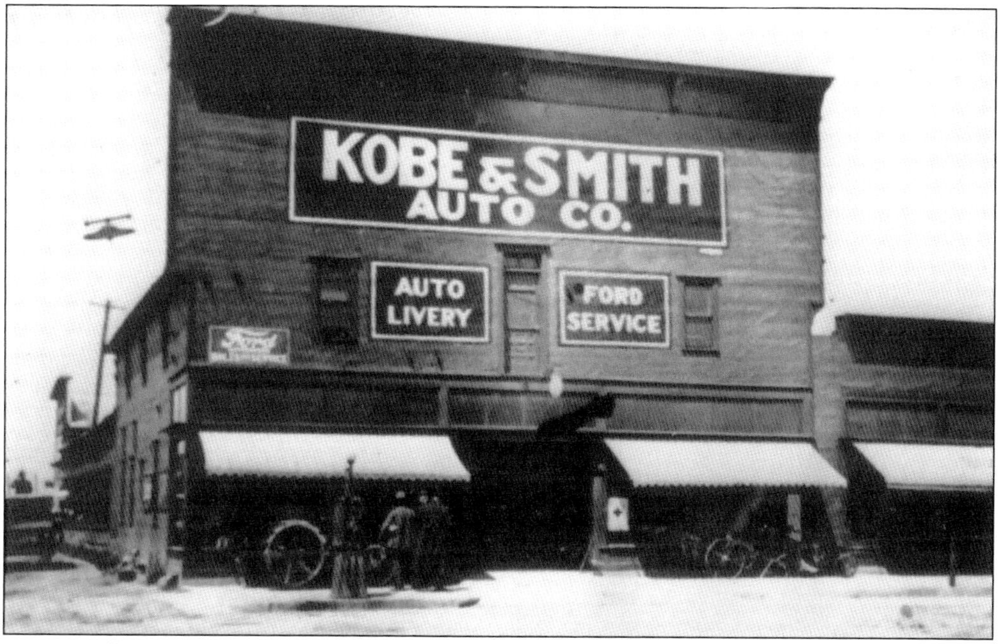

In Scottville, T.D Smith hardware was a major concern, having been established in 1900. By 1915, the store had expanded and was employing 12 men and had annual sales of $100,000. Smith was also a partner in the Kobe and Smith Ford car dealership and had reported in 1915 that they had sold 86 new Fords in nine months and could not keep them in stock because of their popularity. (Author's collection.)

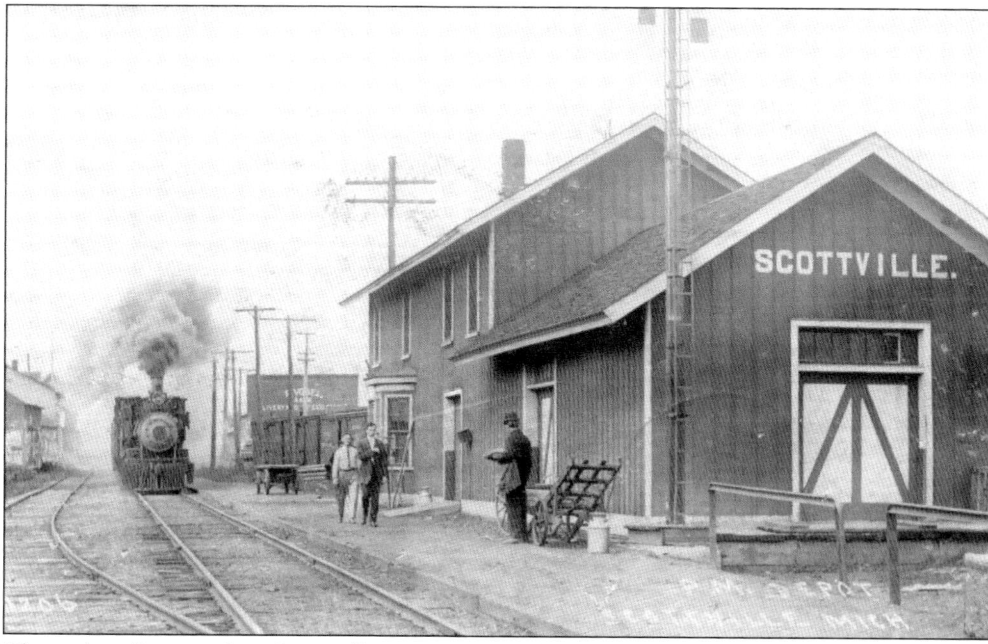

The railroad's arrival in Scottville in 1874 was a boon to local farmers and merchants and contributed greatly to the growth of the region. Scottville was centrally located in the county and at one time was called Mason County Central, a name still sported by the school district. (Author's collection.)

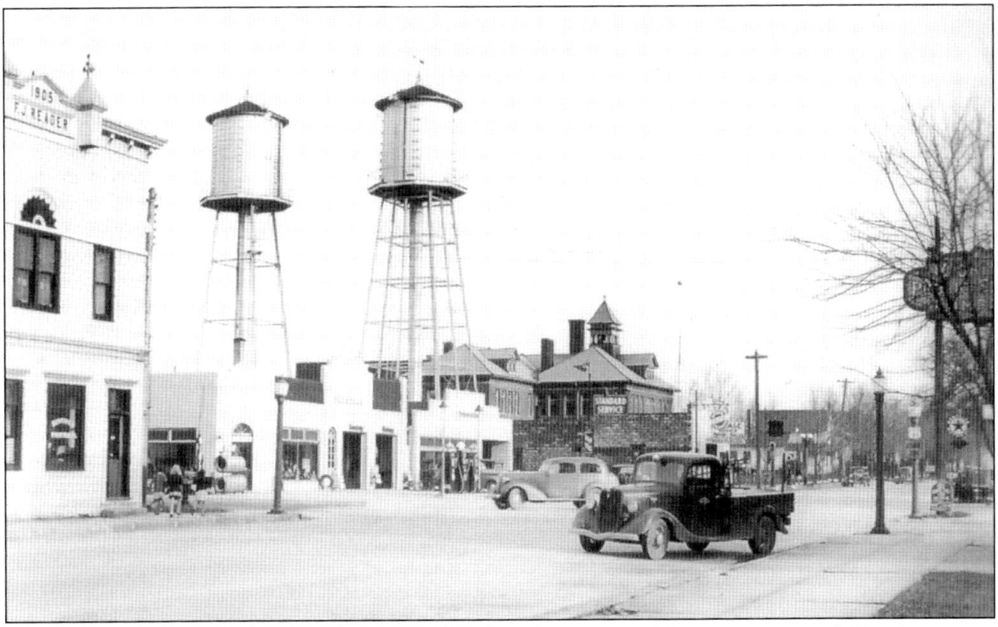

The *Ludington and Its Vicinity 1896* stated, "F.J. Reader is one of the most successful businessmen in Mason County. He conducts a hardware store and an implement store under separate roofs, both of which are admirably stocked, and his customers can always rely on the best bargains to be found anywhere. After receiving a common-school education, he came to Scottville and entered upon the business career." (Author's collection.)

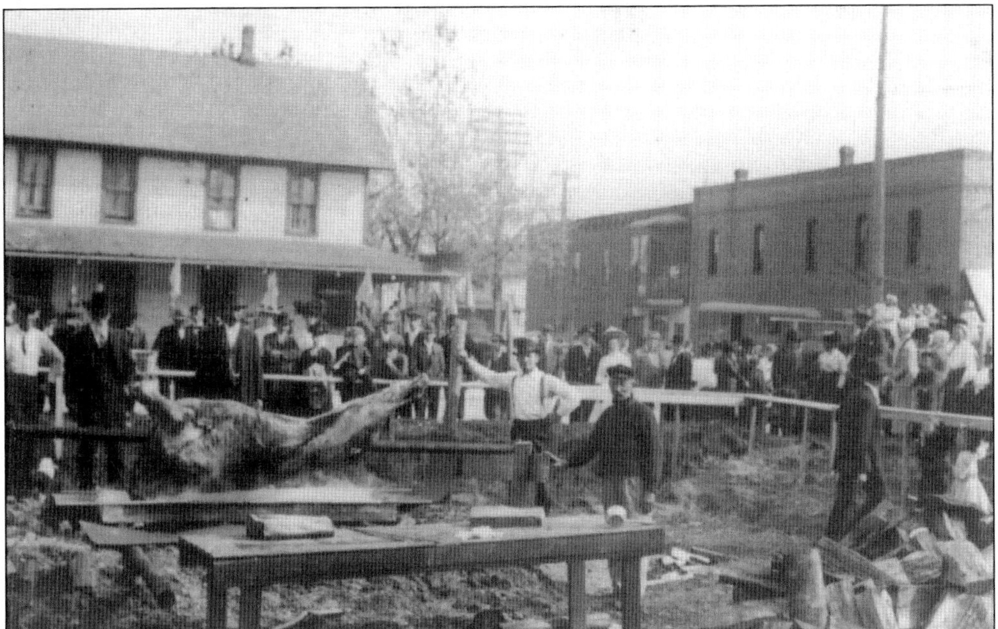

Another longtime tradition is the Scottville Harvest Festival ox roast, which began in 1910. It has continued for most of the past 115 years, and on one recent occasion when there was a discussion about discontinuing the tradition, the community rallied to insure that no one was going to take away their ox burger during the harvest festival. (Author's collection.)

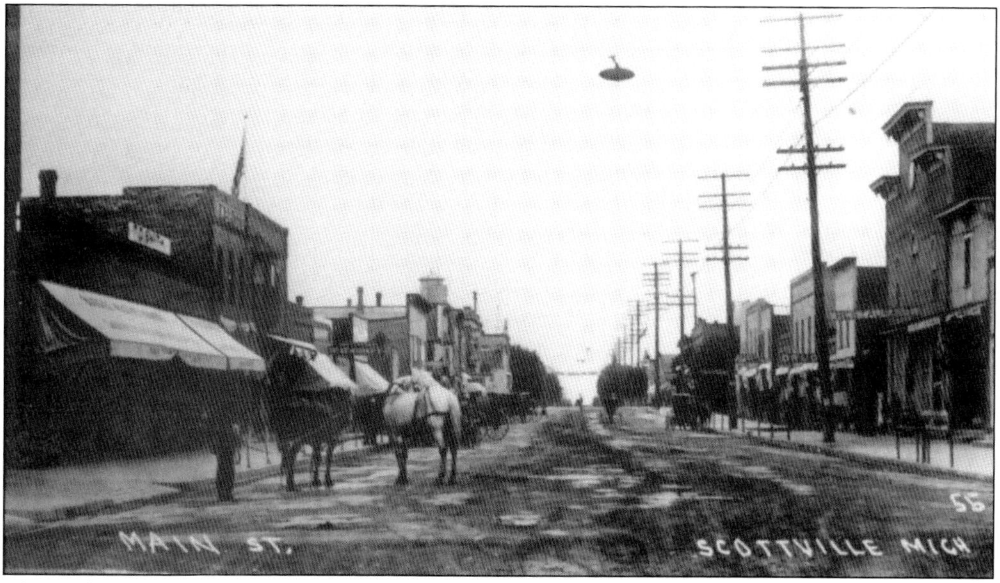

The *Ludington and Its Vicinity 1896* noted, "One of the foremost mercantile institutions in Mason County is the Scottville Hardware Company, with Hon. D.W. Goodenough as its president. The company owns and occupies a large brick store [pictured here] and carries a complete line of general hardware, building supplies, etc. They also deal in agricultural implements, harness, carriages, wagons, and so forth in all of which their customers have a liberal stock to select from." (Authors Collection.)

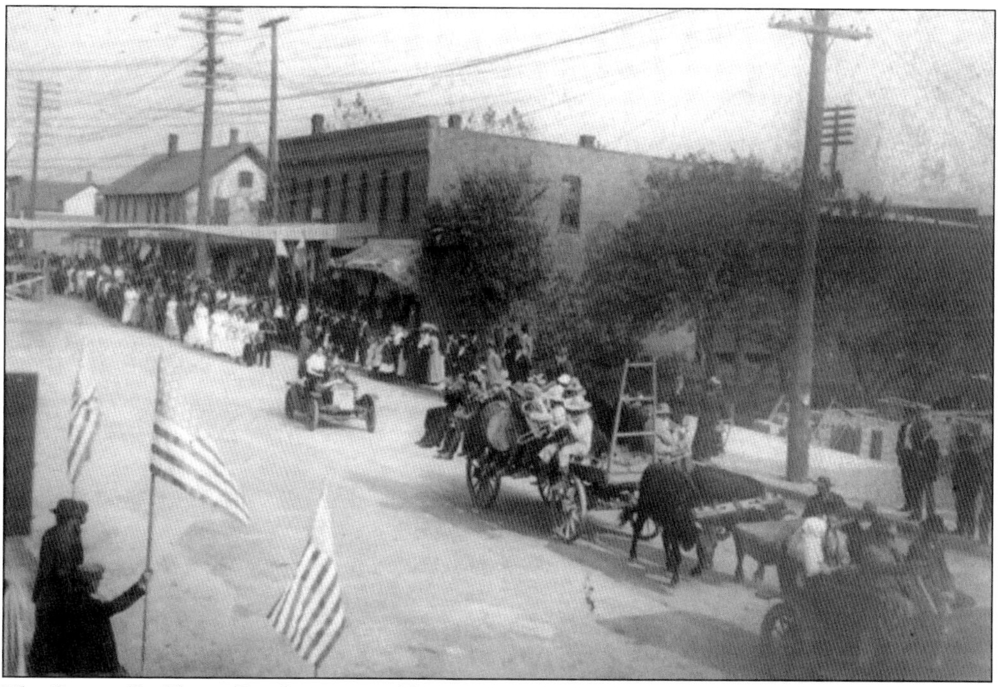

The Scottville Clown Band is pictured here around 1910 at one of its early debuts at the harvest festival parade in Scottville. The Clown Band is synonymous with Scottville and has continued a tradition of entertaining crowds in parades throughout the Midwest. (Author's collection.)

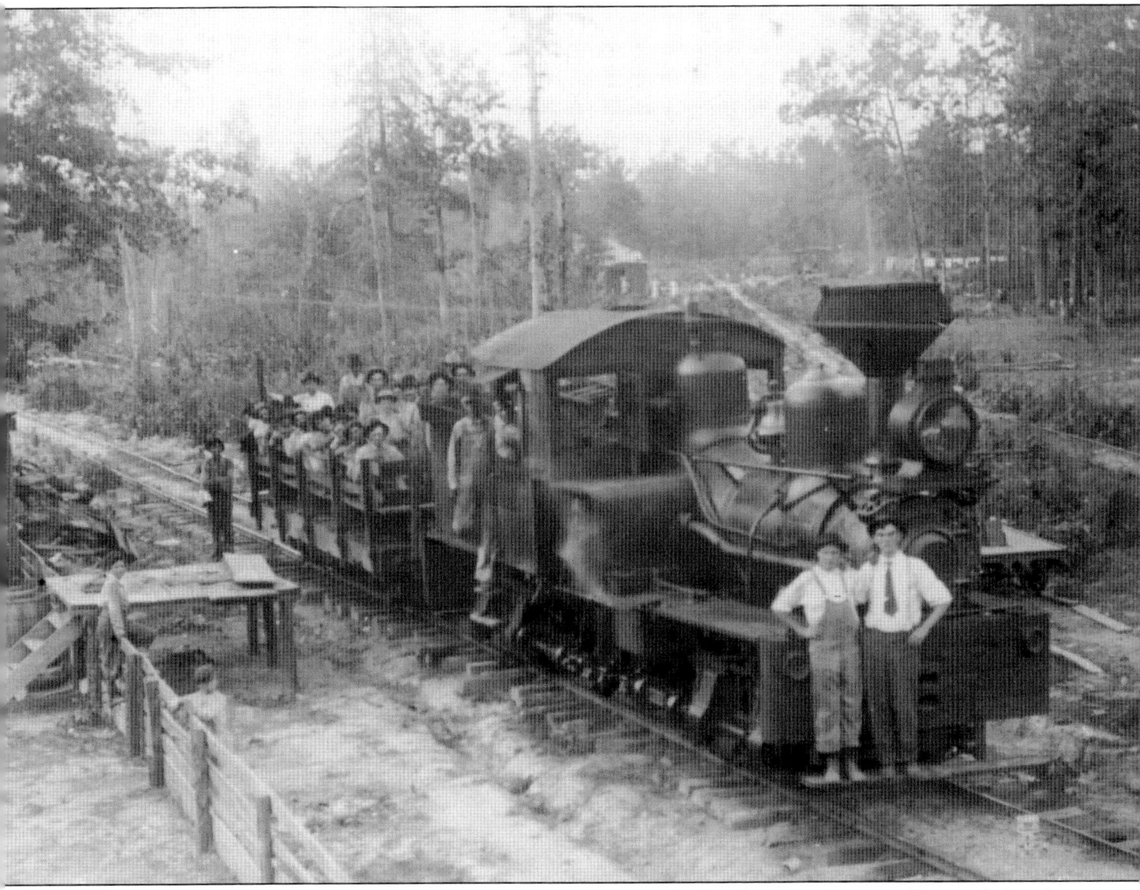

Early on, this area was referred to as Butters Junction (for lumberman Horace Butters), but later when the railroad extended to Manistee, it was called Manistee Junction. The locals referred to the community as Merritt, and in 1905 the post office was renamed Walhalla. Walhalla is defined as the great hall of Odin in Norse mythology, the place where the valiant souls of those slain in battle or who died bravely would go for their eternal rest. In reality, the name change came about after mineral springs were discovered in the area, and Barothy's Lodge was opened to provide that safe haven to those weary souls who would travel north from the cities in search of well-deserved peace and relaxation. Walhalla, like most communities in Mason County, came into being as a direct result of logging in the region. Horace Butters and his son Marshall played an important role in the development of the area. (Author's collection.)

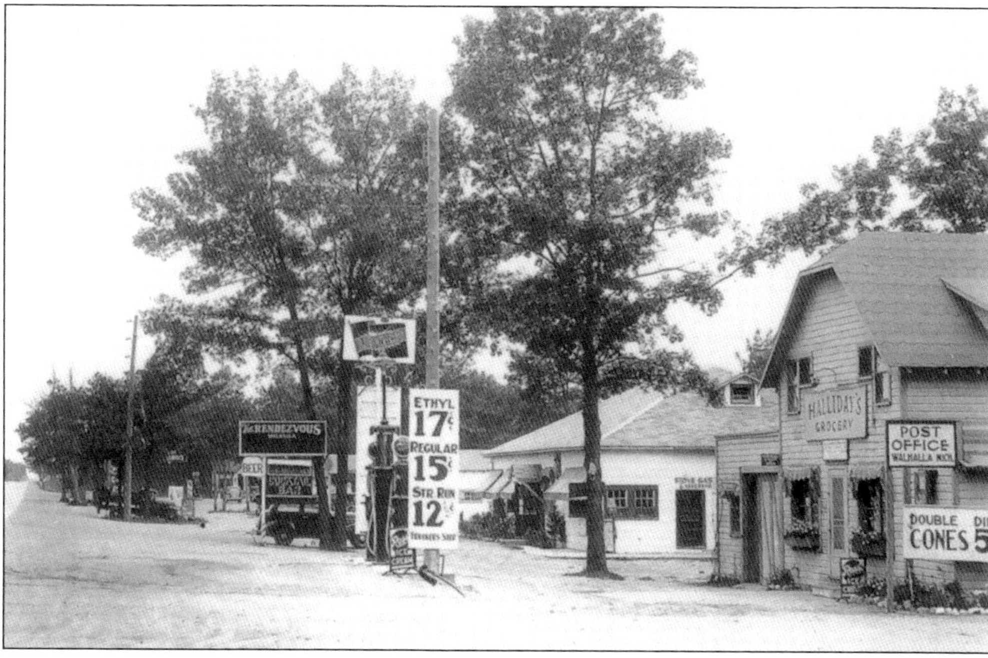

In the 1950s, Halliday's Store stood next to the Rendevous, which was another haunt heavily patronized by the locals. What a great price for gasoline; at 17¢ a gallon, a person could afford premium gas and purchase ice cream for a nickel. US 10 was not much of a road back in those days, looking barely more than a single-lane road. (Courtesy of Wayne Johnson.)

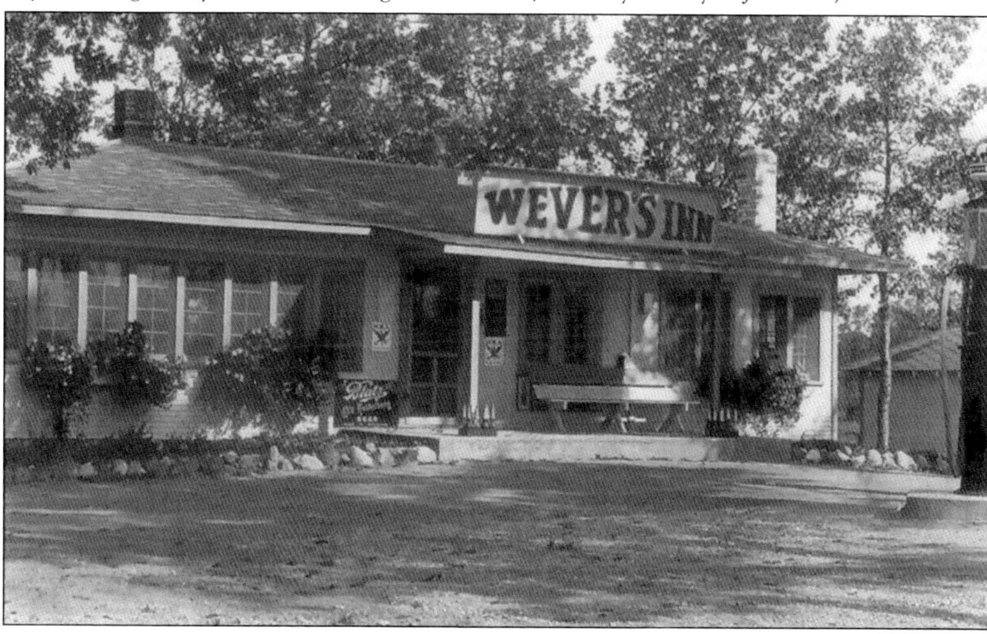

There were no fast-food franchises, but there were a plethora of roadside restaurants and barbeques that one could patronize. Barney's Lunch, built in 1927 by Art Barnhart, provided a living area, housed a lunch counter, and was a service station. Steve Wever later purchased the business from George and Lulu Showers and renamed it Wever's Inn. The building was destroyed by fire in 1940. (Courtesy of Wayne Johnson.)

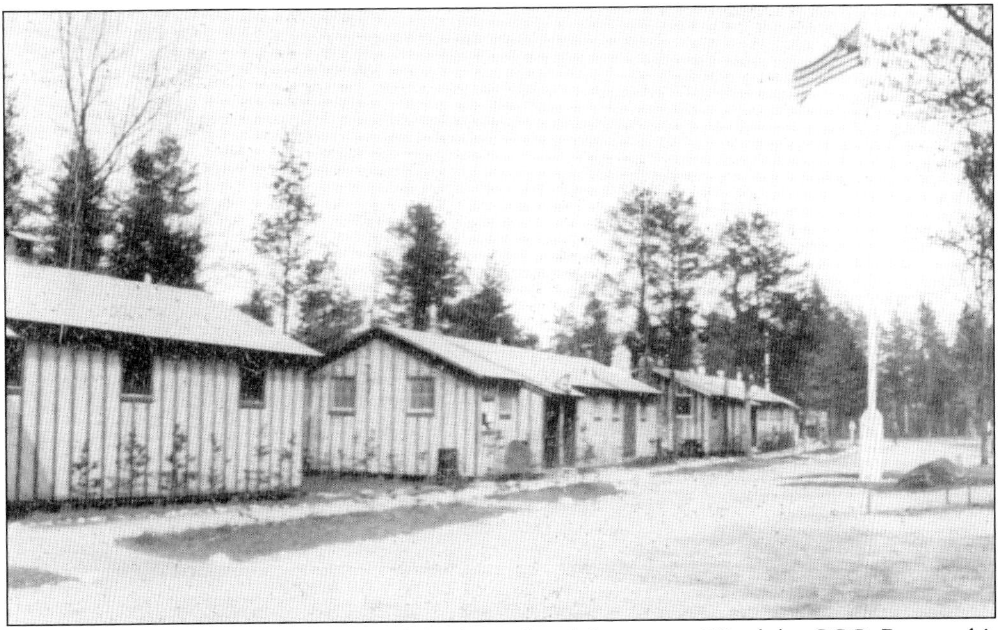

Pictured here are Camp Walhalla and the barracks of Company 687 of the CCC. Roosevelt's plan was to put the great masses of newly unemployed men to work to restore the beauty of the nation by involving them in public-works programs such as planting trees in areas that had been lumbered out and left barren. (Author's collection.)

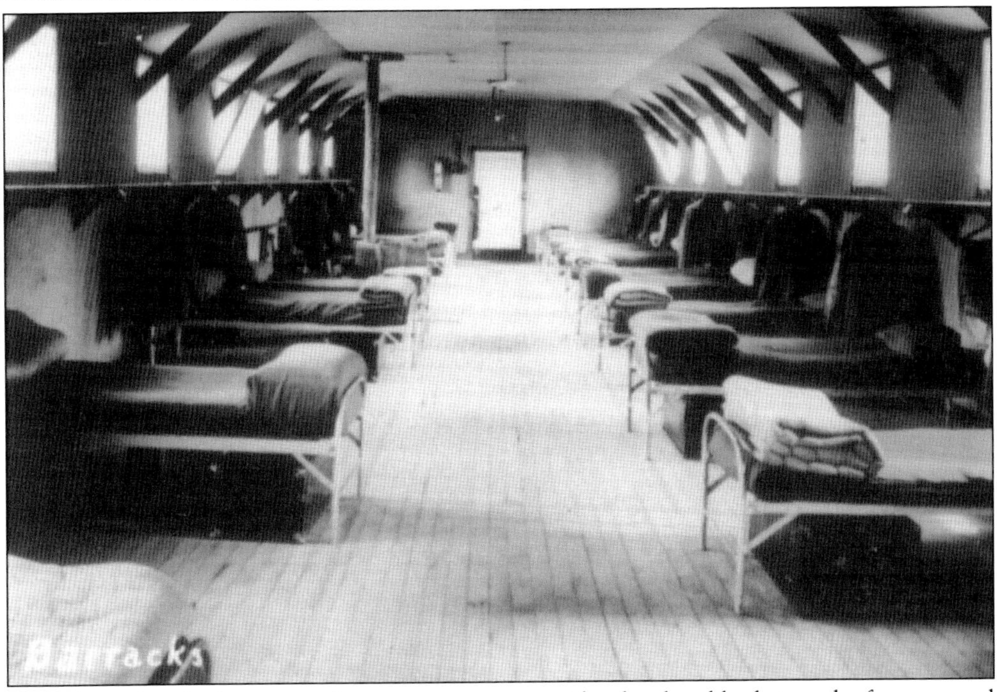

In the barracks, the living conditions were spartan, with a bunk, a blanket, and a few personal amenities. The camps were staffed with a regular or reserve Army officer, and the men who were eligible to apply were single, most between the ages of 17 and 23, and were asked to send $22 of the $30 they received monthly home to their parents. (Author's collection.)

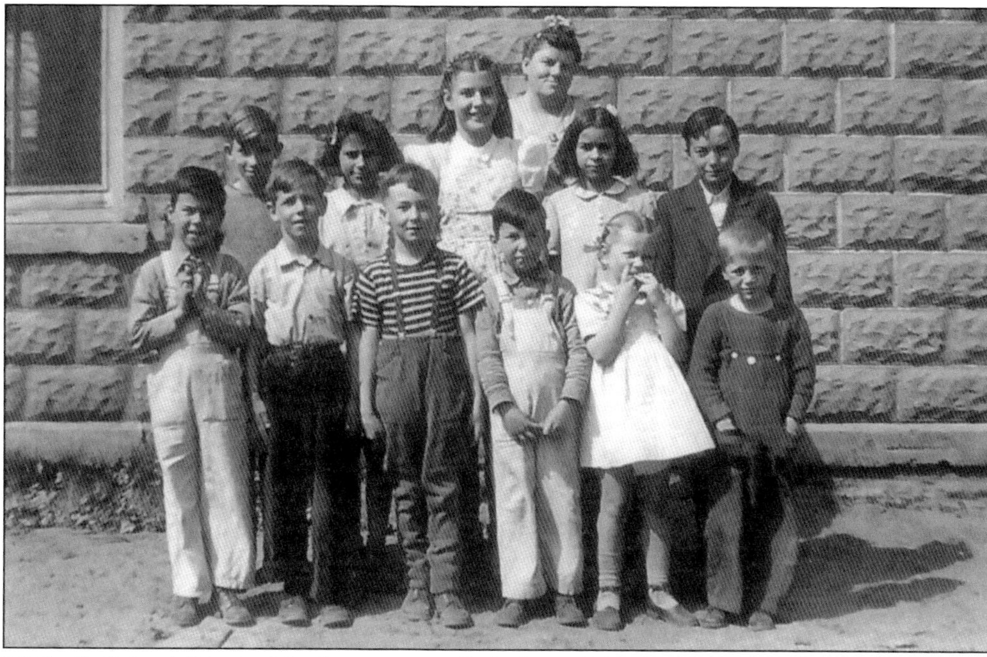

Walhalla School District No. 7 was originally built in 1904 on the corner of Benson Road and US 10. In 1918, a new cement-block building was constructed on First Street. These youngsters are pictured during the 1946 school year. Other schools in Branch Township include Grass Lake, Branch, Comstock, and Tallman. (Courtesy of Wayne Johnson.)

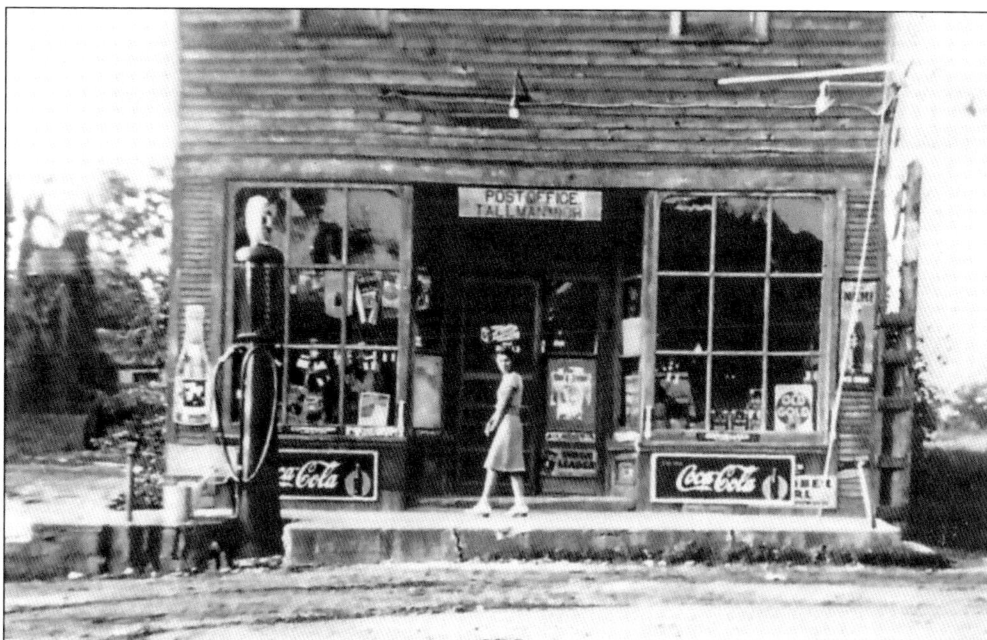

Platted in 1880 by Horace Butters, the village of Tallman was a planned community. Often the shanty towns that sprang up around the mills were haphazardly laid out without much planning or thought. Up to 500 men worked around Tallman, and any of them could build a house on a lot there and live free as long as they worked for the company. (Courtesy Shirley Shoup.)

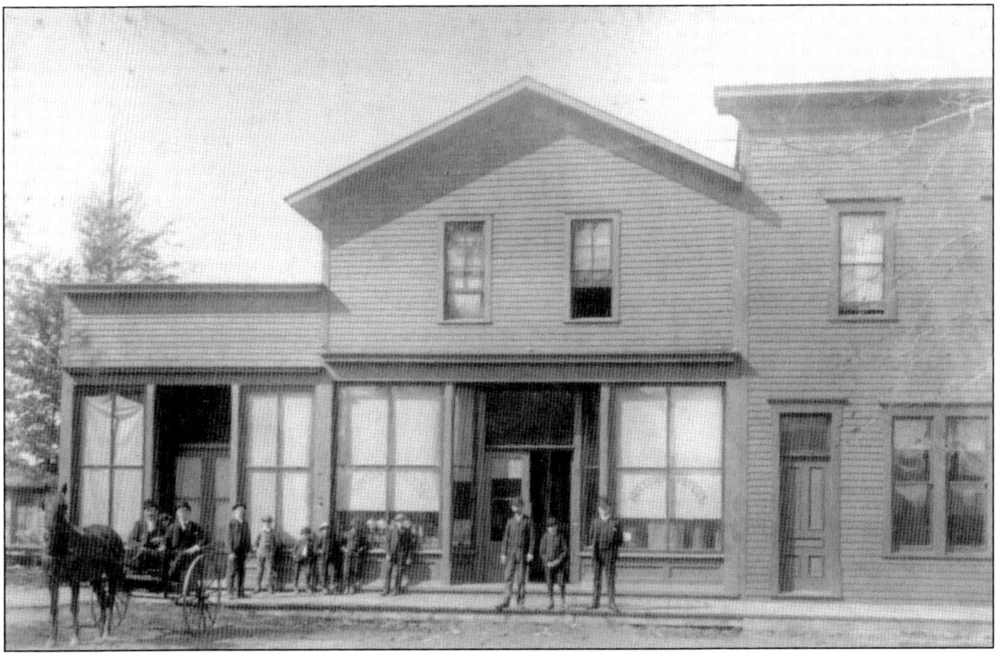

The offices of Butters and Peters can be seen in what appears to be another view of Tallman. Originally named Wever, the name was abandoned because another town had already claimed the name. The village was then named after a cousin, H. Tallman, who loaned the concern the final $10,000 startup capital needed. (Courtesy of Mary Mitchell.)

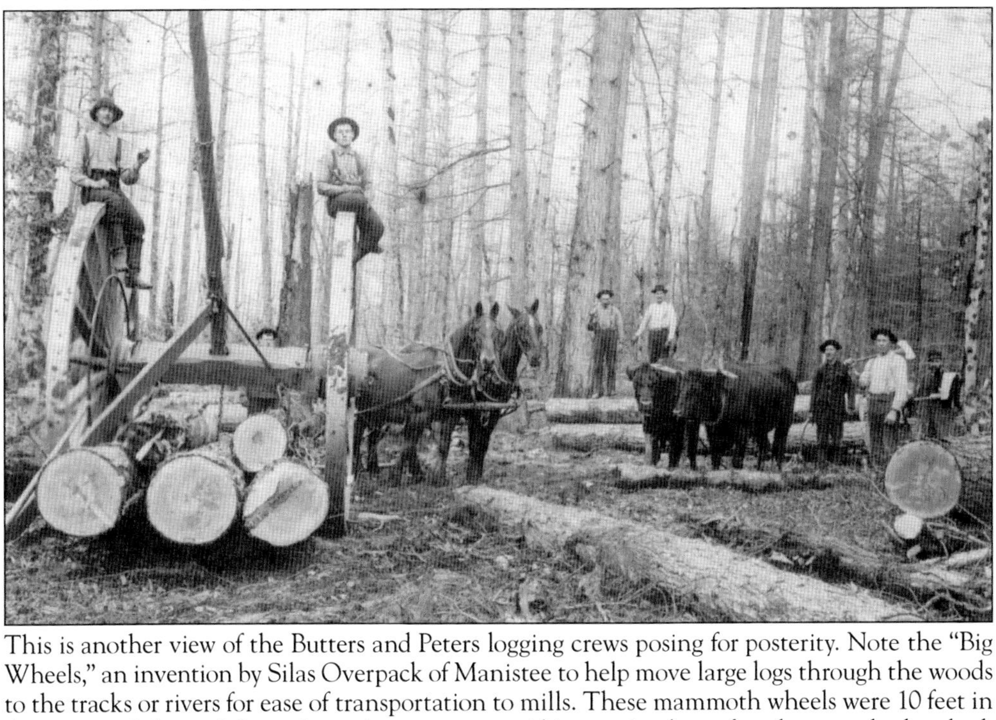

This is another view of the Butters and Peters logging crews posing for posterity. Note the "Big Wheels," an invention by Silas Overpack of Manistee to help move large logs through the woods to the tracks or rivers for ease of transportation to mills. These mammoth wheels were 10 feet in diameter and shipped throughout the country to aid in moving logs after the snow had melted. (Author's collection.)

Four

Ghost Towns and Place Names

There are always areas in communities nicknamed by locals for some specific reason. At times, it is for the people who live there, such as Canada Corners; all four families on Wilson and South Custer Roads had come from Canada. Ethnic naming continued with French Corners in Summit Township, Germantown, and the Swedish Settlement north of Branch. The Fourth Ward in Ludington was in many ways a town in and of itself and known locally as Pollock Town for its Polish inhabitants. Such naming of places created a rich and interesting vocabulary but helped identify not just localities but also the communities there.

Sometimes names have to do with a business, such as Creamery Corner, while other times names often stick in the minds of locals far after the reason for naming it such is gone. In Victory Township, there was Bird Settlement, or Rayne's Corner, but it was also called Forest City. There was a time when a resident might use all three names when giving directions. Manistee Junction was where the Pere Marquette Railroad spur turned north, but it was also known as Merritt, which was just down the road from Tallman.

Then there are the ghost towns, such as Seatonville, Taylorsville, Buttersville, and Finn Town, all on the Buttersville Peninsula. Lincoln and Hamlin were sawmill villages founded and named by Charles Mears for his choices for president and vice president, but what about Abbott, which was founded by W.H. Perring in Logan Township in 1884? In the case of Haire's Rollway, people want to refer to it as "rollaway," which is incorrect (see page 23). There was Rattlesnake Rollway and Chinnery's Rollway on the Conrad Farm in Amber Township. Also, Dead Horse Marsh and Bloody Run are examples of creative and unique place names that come into play for many reasons. How locals make an area known and familiar adds to the rich history of the region.

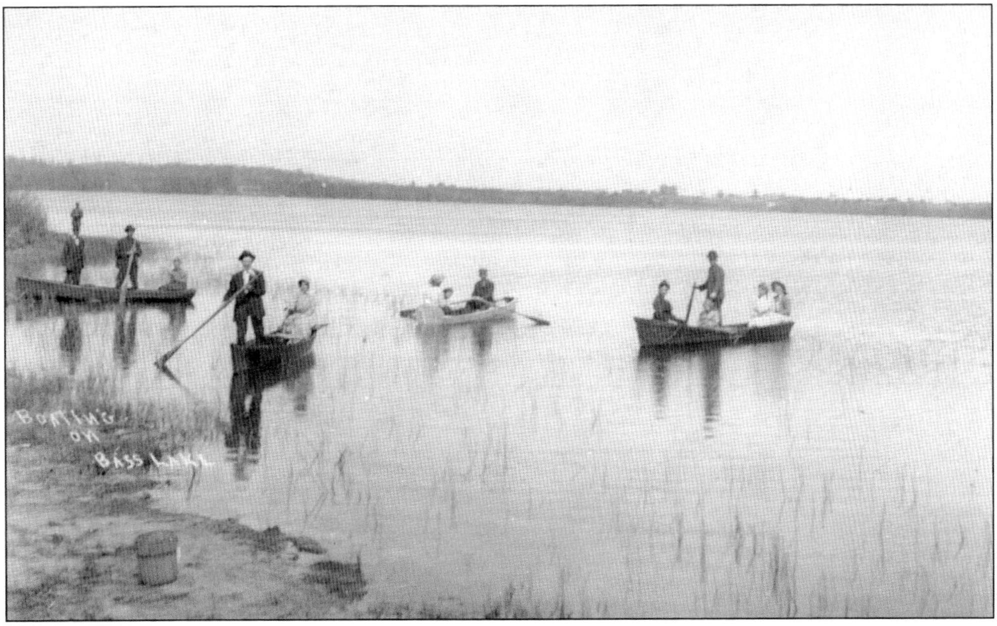

After timber was cut from the area around Bass Lake in southern Summit Township, a few people saw the potential for development of the lake for tourism and recreation. A church choir camp had already been established when in 1911 Georgie "Nana" Mortimer (camp cook) and Arthur "Morrie" Morrison realized the potential for development, and Camp Morrison came into being. (Courtesy of MCHS.)

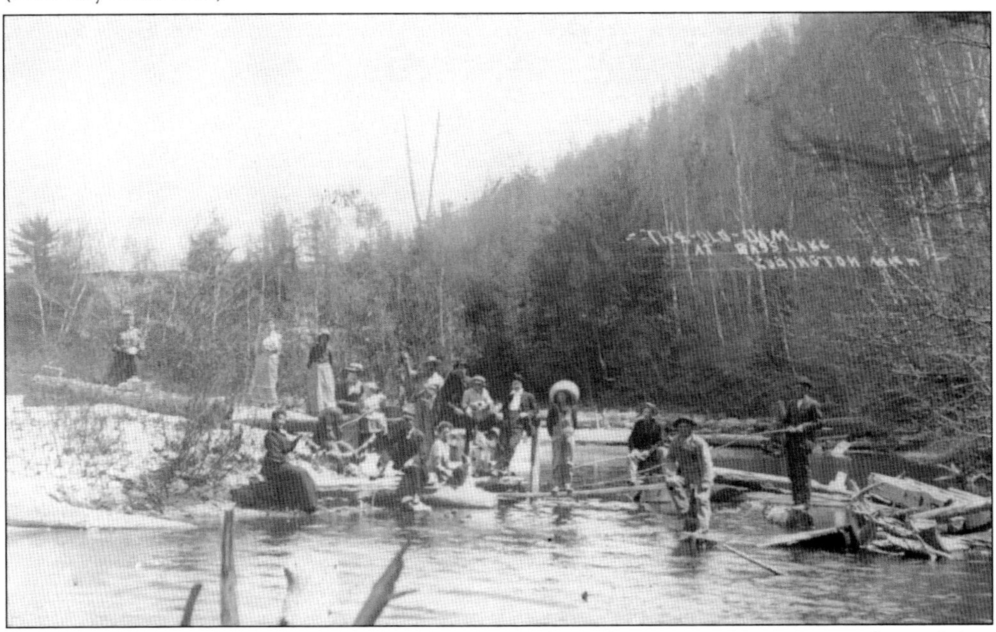

When Camp Morrison at Bass Lake first started, roads in the state were in poor condition. Most travel was by passenger boats and steamers. Visitors would arrive in Pentwater by steamer or by rail and would then travel in small launches or by buggy to their destination. Bass Lake also had a post office established on June 17, 1897, with Hattie L. McKee as the first postmaster; the office closed in 1902. (Courtesy of MCHS.)

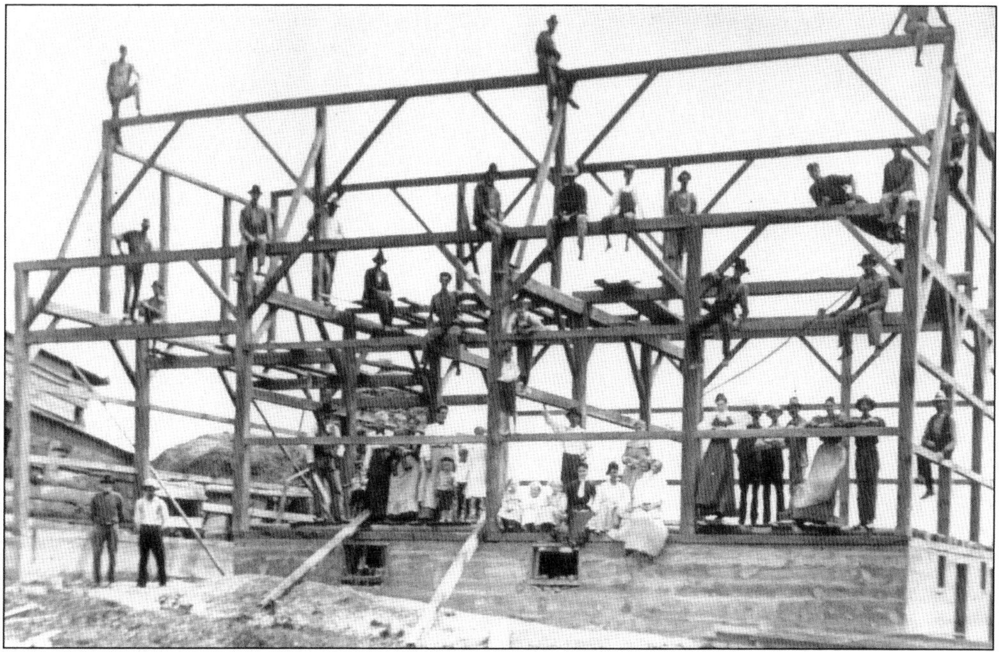

This image is simply titled "Bacheller Barn Raising." It illustrates the tight-knit fabric of small communities of settlers coming together to help each other weather the storms of life as they worked to meet the challenges of what at times could be a harsh life, but one made easier by deep and lasting friendships that spanned generations. (Courtesy MCHS.)

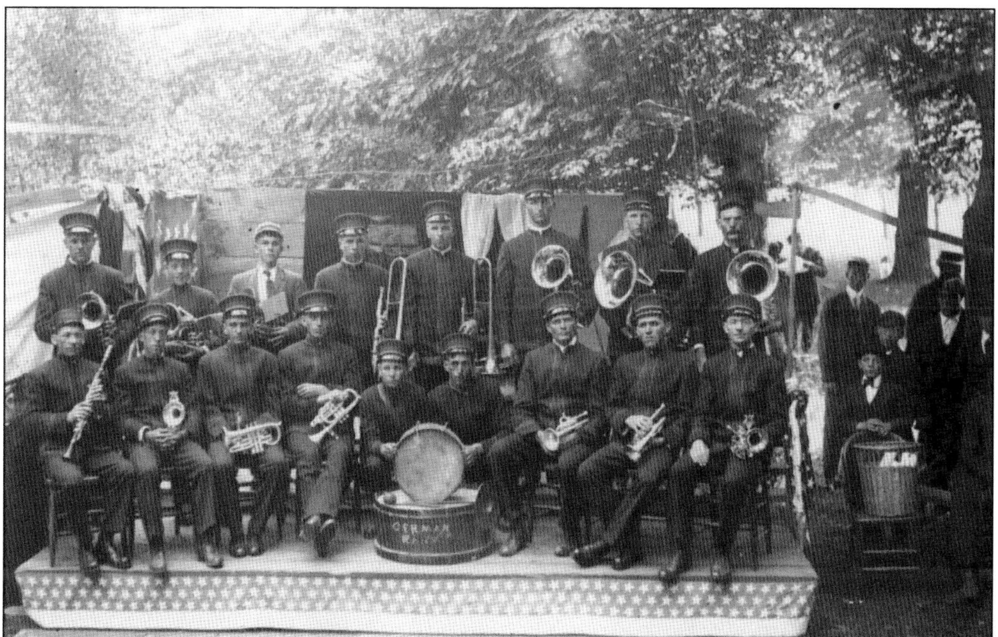

Originally a stop on the Pere Marquette Railroad, Bachelor was named after a local sawmill, owned by the Alden A. Batchelor Company. It was granted a post office on February 14, 1884. The German Band is getting ready to provide some entertainment for a community event. (Courtesy of MCHS.)

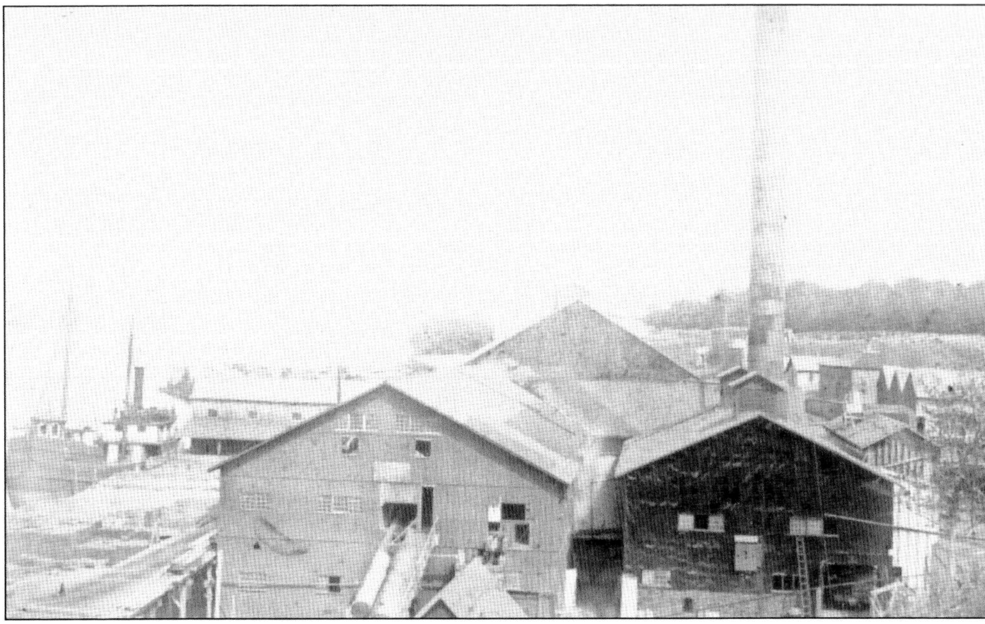

The Buttersville mill was built by Vahue Hustis and Company in 1872 and changed hands several times, going from Foster and Stanchfield to Cartier and Filer before Horace Butters and G. Peters bought the mill in 1882. In 1887, a post office was established and operated until January 7, 1907. Work continued at the mill until the fire of 1909 destroyed it, and Buttersville ceased to exist. (Courtesy Mary Mitchell.)

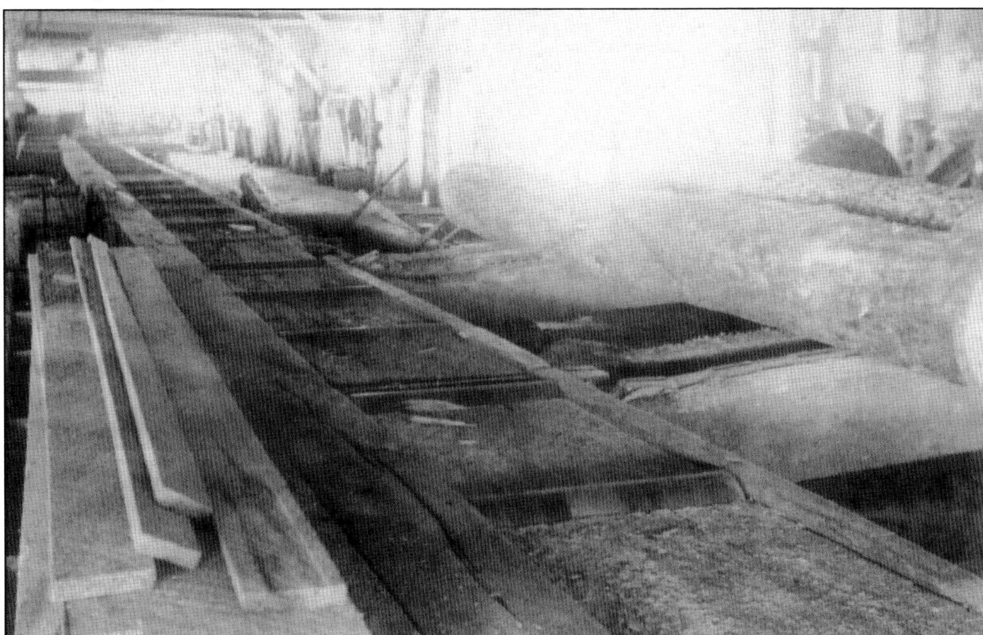

Interior views of the mills in the Ludington area are a rare treat. Buttersville had nearly 1,000 residents at one time, living in the vicinity of the mill. After the mill burned and the village was deserted, a number of the houses on the island were moved across the iced-over lake and placed on new lots in the city of Ludington. (Courtesy of Mary Mitchell.)

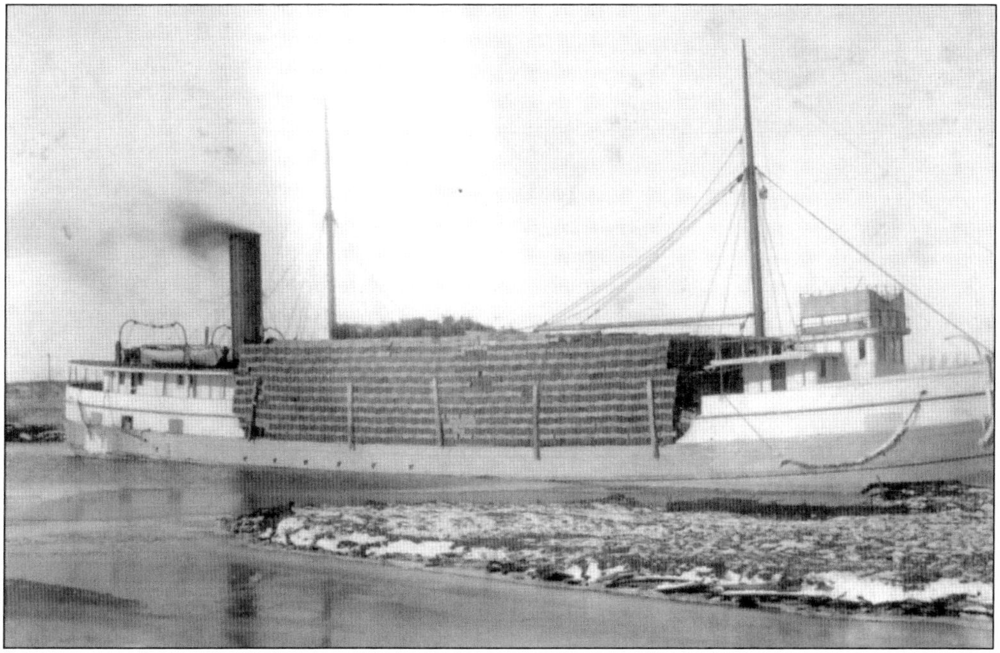

After 1885, the Butters firm branched out into the manufacturing of salt and built a cooper's shop on-site to manufacture the barrels needed to ship its products. The salt well produced 1,500 barrels a day. A lumber hooker, named the *Marshall F. Butters* after Butters' oldest son, carried salt, lumber, lathes, and shingles to market. (Courtesy Mary Mitchell.)

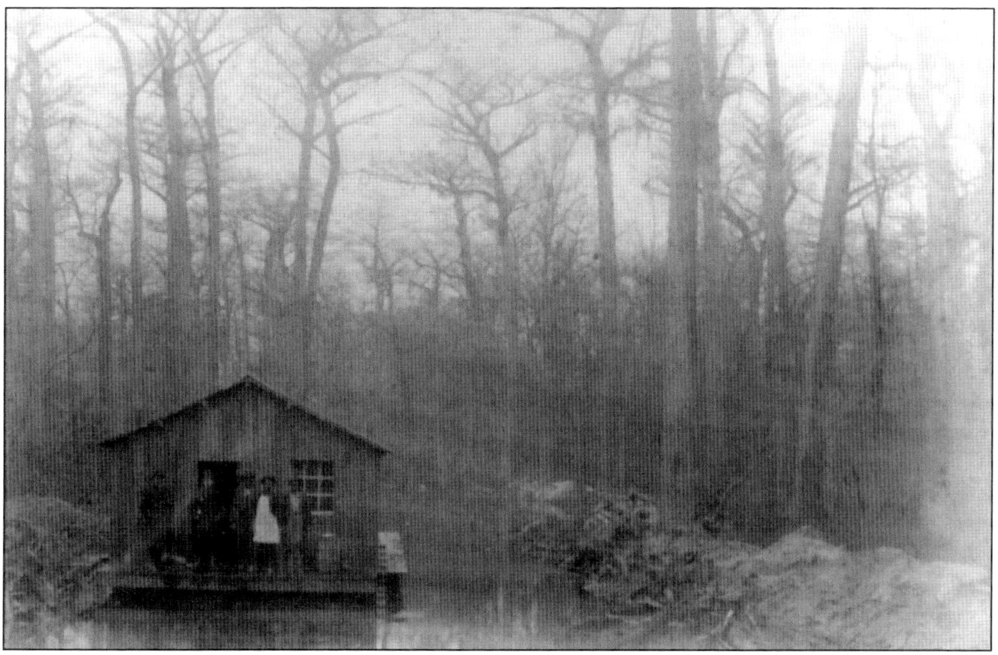

There was a lot of lumber to be harvested near the Pere Marquette River, and the need was great to be able to feed the crews near where they would be working. This floating mess hall provided a warm place to dry out and grab a hot meal in a wet and cold working environment. (Courtesy Mary Mitchell.)

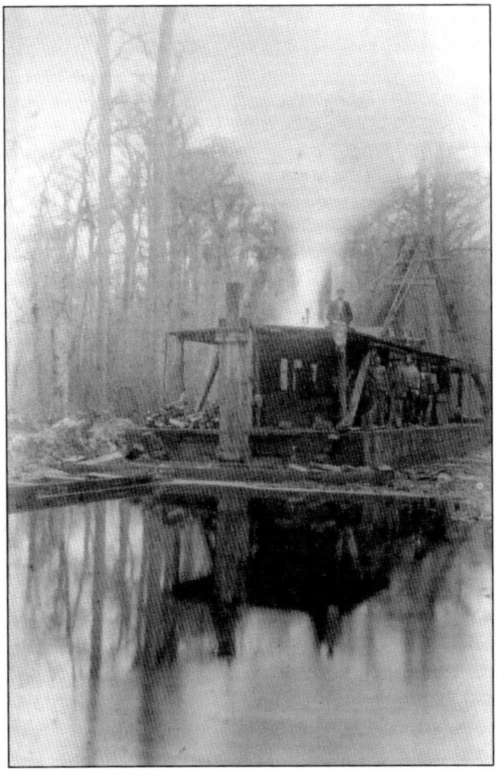

The Horace Butters Patent Steam Skidder was devised to help cut the costs involved in the labor-intensive skidding of logs. The machines cost $5,000 each, which was a great deal of money at the time, but they were popular in the South and Western states. When harvesting logs in the swamps and rivers, sometimes "canaling" was required to open an area up for easier access, as this steam dredge seems to be doing. (Courtesy of Mary Mitchell.)

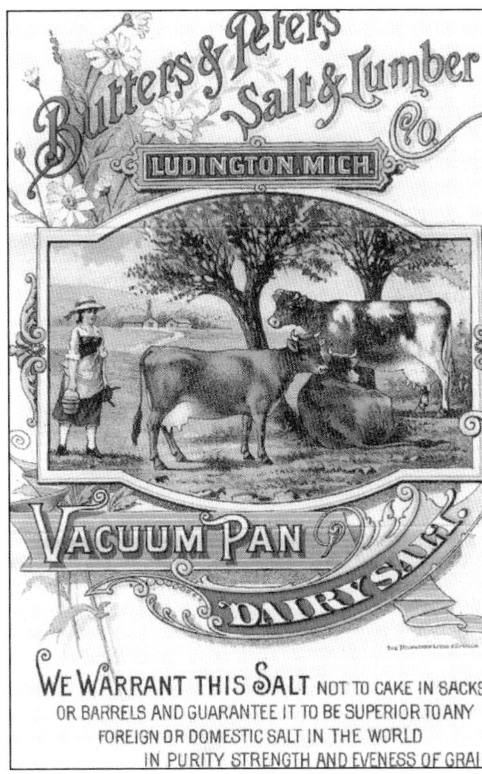

This period advertisement extols the virtues of the Butters Company salt produced from its wells at Buttersville. When the lumber started to become depleted, Stearns and Butters both invested in brine wells to begin the manufacturing of salt as a means to keep the business active and replace revenues that they would soon lose as the timber was depleted. (Author's collection.)

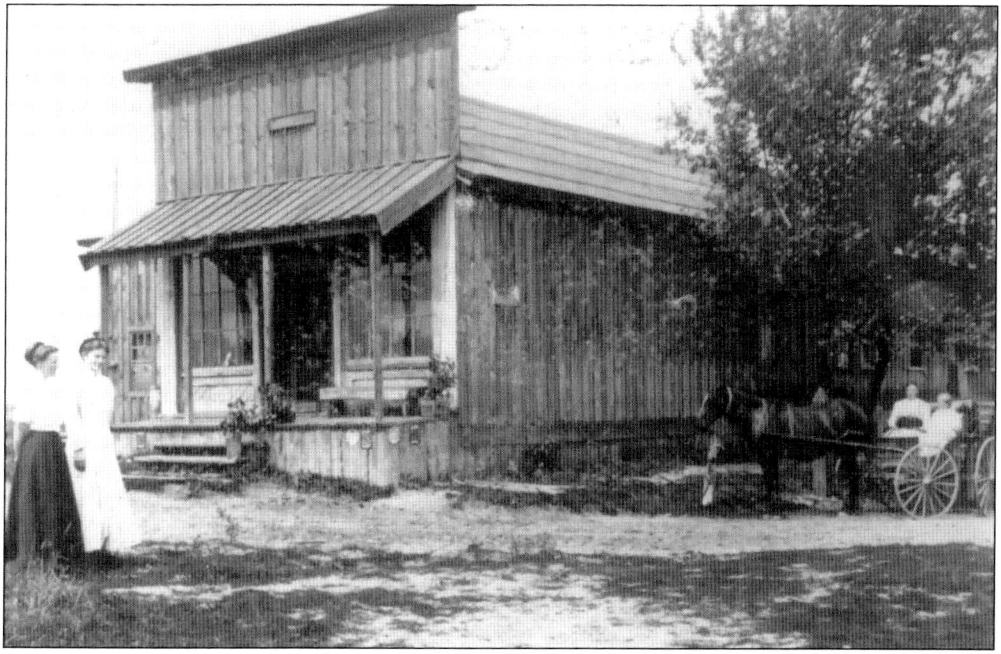

From left to right, Bessie Anderson, Ann ? , and Carrie Adams are pictured here outside of the Fern Store south of Custer. Fern was a little community that built up near the J.S. Adams Sawmill in Eden Township. In 1886, the Mason and Oceana Railroad opened a station there, and in 1888 a post office was established with Carrie L. Adams as the first postmistress. (Author's collection.)

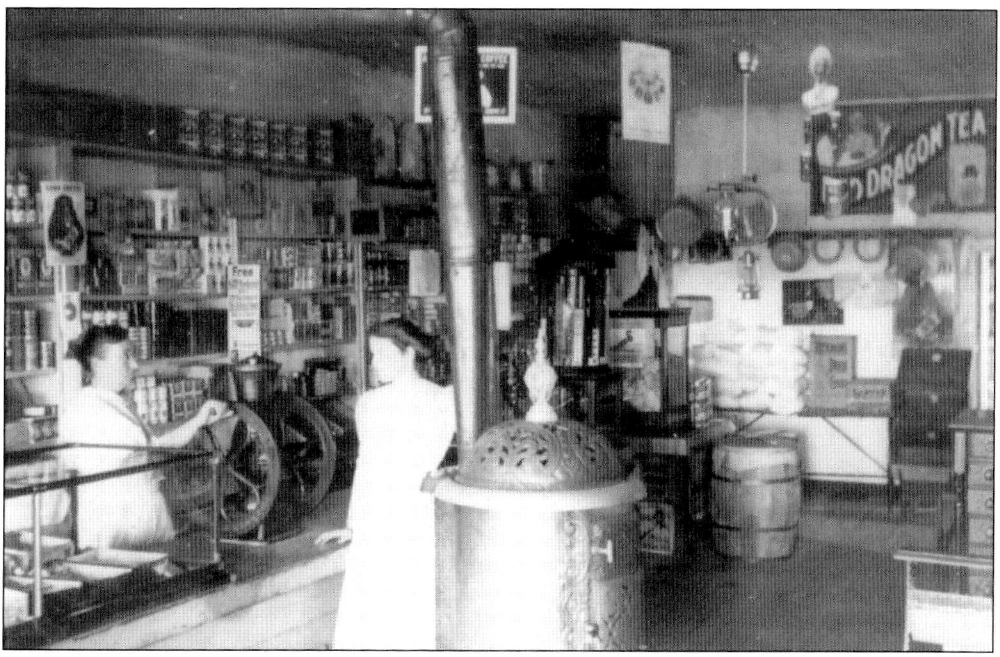

Anna Anderson (left) and Christine Hoffman are inside the General Store at Fern in Eden Township. The Mason and Oceana Railroad had a station at Fern until the railroad closed after the timber played out. There is a large section of the township that is part of the Manistee National Forest; Sippy Swamp is near Fern to the east. (Author's collection.)

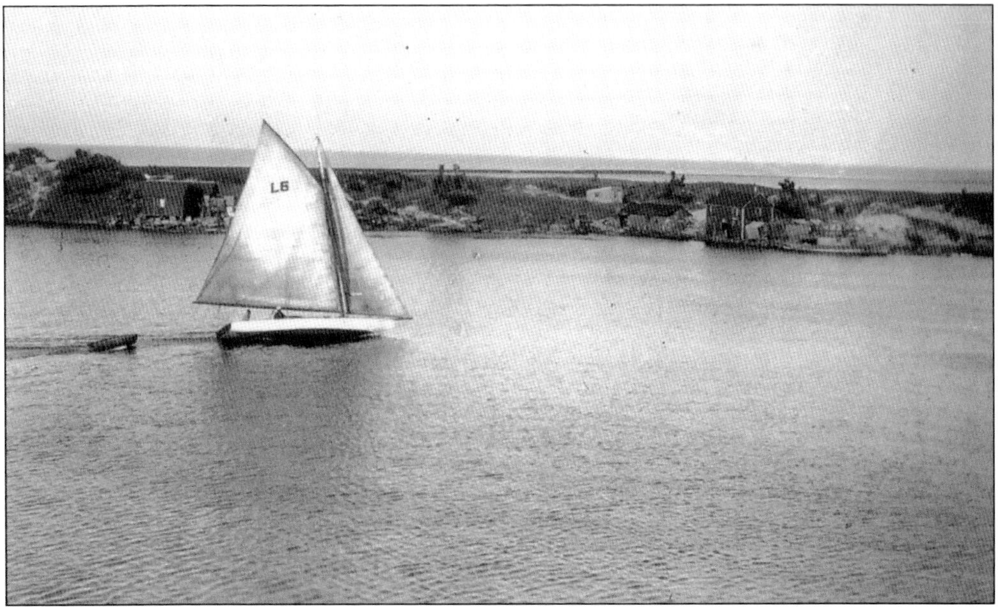

The spike of sandy peninsula that was referred to as Buttersville once had a small creek on the south end, hence the nickname "The Island." It was once a community, actually several communities—Buttersville, Taylorsville, Seatonville, and Finn Town—that are all ghost towns but were once alive with activity from the sawmill, schooners at the dock, fish tugs going in and out of the harbor, and to over a thousand souls who called the area home. (Author's collection.)

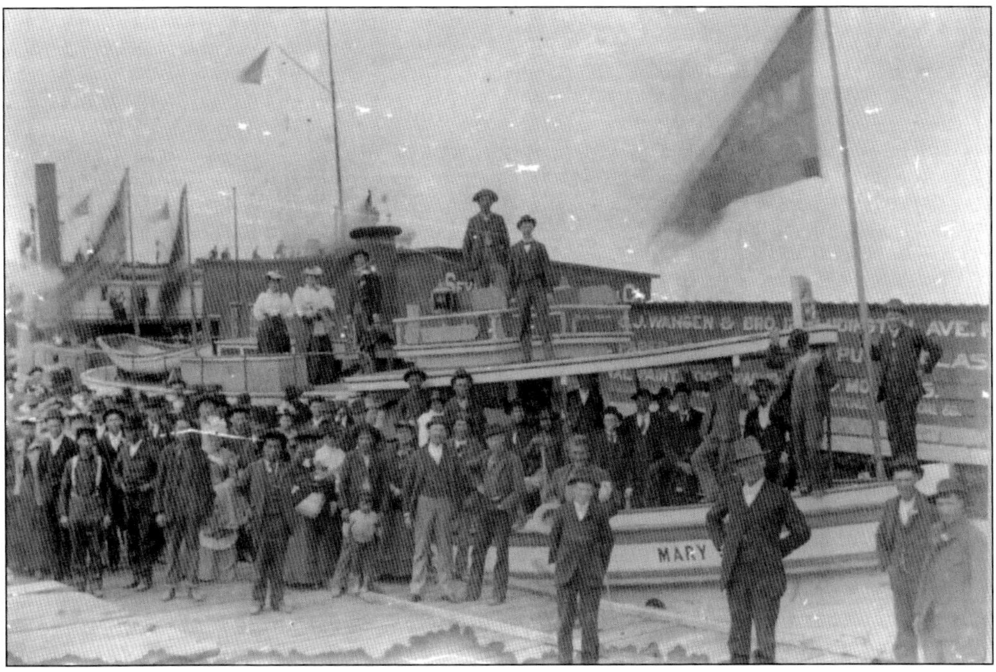

The schooner *Mary A. Gregory* is shown here docked at the Buttersville Peninsula at Finn Town. Several locals are shown standing on the beams to show off for the cameraman. Built in 1875 in Chicago by John Gregory, this schooner served on the Great Lakes until being abandoned in 1925. (Courtesy of James F. Fay.)

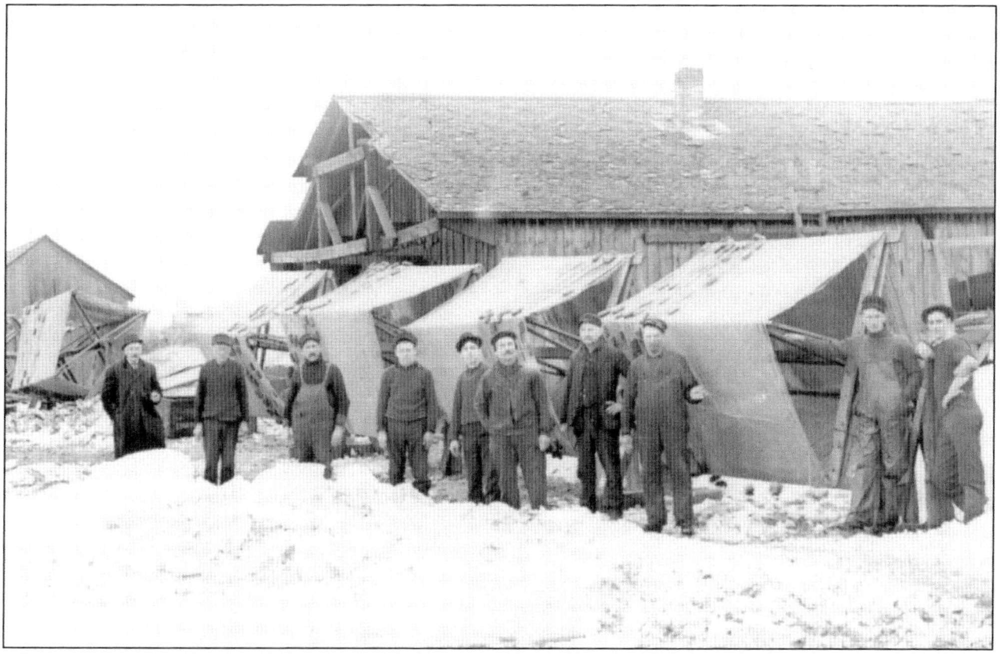

There were many fishing families living in Finn Town; at one time there were up to 50 dwellings and businesses built around the community on the sandy spike of dune. There was a dance hall that afforded entertainment and room for the commercial fishermen to dock their tugs and set up racks for drying their nets. (Courtesy of Margaret Gustafson.)

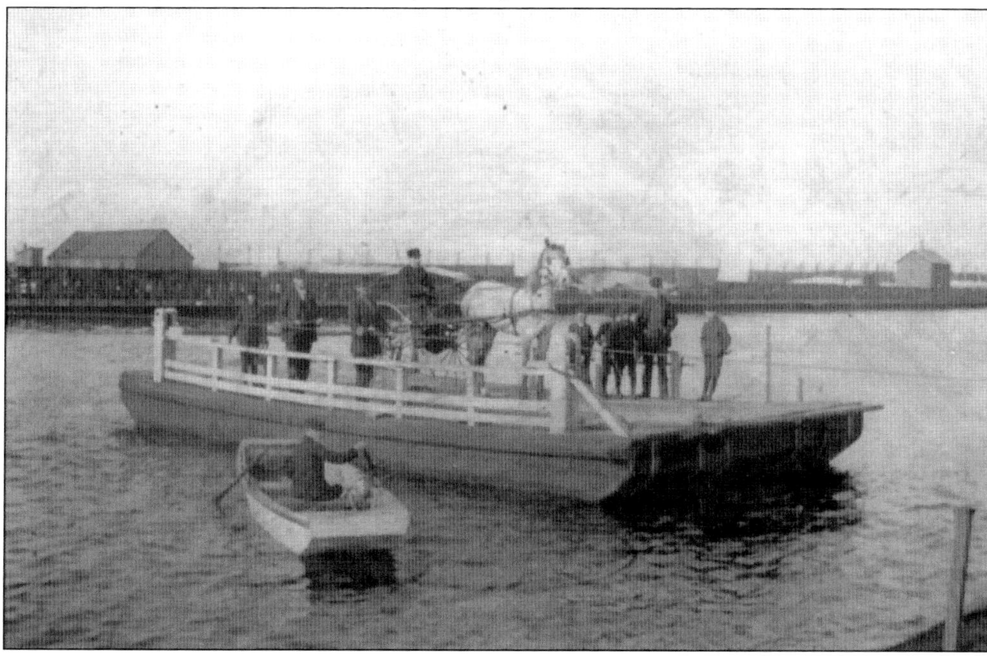

By virtue of the Buttersville Peninsula's situation, there was a need for Ludington residents who worked in the mills to get back and forth without having to take the long way around to south Lakeshore Drive. The ferry could be taken for 5¢, and during the winter months it was not unusual to see groups crossing on the frozen lake in order to get to work. (Courtesy of MCHS.)

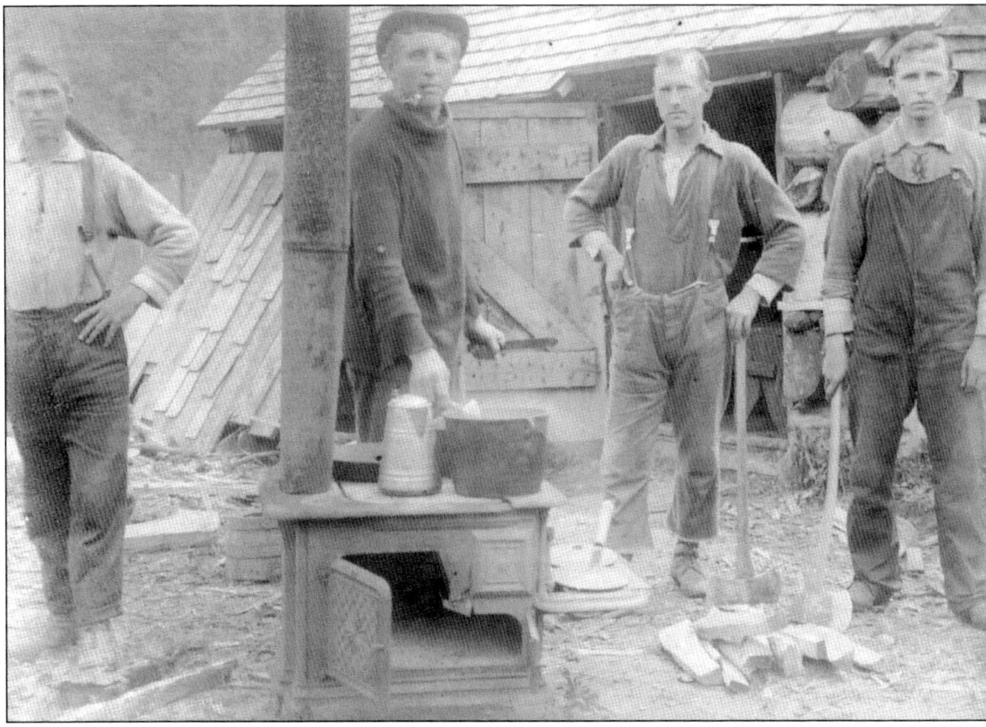

Gurnee was a lumber camp in northern Meade Township that was granted its own post office. The image here of the camp illustrates the spartan lifestyle and lack of amenities in the woods and these rural communities. When they were finished with logging, there was very little to move out, and the communities blended into the landscape. (Courtesy of James F. Fay.)

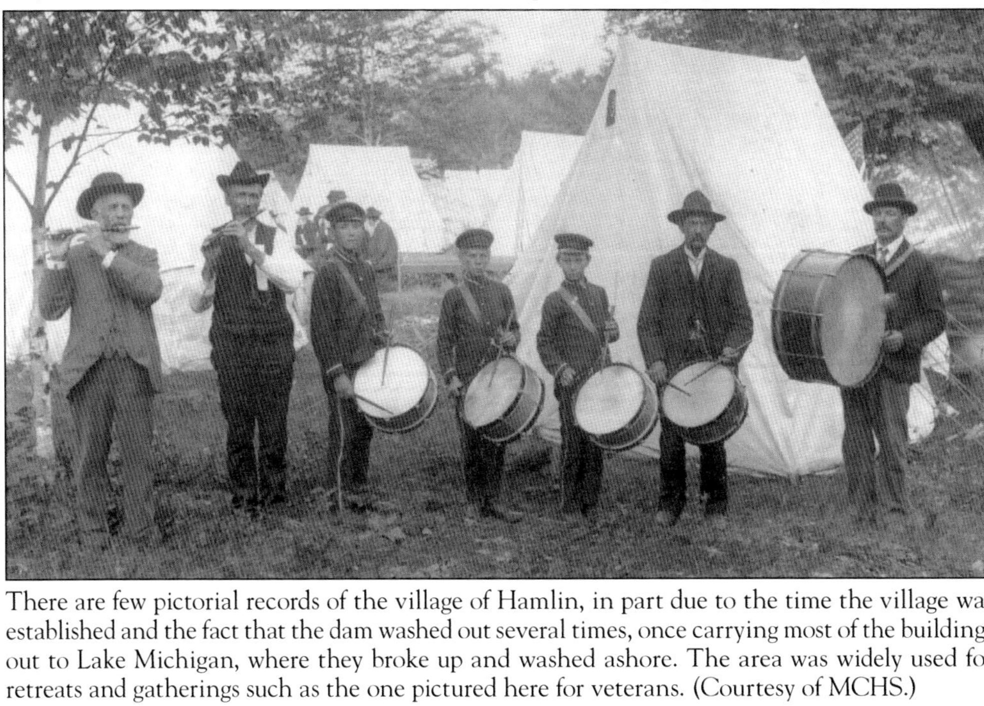

There are few pictorial records of the village of Hamlin, in part due to the time the village was established and the fact that the dam washed out several times, once carrying most of the buildings out to Lake Michigan, where they broke up and washed ashore. The area was widely used for retreats and gatherings such as the one pictured here for veterans. (Courtesy of MCHS.)

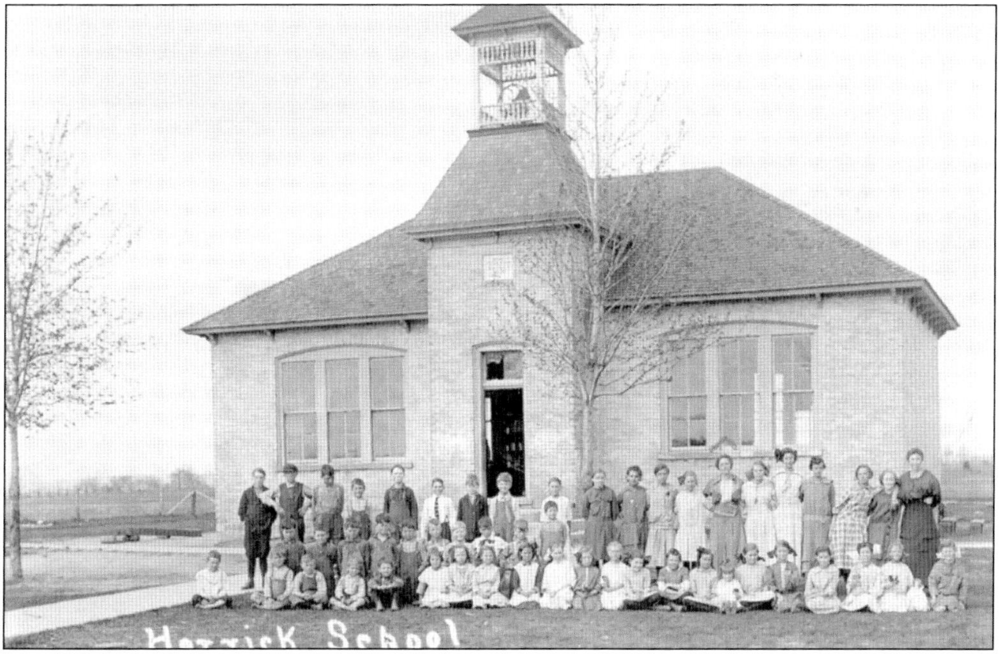

The Herricksville Mill was near the south bank of the Pere Marquette River, south of Custer, and Herricksville at one time had a post office. Brothers Fred and Frank Herrick began lumbering operations there after coming to Mason County. The area referred to as Herricksville was located in the area of the last Native American settlement in Mason County. (Courtesy of James F. Fay.)

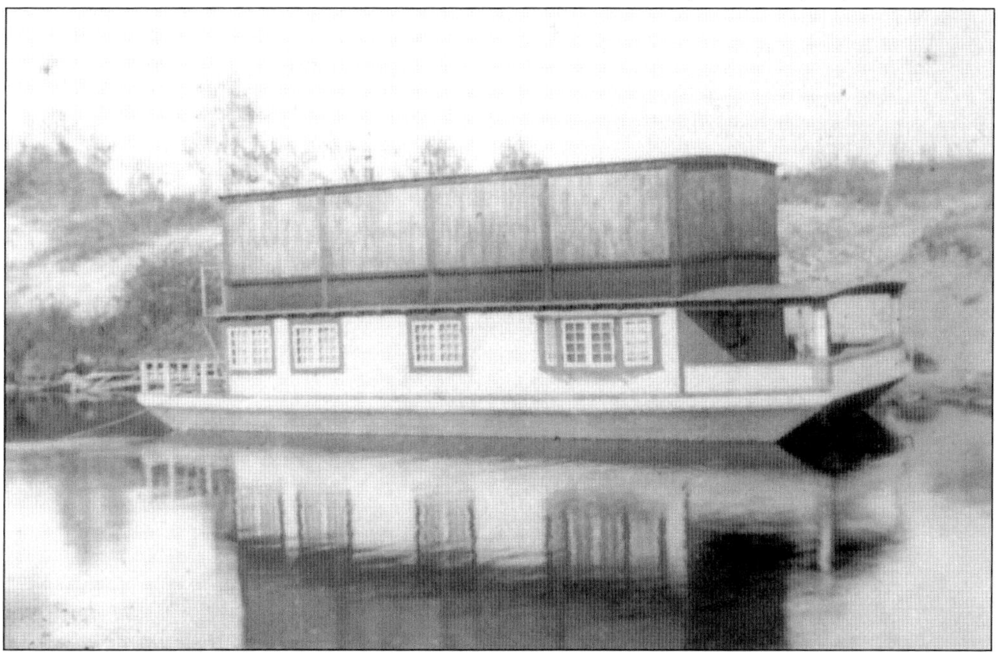
The *Hostess*, as she was called, was built on Hamlin Lake (just below Sable Inn) by M.F. Butters and launched July 16, 1908. It was, as the paper extolled, the social event of the season; Mrs. Margaret Butters arranged for the Dummy Train to transport 125 guests out to the lake for the festivities. After the dam burst, the boat was moved to Pere Marquette Lake. (Author's collection.)

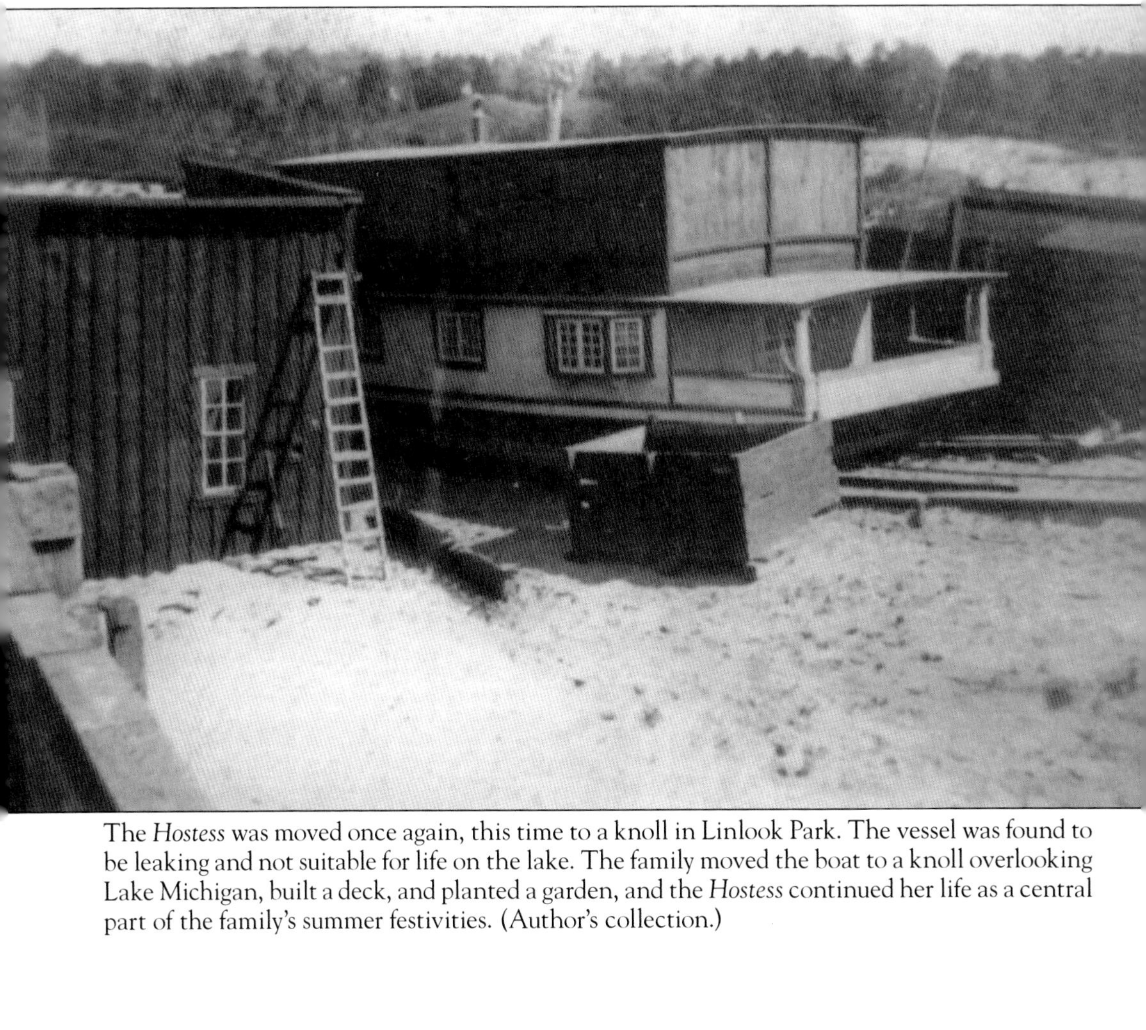

The *Hostess* was moved once again, this time to a knoll in Linlook Park. The vessel was found to be leaking and not suitable for life on the lake. The family moved the boat to a knoll overlooking Lake Michigan, built a deck, and planted a garden, and the *Hostess* continued her life as a central part of the family's summer festivities. (Author's collection.)

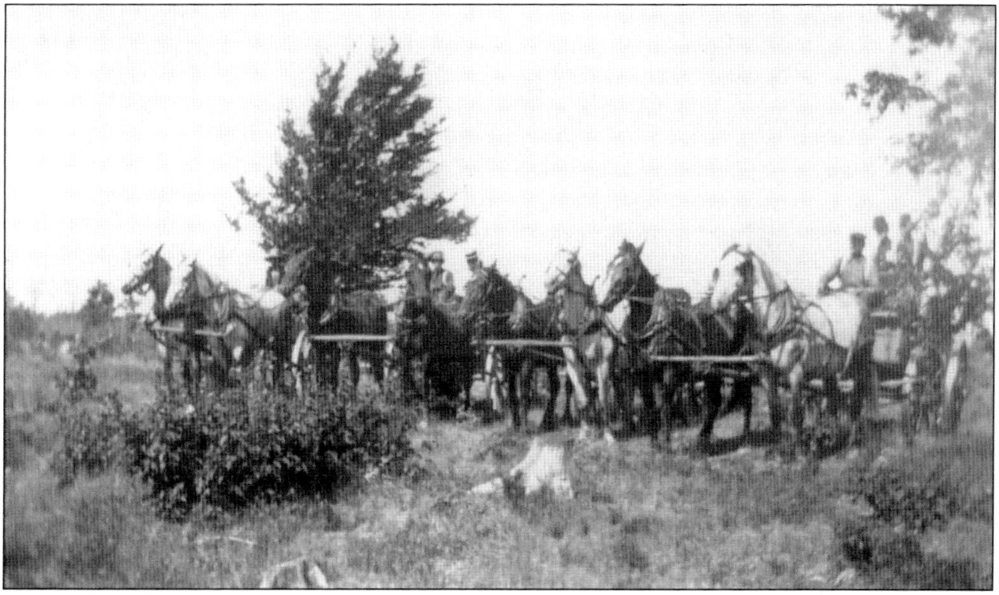

Meadeville has a history reminiscent of tales of Florida swampland buyers, except this took place here just north of Freesoil. George Swigert, a realtor from Chicago, bought land for $1 an acre and then sold it to unsuspecting buyers for $25 an acre after convincing them that it was lucrative farmland. He hired local drays to ferry customers out to survey the land. (Courtesy of Benita Eddy Hurd.)

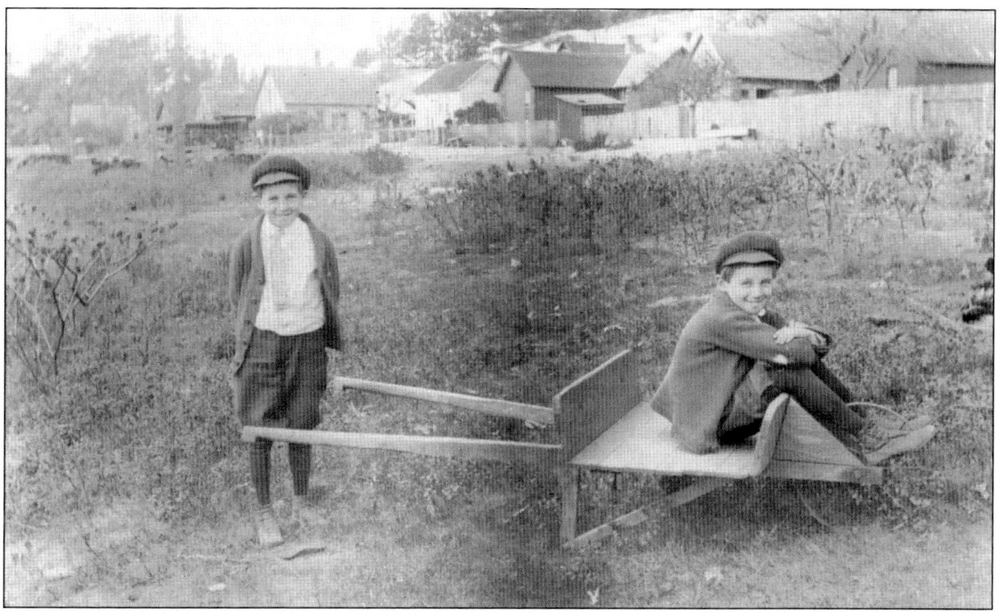

These youngsters are playing on the south side of Smokey Road, a short thoroughfare that ran along the shore of Pere Marquette Lake. The road had extended west from US 31 but was abandoned by the county after the land was purchased by Dow Chemical during World War II and the homes razed as Dow expanded to meet the needs of the war effort. (Courtesy of Robert Tushek.)

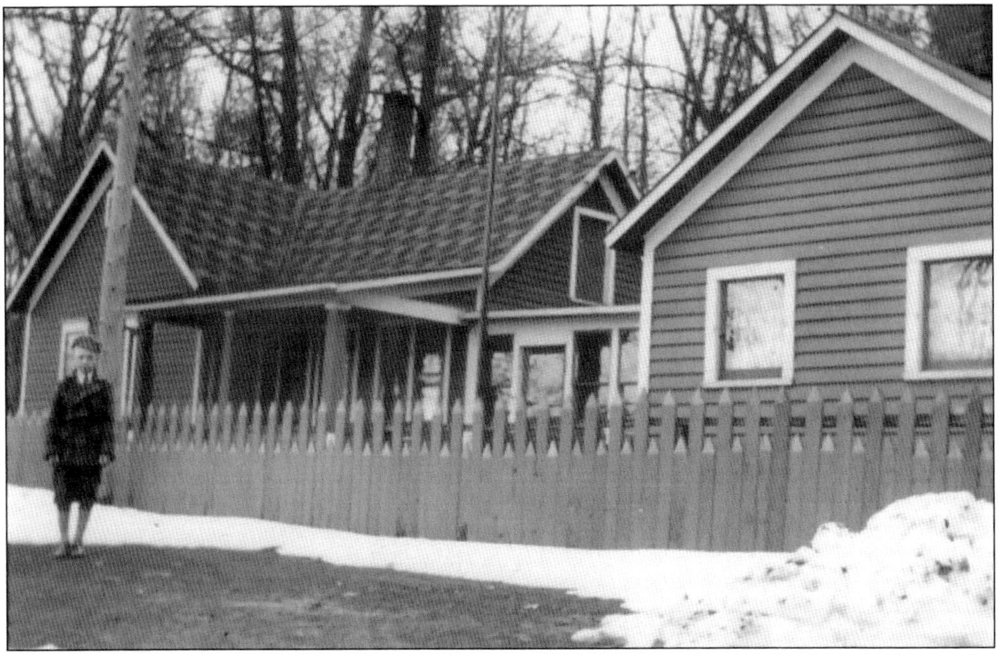

In the early history of the area, Smokey Road was one of the main routes into Ludington during the lumbering years. Pictured here is the Michael and Anna Tushek home. It was not bulldozed as the first 10 houses were, but rather Austin Construction took it apart. The homes of George Brooks, Jim Mitchell, and Ed Petzak's were the first three to be bulldozed. (Courtesy of Robert Tushek.)

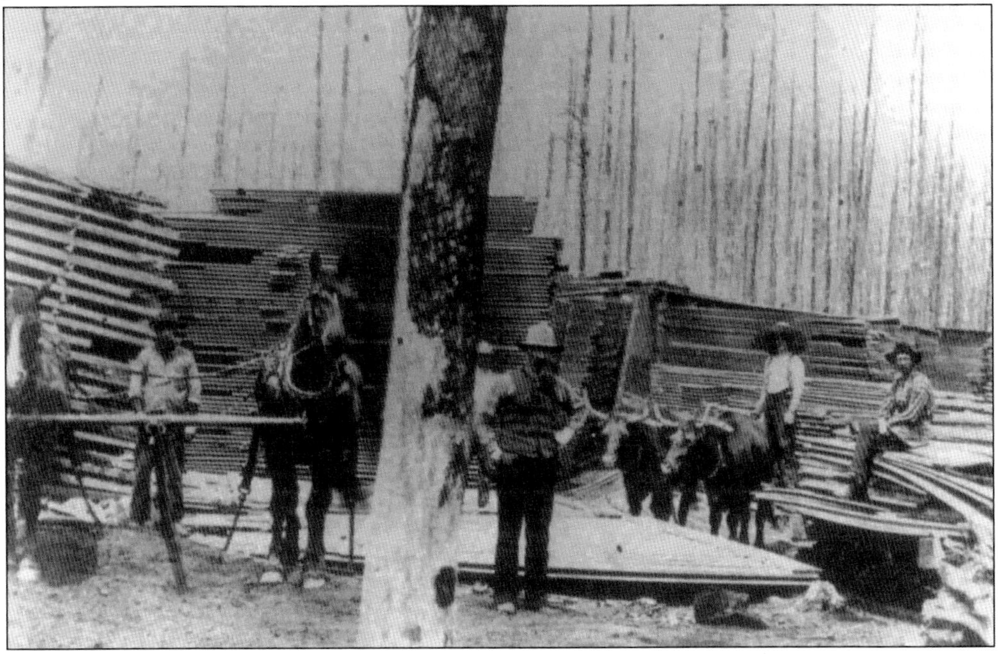

Stearns Siding, founded by Justus Stearns, was just over the county line in Lake County. A post office opened there in 1882 named Wingleton, and for a while the village thrived with upwards of 2,500 people living and working in the vicinity. Today, only depressions remain in the ground to indicate what was once there. (Courtesy of Lake County Historical Society.)

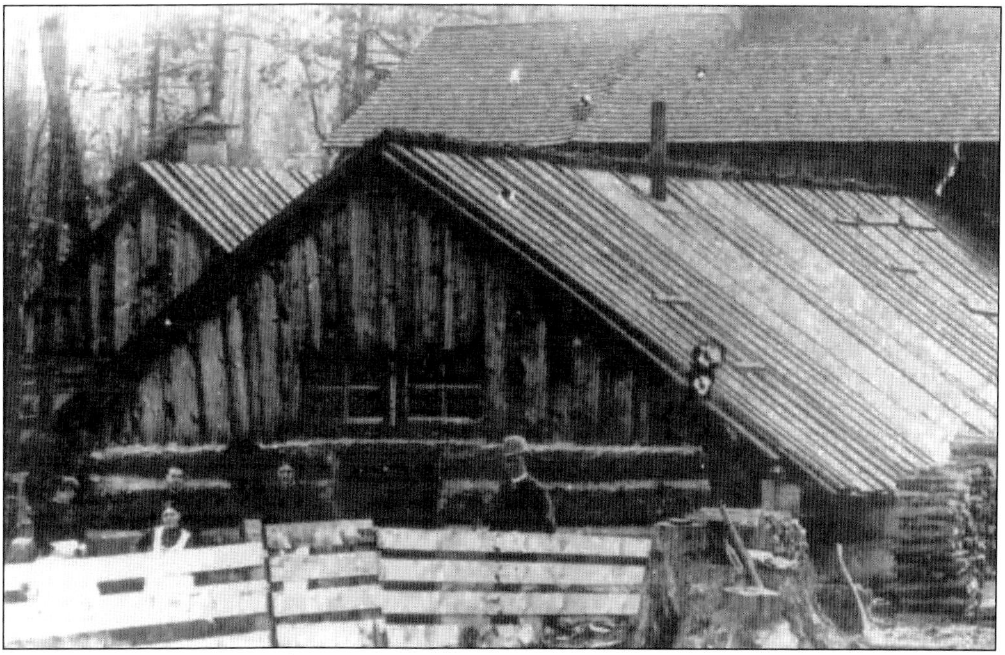

Justus Stearns married Paulina Lyons of Conneaut, Ohio, and came to Michigan to work near Big Rapids with a portable mill. That venture failed, and after a while Justus was able to purchase lands east of Ludington to start again and founded Stearns Siding in 1880. He then began building what would become a vast lumbering empire. (Courtesy of MCHS.)

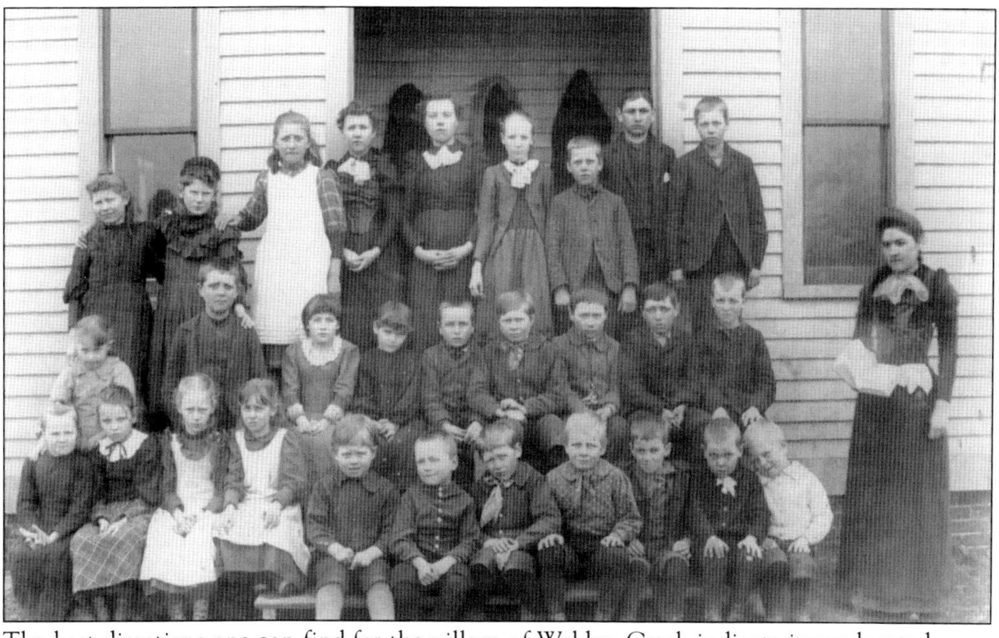

The best directions one can find for the village of Weldon Creek indicate it was located upon the west bank at the point where the stream is crossed by the railroad. John Wells settled here and opened a store on what was called Indian Creek about 1875. Weldon Creek had a station on the Flint and Pere Marquette Railroad, a school, and a post office, which by 1892 had closed. (Courtesy Lake County Historical Society.)

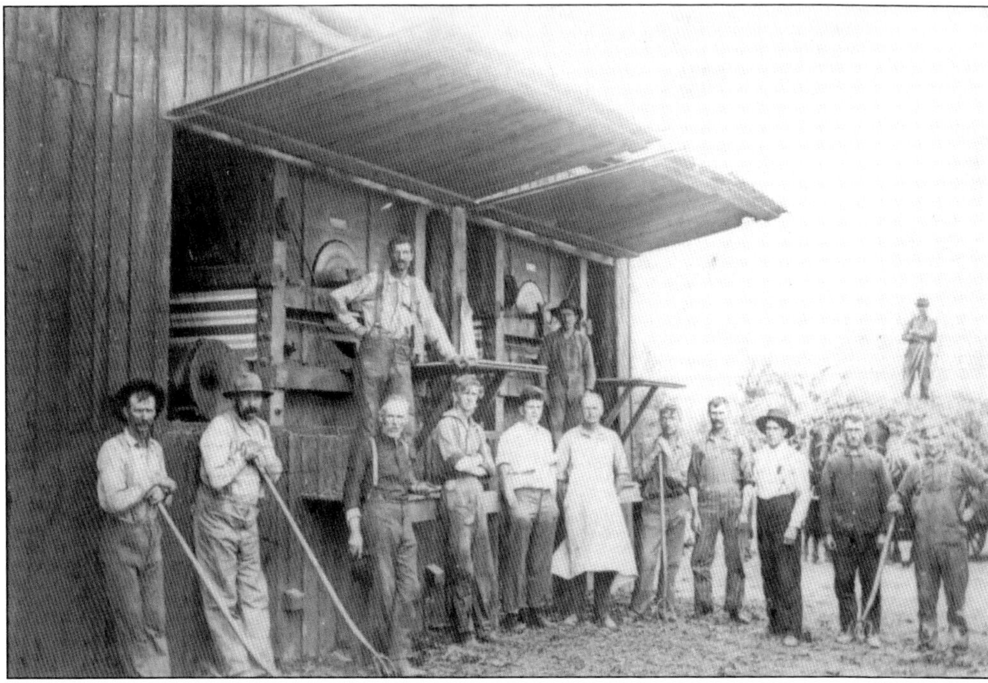

The Wiley Pea Vinery was built in 1907 by the Sears and Nickels Canning Company of Pentwater. At that time, it was feasible to process some produce near where it was grown before transporting to markets to the south. The vinery operated until 1912, when it was closed, but by 1917 Roach Canning Company of Scottville opened another vinery in Wiley. (Courtesy of MCHS.)

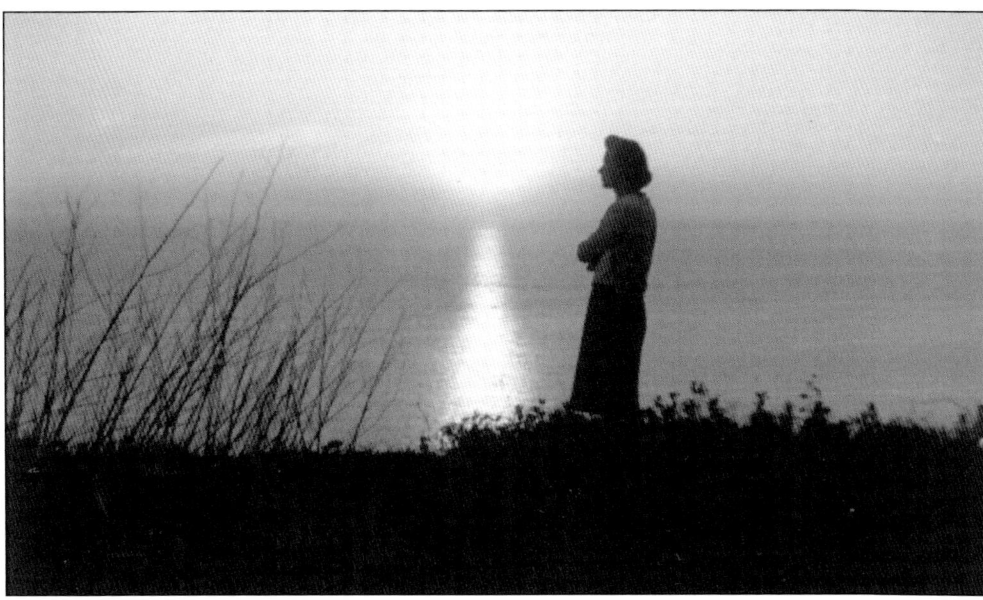

A young woman looks off to the west as the sun sets on Lake Michigan. Mason County is rich with natural resources and miles of sandy beaches. There is also a rich history of an area that was settled by immigrants searching for a new life in a new land. *Mason County 1850–1950* attempts to give readers a glimpse into that past and the lives that came before. (Author's collection.)

About the Mason County Historical Society

The Mason County Historical Society is a private, nonprofit educational organization, formally organized on November 30, 1937. It is a tax-exempt 501(c)(3) that operates from Historic White Pine Village, currently hosts the Mason County Sports Hall of Fame, is developing the Port of Ludington Maritime Museum, and maintains an extensive research library. The society is led by a nine-member board of directors and staffed by an executive director, financial manager, operations manager, project manager, and several part-time positions, along with hundreds of dedicated volunteers. The MCHS mission is to foster a deeper understanding of and appreciation for Mason County history; to collect, preserve, and present for viewing and experiencing historically important artifacts, archives, and buildings of the inhabitants of Mason County; to stimulate and encourage the interpretation of Mason County's past through publications, educational programs, and related historical programs; and to cooperate with individuals, organizations, and institutions on the local and state level in projects and activities that promote and sustain a general interest in history and preservation. The MCHS strives to develop an expanded array of exhibits, programs, and attractions to significantly enhance the visitors' awareness of all the diverse experiences, occupations, hopes, and dreams of county residents, thereby awakening visitors to the importance of being involved in the civic life of their community.

Historic White Pine Village is an exciting interactive historical and educational experience in a beautiful and serene setting overlooking Lake Michigan just south of Ludington. The village is open to the public six days a week from early May through mid-October. Thousands of visitors have been coming to the village since 1976 to see and experience what life was like more than 100 years ago in Mason County. Visitors tour 30 buildings and sites displaying items from Mason County's rich and storied past. Historic White Pine Village is truly a place where history lives. The multimillion-dollar, state-of-the-art Port of Ludington Maritime Museum is slated to open in 2016. It is situated in the former Coast Guard station at Ludington, a landmark of that city's waterfront for over three-quarters of a century and in the National Register of Historic Buildings. The MCHS Research Library is located at Historic White Pine Village. An online research database is currently under construction to aid family historians in their research. The Mason County Historical Society is committed to engaging its community and visitors with dynamic interactive experiences that enhance understanding of our county's past and help build a better future.

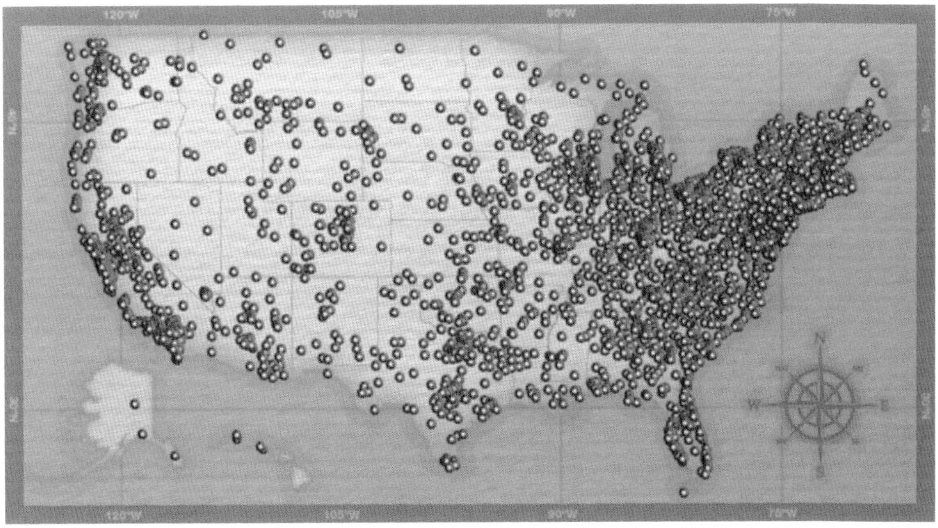